To Sharon

Very be

Dermot.

The Man with the Camino Tattoo

Searching for sanctuary on the Camino de Santiago

Dermot Breen

Dedicated to Matthew and Hannah.
Your mother lives on through you.

Published in 2018 by Shanway Press,
15 Crumlin Road, Belfast BT14 6AA

Cover design: David-Lee Badger

ISBN: 978-1-910044-17-9

"Grief is like a long valley, a winding valley
where any bend may reveal a totally new landscape."

A GRIEF OBSERVED by CS Lewis
© copyright CS Lewis Pte Ltd 1961

About the author

Dermot Breen was born in Omagh in 1960, but now spends his time between Belfast and Portrush. He graduated in Civil Engineering at Queen's University Belfast in 1983 and then followed a career in occupational health and safety for over thirty years. He took early retirement from a senior management post in 2016 following the death from ovarian cancer of his beloved wife Jacqui. He has since devoted his time to raising funds for cancer research and has undertaken several long-distance walks in Ireland, Spain and China as part of his fundraising efforts. He has previously written *The Edge, Walking the Ulster Way with my Angels and Demons*. This is his second book.

CONTENTS

Prologue

It wasn't too late to turn away. Nobody was forcing me to do this after all. Nevertheless, I stepped forward and pushed the button on the door panel outside the four storey Georgian mid-terrace on Belfast's Stranmillis Road. The intercom crackled and, after announcing myself, the door was unlocked from some hidden location within. I stepped into the warmth of the lobby, leaving the cold, damp October day outside. I climbed the stairs to the third floor and made my way to the door of the tattoo parlour at the rear of the building. It looked reassuringly clean and modern as I stepped inside and was greeted warmly by Jenna, who I had arranged my appointment with a few weeks previously. It was the first time I had ever set foot inside a tattoo parlour and, to be honest, I had never expected nor imagined that I would ever become a prospective customer of such an establishment. I had always been such a conformist and conservative with a small 'c'. Jenna was very chatty and friendly and put me at ease right away by assuring me that I wasn't the eldest customer she had ever had, not by a long shot. I could only imagine that there were some very wrinkly tattoos on the streets out there.

After signing the necessary consent forms, it was straight down to business. I sat in the comfortable arm chair – not unlike a dentist's chair – and rolled up the right sleeve of my tee-shirt to expose my shoulder, which I had chosen as the site for my body art.

"A good place for your first tattoo" Jenna said, as she began to shave the already smooth area smoother with a disposable razor.

"My first and only tattoo" I said resolutely.

"Oh, if I had a pound for every customer who said that, I can tell you I wouldn't be sitting here in Belfast with winter approaching," she responded with a laugh. She cleaned my shoulder with a little alcohol and then applied a transfer of my tattoo design onto my skin. I had already sent Jenna a copy of the design when I had arranged my appointment. From that she had produced a temporary transfer to act as her template or guide. "See what you think," she said.

I stood up and walked over to the wall mirror to check the position of the transfer. This was the first time I had seen the tattoo, or replica of it, actually on myself. Although only a transfer, the image was still pretty clear. It depicted a path winding between forests and mountains and meandering towards a horizon under a setting sun. This was all contained within the outline of a scallop shell, the iconic and potent symbol of the Way of Saint James. Beneath this was an arrow, the *fleche* of the Camino, containing the figures '1000 - 2000', with 'K4J' immediately above, representing the kilometres I had walked for Jacqui, both in Northern Ireland and Northern Spain.

"Looks good," I said, taking my seat again and watching nervously as Jenna prepared her pen and inks.

"Ready?" she asked.

"As I'll ever be" I replied and, before I had an opportunity to change my mind, she got to work.

The needle of her pen started to buzz incessantly, and I tensed as I waited for skin contact to be made. It certainly stung to begin with, but it wasn't nearly as bad as I had imagined it might have been – more of an irritation than anything else really. But as Jenna proceeded to work on the tattoo, and particularly when she began to fill in some of the darker areas, it began to feel more like my skin was being slowly and methodically scraped away – quite unpleasant. But nevertheless bearable – just. I don't think I cried once.

"You're a real trooper; you're doing really well" Jenna said more than once, in a voice that was obviously well accustomed to making wimps feel that they were being really tough and brave.

Being tough and brave – facing a little needle while sitting in a tattoo artist's chair. What a joke. How would I have fared if I had had to face numerous attempts at surgical needles being forced into elusive veins by well-intentioned but busy nurses; all while sitting in a cancer ward awaiting the next round of chemotherapy? Not very well at all I reckoned. But that was what my wife had had to face on many occasions. That and worse, much, much worse, as she had courageously fought against ovarian cancer; the cruel disease that had taken her life less than two years before.

"I really love this design," Jenna said, thankfully interrupting my dark train of thought. "What's the story behind it?"

Good Lord, I thought. Where do I begin?

Chapter One: Signs
(Days one to five - Irún to Deba)

It had been exactly one year, three months and seventeen days since my world had been blown apart. Of course, I could have chosen any number of words to describe how my life had changed so dramatically and permanently on the day Jacqui had died. However, as I stood at the Belfast Bus Station, located directly behind the Europa hotel, once famous for being the most bombed in Europe, the words 'blown apart' seemed more appropriate than ever.

It was 5am on a cool morning in early May and I was waiting to board a bus to take me "down South" to Dublin Airport, where I was booked on a flight to Biarritz in France. This was the beginning of my second 1,000km challenge in memory of Jacqui and to raise funds for cancer research. After walking the Ulster Way the previous year, I was now setting off to tackle the Camino de Santiago, the Way of Saint James, in Northern Spain.

What was it that drove me to embark on yet another long-distance odyssey just eight months after my Ulster Way pilgrimage? Good question, I thought, as I climbed on board the Dublin Express and settled into my seat by the window. The truth is; I was still searching for something. Something that had eluded me on the Ulster Way and something that had obstinately remained out of my reach ever since. That something was sanctuary.

Ever since Jacqui had been taken from me, I craved some sort of sanctuary. Somewhere that I could find peace and finally escape the demons that still tormented me. What this sanctuary looked like or where it was, I really had no idea, but I felt that I had to keep searching until I found it. Without it, I felt that I would never truly escape the clutches of grief and my shattered heart would never have a chance to mend. Deep down, of course, I knew that there was every chance that such sanctuary simply did not exist and that I was deluded for even imagining that I could ever reach such a place. But I also knew that I had to at least try. If I kept searching, there was still hope. And I felt that the Way of Saint James was particularly suited to my quest, for the path to Santiago is also known as the Way of the Sword. It's reputed to be the path where you fight your demons and find your strength.

The coach journey to Dublin Airport was pleasant and uneventful and, two hours later, I was stepping into Airport Departures and seeking out my check-in desk. I had booked a one-way ticket to Biarritz as I wanted to have flexibility as regards my return date. This walk was going to take as long as it would take. I had taken a one-year career break from work and so I had the luxury of not being under any time constraints. After locating my check-in desk, I headed over to a nearby row of metal seats and began the cocooning process. I removed a roll of cling film from one of the side pockets and began to wrap it repeatedly round the rucksack until it was totally encapsulated in a semi-transparent skin. This provided the rucksack and its contents with a little more physical protection against the inevitable rough handling it would face from both Irish and French baggage handlers. I lifted my rucksack, which now looked like a huge insect that had been captured and encapsulated in the web of some equally huge spider, and headed over to the check-in desk.

One hour later and I was boarding the 9.30am flight to Biarritz. There was a young guy from Limerick in the seat beside me and we soon discovered a common bond in that we were both travelling on to Spain from Biarritz to walk the Camino de Santiago. Like me, Rory was planning to walk the less travelled Camino del Norte route, which closely hugs the north coast of Spain for the first 625 kilometres before turning inland towards Santiago. We both clutched the same guide book, which was one of the very few guides for the Camino del Norte published in English and therefore a dead giveaway as to our intentions. In an early introduction to what would become a standard ice breaker between Camino pilgrims, we exchanged information about why we had decided to walk the Camino de Santiago. Rory just wanted to do something challenging with his life and when he had heard about this Spanish walk he researched it a bit more and then quit his job in sales and just went for it. Rory was less than half my age and I was really impressed with the determination and sense of adventure displayed by this young man from the West of Ireland. I skirted round the real reasons for my pilgrimage by simply saying that I had heard about the Camino from friends and had decided to walk it to raise funds for a charity. The rest of the time on the flight passed easily in Rory's company and before long we were securing our seat belts once again for our descent into Biarritz.

We arrived in Biarritz Airport at just before 1pm, pretty much on schedule. It had all been going like clockwork up to this point, but I knew it couldn't last – and it didn't. I had been hoping to get a bus from Biarritz Airport to Hendaye on the French/Spanish border at just after 3pm. I had taken great care to obtain the bus times before setting off. However, for some reason – maybe my 'spider senses' – I decided to double check the bus times to Irún at the information desk.

"Are you sure?" I said, when the lady at the desk told me that the next bus was not until 5pm, "I thought there was one at 3.05".

"There is usually," she said, "but this is a Bank Holiday and not all the buses are running today".

"Bugger." I didn't actually say that; I just thought it.

I thanked her and turned away, now resigned to a longer wait than expected. After investigating further, I found out that it was in fact a Holy Day, the Feast of the Ascension. Oh dear, I really had betrayed my good religious upbringing.

I grabbed some lunch and then waited outside the terminal in the bright afternoon sunshine for the 5pm bus to arrive. It was pretty deserted outside the terminal – just a handful of locals really. There had been a sizeable number of backpackers on my flight, but they had all vanished pretty quickly from the airport. I could only assume that, if they were planning to walk the Camino, then most, if not all, had headed for the trains to Saint Jean Pied de Port, where they would join the start of the inland Camino Frances route. I hadn't spotted Rory since I had last seen him heading through customs and I hoped that he hadn't inadvertently followed the crowd to Saint Jean.

*****

It was after 6pm by the time I arrived in Hendaye and from there it was only a short journey across the River Bibasoa, and the French/Spanish border, to Irún, the official starting point for the Camino del Norte. Although it was a lot later than I had anticipated, I nevertheless decided to stick to my original plan and walk the first five kilometres of the Camino, which would take me out of the town to a private *albergue* (a pilgrim hostel) near Guadalupe. I felt that it might give me a psychological advantage the following morning to know that I already had a head start and it would certainly reduce the distance I had to cover the following day. However, in order to get there, I had to first make my way out of the busy town of Irún.

I looked around for one of the famous Camino signs to point me the correct way, but I couldn't spot any. I tried asking a few passing locals, but they had either never heard of the Camino or simply couldn't understand my rudimentary Spanish. I called into a small patisserie beside the train station and the lady there got the gist of what I was looking for. She led me back out onto the street and pointed me in the direction of a road junction in the distance. I thanked her and set off as directed and upon arriving at the junction I came across my very first Camino sign. The feeling of reassurance provided by this first sign was a feeling that would be repeated countless times over the coming days and weeks.

The Camino del Norte turned out to be, for the most part, very well way-marked over its entire length. The variety and variations of signs used on the Camino were quite numerous, but the two most common were the yellow arrow, known as the *fleche,* and a graphic representation of the scallop shell. The reasoning behind the *fleche* is quite obvious in that it is simply a directional arrow, painted in a vibrant colour to stand out from the background and be easily spotted from a distance. The reason for the scallop shell symbol is perhaps not quite so obvious. There are many legends and myths attempting to explain the ancient link between the scallop shell and the Way of Saint James. One such legend says that, while the remains of Saint James were being taken from Judea to Galicia a knight's horse fell into the water and emerged covered in scallop shells. The shell is also claimed to have links to the end point of the original pagan pilgrimage route in Finisterre, where there are many scallop shells washed up on the local beach. The converging lines on the shell happen to quite neatly symbolise the various Camino routes that start at different points throughout the world, but all drawing towards a common point, originally Finisterre and subsequently the tomb of Saint James in Santiago de Compostela.

Having located this first Camino sign, the *fleche* now started to appear at fairly regular intervals; painted on lampposts, the corners of buildings and even on the pavements. So I was able to negotiate my way through the busy streets relatively easily, checking with the occasional local to ensure that I didn't stray too far off route. It wasn't too long before I picked up a quiet pathway through a public park that followed a tranquil tributary of the Rio Bidasoa. The pathway eventually brought me to a narrow rural road, which climbed gently and provided nice views back over the town and the eastern peaks of the Pyrenees behind.

I was about one and a half kilometres from the hostel, when I noticed a dark van coming down the road towards me. On drawing level, the van stopped and the young Spanish man driving asked me if I was on my way to the hostel. When I said that I was, he told me that he ran the hostel and that unfortunately it was now full.

Bugger, I thought for the second time today! What was I to do now? It was getting late and starting to get dark. It was then that I had my first experience of the much-celebrated hospitality that the locals show towards pilgrims, or *peregrinos* as they are called in Spanish. The driver introduced himself as Gabriel, told me to get into the van and he then very kindly drove me back into Irún. Gabriel explained that he had passed me on the road earlier and, upon learning that his hostel was full, he had driven back to tell me. It was certainly disappointing to have walked all that distance only to be brought back practically to the start, but it was very fortunate that Gabriel had spotted me and very kind of him to help me out. He even got me fixed up in another *albergue*, the *Convento de los Capuchinos*, and left me right to its door.

I thanked my 'Angel Gabriel', before climbing out of the van to ring the doorbell next to the side entrance of the seventeenth century convent. After what seemed like an interminably long wait, the heavy wooden door creaked open and I was met by a small woman with a kindly face. Maria, the caretaker, or *hospitalero*, was expecting me. She invited me in, showed me round the guest facilities and then led me upstairs and along dark corridors, before handing me a large, rusty key that let me into my 'cell' for the night. On the way to my room, María had informed me that the convent had been home to a small number of nuns up until just a few years ago, but after the last one had passed away, it had been used as an *albergue* for pilgrims. Being a former nuns quarters, my three-bed room was certainly pretty basic, but I had it all to myself and it turned out to be fairly comfortable. As I settled in, I wondered how pairs of pious knees had endured the dark, bare, wooden floorboards in the room since the convent had been established back in 1638. Quite a few no doubt, but my knobbly, agnostic knees certainly wouldn't be adding to the number. However, before going to sleep that night, I did consider performing an act of contrition. For, although there were no nuns in residence any more, my imagination conjured up the possibility of the ghost of one returning in the night to re-educate me in the dates of holy feast days. There's nothing like the guilt felt by a lapsed Catholic to fire the imagination.

*****

My long day of travelling helped ensure a sound sleep at the *Convento de los Capuchinos* and thankfully I was spared any visitations from nocturnal nuns during the night. I woke up early and felt refreshed, although my enthusiasm was slightly tempered by the realisation that I had to start my day's walk by retracing steps I had already taken. It was a case of 'rewind and start again'. After breakfast I said my goodbyes and set off, once again rejoining the Camino del Norte route on its gradual ascent towards Guadalupe.

It took me just over half an hour to reach the point where my 'Angel Gabriel' had picked me up the previous evening. I was now back to where I was, so to speak. It wasn't too much longer before I reached the *Santuario de Guadalupe*, a sixteenth century church on a hillside overlooking the Bidasoa valley below. Unfortunately the church was closed at the time of my visit and so I wasn't going to obtain any sanctuary here. Nevertheless, the views from outside the church back down to Irún, the Rio Bidasoa and the eastern end of the Pyrenees behind, were quite spectacular. Some of the blue-grey hills of the distant Pyrenees were nicely highlighted, as shafts of bright sunlight, buscular rays, cut through gaps in the grey cloud cover above and reached down to illuminate the earth below. Looking out on this heavenly scene, it was possible to forget about my loss for a while and simply enjoy the feeling of being alive in such a wonderful world.

From the *Santuario de Guadalupe*, I had a choice of two routes that would both lead me to Pasajes, the next town on the route. I could either follow the official Camino route, marked out by the Camino specific yellow arrows, or I could be adventurous and follow the GR (Gran Recorrido) path, marked with GR specific red and white

One of the 'Spanish Ten' taking in the view over Irún, the Rio Bidasoa and the eastern end of the Pyrenees from Mount Jaizkibel

markings. The GR routes comprise a network of more than 100 long-distance walking trails across Europe and they are found mainly in France, Belgium, the Netherlands and Spain. In general, the GR route in Northern Spain tends to follow a more mountainous and/or coastal route and therefore also tends to be more scenic. This was the route I decided to go with. I had chosen to walk the Camino del Norte due to its coastal and scenic nature, so it seemed logical to get the best out of it. However, although this came with benefits in terms of scenery, it also came at a cost in terms of difficulty.

This was immediately apparent shortly after leaving the *Santuario de Guadalupe*, when a sign pointing in the GR route direction referred to it as the way for 'Alpinist Pilgrims'. It was certainly a tough climb to the ridge of Mount Jaizkibel and I was very glad that I had used the Mourne Mountains back home in Northern Ireland as my main training ground before embarking on my Spanish pilgrimage. Even though, I was sweating profusely by the time I reached the top. I met a very friendly group of ten Spaniards here who were at the start of a week's walk to Bilbao. I walked with one of the group, Toni, for a while, but

The treacherous path around the rocks at the end of Mount Jaizkibel before descending into Pasajes

they were all much more seasoned walkers than I was and they soon left me behind. Anyway I preferred to take my time to savour the experience and the superb views whilst traversing the ridge of Mount Jaizkibel.

Somewhere along the way though, I think I must have missed a turn, because the final stage of my trek along the mountain ridge was more challenging than I was comfortable with. A few sections had quite a narrow dirt track skirting round the base of rock faces high above the valley below. One foot misplaced or one careless slip could easily have brought my Camino to an abrupt and premature end. Fortunately there were wire ropes secured to some of the rock faces to provide a handhold at the trickier sections, but it was still a lot more treacherous than I had been expecting. It certainly made no mention of such Indiana Jones type escapades in my guidebook, hence my reasoning that I must have strayed off course. Perhaps this was what had been meant by that earlier 'Alpinist Pilgrims' sign. Anyway, it certainly made for a very dramatic and picturesque approach to the town of Pasajes and the very deep, fjord-like inlet in which it nestled. The clear blue sky, the azure coloured water and the sheer cliffs on either side of the inlet leading into the pretty port were the very epitome of the coastal beauty I had yearned to experience on the Camino del Norte. I slowly picked my way down off the mountainside and, with some relief, soon met up with proper pathways and then roads that led me into the town.

Due to the deep-water inlet in which it is located, Pasajes has been a prominent port for centuries. Part of the Spanish Armada fleet was even built here and, as I made my way into the town, thoughts of the Causeway Coast back home came to mind. For it was along the Causeway Coast, close to the famous Giant's Causeway rock formation, that one of the ships of the Spanish Armada, the Girona, was shipwrecked in 1588. In the 1960s, a team of divers investigated the wreck of the Girona and they salvaged the greatest haul of Armada treasure ever recovered, which is now on display in Belfast's Ulster Museum.

Entering Pasajes, I ran into the 'Spanish Ten' again. They were finishing off their lunch at a lovely little restaurant close to the water's edge. After enjoying a bit of good natured banter with them, which was mainly at my expense given my late arrival, I joined another couple of walkers at a nearby table who were still waiting to be served. I had also met Pierre from France and Kelly from Australia on the way over Mount Jaizkibel and they readily invited me to join them for lunch. The strong sense of comradeship between pilgrims walking the Camino was already becoming very apparent.

After lunch we headed for the small pedestrian ferry to make the short crossing to the other side of the port. The captain was just about to push off when we heard someone shouting and I looked up to see Rory, the young guy from Limerick, running towards the ferry. The captain waited for him and Rory boarded with great relief. The crossing only took about five minutes, but it was very pleasant in the afternoon sunshine with fabulous views of cliffs on either side of the port.

When we alighted at the other side, Rory suddenly said, "Well that wasn't too bad a day's walk, was it?" When he saw the questioning looks on our faces, he asked, "We are finished for the day, aren't we? This is San Sebastián, isn't it?"

Poor Rory had misread his guidebook and when he realised this, he let out an expletive or two. Resigned to the fact that he now had yet more distance to cover, Rory said that he had better get something to eat before continuing. We left him to seek out somewhere to grab lunch and Pierre, Kelly and I walked on together for a while along a flat promenade taking us out towards the coast. There then followed an extremely long and steep climb up a set of stone steps to the top of the next headland. However, our paces didn't match on this climb and on this occasion it was me who pushed ahead.

It gradually got hotter as the day went on and I was absolutely sweltered by the time I started the long descent into the stunning beach city of San Sebastián. I watched with envy as surfers enjoyed the fabulous waves at the first of the city's two beaches, Playa de la Zurriola, as I began my walk along the three kilometre long promenade to the other side of San Sebastián and to the pilgrim hostel. When I finally got there, and for the second day in a row, I found that the hostel was full. I couldn't believe it. I spent the next two hours searching for somewhere else to stay in the city. Everywhere I tried was full and it was the same story wherever I went – it was a holiday weekend in France. It seemed like the whole country had descended on San Sebastián.

As I was unsuccessfully tramping the city streets, I met a lot of other pilgrims who were also desperately searching for somewhere to stay for the night, which wasn't an encouraging sign. After being turned away from numerous hotels and guest houses, I was advised at one that it might be easier to find a place to stay in the old part of the city, which was essentially back close to where I had first entered San Sebastián. So, I got a bus back to the other side of the city again and, after much searching, I finally managed to secure a 4x2m cell in a dingy pension at an over-inflated price. San Sebastián was a beautiful place, but it was definitely not a good time to be passing through as a pilgrim. Having said that, I had a really great tapas, or '*pinchos*', meal at the Bar Cera just around the corner from my pension. The bar was full of locals, the food was wonderfully authentic, the beer cold and refreshing and the atmosphere really buzzing.

However, the Bar Cera got much too busy after a while and when a large English group descended on my table, literally surrounding me, I finished up my beer and surrendered my seat to one of them. It was still too early to return to my lonely cell, so I instead headed across the street to a quieter tapas bar for a coffee. Here I was served by an older member of the bar staff with unruly dark hair and very swarthy skin. He introduced himself as Carlos and he was delighted to learn that I was from *Irelanda del Norte*. He leaned forward and whispered in my ear, in conspiratorial tones, that he wasn't Spanish, but that he was in fact Basque. And he was obviously very proud of it.

"*Moy importanti,*" he said as he grabbed my hand in a firm handshake. He clearly thought I was a 'brother in arms'.

"*No comprendi,*" was my avoidance strategy, when he persisted with his revolutionary talk.

Taking my coffee, I quickly headed to a table at the back of the bar, where I had a bit of peace from Carlos to catch up with the blog I was preparing for my Facebook page. He kept glancing over at me though and, although I might have been reading too much into his expression, I started to feel a little bit uncomfortable. I finished my coffee and made for the door, my cheery "*Buenas noches*" being met with little more than a gruff 'humph' from Carlos.

*****

The next morning, I was on the road by 7.30am. Whilst it was certainly good to have had a roof over my head for the night, I didn't manage to get much sleep. The room I was in was the only one in the pension that had a window above the door. I honestly think it might have previously been used as a storeroom. Unfortunately the window had no blind or curtain, so every time the light went on in the hallway outside (which seemed to be every ten minutes) my room was lit up like a landing strip. The window also didn't close properly and the noise throughout the night from other guests returning after a night out partying was truly awful. I think it finally died down at about 4am. So even though I was on the road bright and early, I certainly didn't feel bright-eyed and bushy-tailed.

The location of my pension back in the old part of the city, meant that I had to once again retrace my steps for the second morning in a row – "rewind and start again" again. But at least I also had the opportunity to take in the beauty of San Sebastián once more. It really was a beautiful city and, even though it was quite a damp start to the day, the early morning calm as I made my way through the cobblestoned old town, Parte Vieja, and then along the wide seafront promenade certainly helped compensate for my lack of sleep. I even stepped off the promenade for a time to walk along the crescent of the city's second and largest beach, Playa de la Concha. Here I enjoyed the almost deserted sands with views out across the wide sweeping bay that held the small island of Isla de Santa Clara in its embrace.

After reluctantly leaving the beach, it only took about another ten minutes to get back to where I had reached the previous day, close to the pilgrim hostel. There I began a long climb up and out of the city along a mixture of roads and footpaths. It wasn't too long before the light drizzle I had experienced walking through San Sebastián became heavier and then the rain was on for pretty much the rest of the morning. And so I donned my new cape fairly early on in my Camino. Gone was the old, torn, blue cape I had worn the previous year on the Ulster Way. This year I had acquired the latest fashion in capes, which came in a range of colours. I had opted for the rather fetching black, which I had rather sardonically labelled 'pilgrim black'. As well as helping to keep me dry, the cape also importantly covered any washing hanging from my backpack. It would become a regular routine for most pilgrims on the Camino, including myself, to wash socks, pants and tee-shirts at the end of each day's walk and then hang them out overnight to dry in whatever suitable place could be found. If my laundry was still not dry in the morning, then any damp items would be attached to the exterior of my rucksack with a few safety pins and allowed to continue drying as I walked. I hasten to add at this point that I had at least a second pair of everything. I never became a 'naked rambler'.

The rain gradually became more persistent and made for miserable walking conditions, but the lush, green, rolling hills of the Basque countryside certainly made the journey a little more agreeable. Near Orio, which was nine and a half kilometres from San Sebastián, the rain finally eased and the sun gradually appeared again to brighten and warm all in its path and the remainder of the day was quite beautiful.

On the outskirts of Orio, I came across the *Albergue San Martin* and, not wanting to be caught out accommodation wise again, I considered the possibility of finishing today's walk here. However, the *albergue* was closed and wouldn't be opening for another hour. I took a seat in a little covered area at the rear of the *albergue* and searched online for accommodation in Zarautz, my original intended stopping point for the day. My guidebook described Zarautz as having the longest beach in the region, which sounded very attractive indeed, but as a consequence it also had a population that tripled during the summer months. So I wasn't going to venture on to Zarautz before I was assured of having somewhere to stay. I was in luck. I booked myself into a private hostel for the night and also a hotel for the following night, as I had planned to stop over in Zarautz for a rest day.

No sooner had I sorted out my next two nights accommodation, than another pilgrim appeared around the corner of the *albergue*. I immediately recognised him as Miguel from Mexico. Our paths had crossed a number of times on today's walk and, although we had only exchanged a few words, I knew that he was from Mexico originally, but now lived in the US. Like Rory the day before, Miguel thought that he had reached the end of today's stage and I had to burst his bubble and tell him that it was still another 6km to Zarautz. Like me, he had found it difficult to get a place to stay in San Sebastián the previous night. I told him my plans and he asked me if I would book ahead for him for tonight also. He was lucky as I got him the last bed available.

We then walked on in towards the centre of Orio. It was quite slow going as Miguel was a self-proclaimed devout Catholic and he therefore took his religion very seriously – too seriously for my liking. Every 100 metres or so along the roadway we were on, there was a roadside cross erected. This was quite common in Spain along roads that led to or from a church. In this case it was the pretty pre-thirteenth century San Martin's Chapel, which was quite close to the *albergue* we had stopped at earlier. It was aptly named, as Saint Martin is the patron saint of pilgrims. Unfortunately, Miguel felt obliged to stop at practically every cross, bless himself and then take a picture of the cross. It became rather tedious waiting on him each time, but he was such a pleasant chap that I just endured it and accepted it as part of the suffering a pilgrim must absorb as penance, or whatever.

Thankfully, we didn't have too far to travel until we reached the town centre. On entering an open plaza area next to the River Oria, I spotted the 'Spanish Ten' and Pierre and Kelly all having lunch outside a busy little cafe. I stopped here also while Miguel decided to keep going. I joined Pierre and Kelly for a tasty lunch, after getting some great recommendations from Spanish Toni about what was best to order.

After a leisurely lunch, Pierre, Kelly and I crossed the bridge over the River Oria and set off together towards our final destination for the day. Our paces seemed to be much better matched today and we ended up walking almost the whole way to Zarautz together. They were great company and we sang some well-known songs from our respective countries along the way to help distract attention from our now tired legs, like "Frère Jacques", "I Come From A Land Down Under" and "Danny Boy". Well, truth be told, they sang and I did my usual impression of a cat being put through a mangle. The skies were now blue, with just the odd white cloud helping to occasionally temper the strength of the sun's rays, as the temperature began to rise. And the ground before us also began to rise, as we climbed out of the valley in which Orio rested. The landscape around us now had an opportunity to look resplendent in the afternoon sunshine and it certainly didn't disappoint. At one point we stopped at an elevated position to drink in the beautiful view over vineyard upon vineyard stretching back down the valley towards Orio. Pierre, being a stereotypical Frenchman, knew a thing or two about wine and he informed us that some very fine wines came from the Basque region. He recommended that we try *"chacoli"* at the first available opportunity. With mouth-watering relish he described it as a light and crisp white wine that was not too strong and very refreshing. It was only then that I realised that this was what Spanish Toni had been trying to advise me to drink at lunchtime. Ah well, there would, no doubt, be plenty more opportunities to sample it along the way.

Regrettably, our happy trio parted ways just before Zarautz, as I wanted to take the coastal route into the town, which would join the two and a half kilometre long beach at its eastern end, while Pierre and Kelly were keen to take the shorter and more direct route by road. Zarautz was another beautiful spot and I was glad I had chosen it for my first rest day. I had only been walking for two days so far, but following my experiences of walking the Ulster Way the previous year, I knew that it was best to build things up gradually. I waved goodbye to Pierre and Kelly and headed towards the coastal path that wound around the top of Mount Talaimendi. At the top of the hill there was a lookout point, which originally was a watchtower for whale hunting. Thankfully it now simply provided superb views down over the beach and town. The path eventually led me down off Mount Talaimendi, where I picked up a long boardwalk along the top of the wonderful sandy beach that stretched the length of Zarautz. As was the case when I arrived in San Sebastian, I watched with envy as a number of surfers made the most of the beautiful, peeling waves that were rolling into the wide bay. I promised myself that I would seek out a surf shop the following day and rent a wetsuit and surfboard if the waves held up. I followed the beach to around its midpoint and then reluctantly turned my back on the sea and headed into town in search of my accommodation for the night. It had become very warm at this late afternoon stage of the day and my energy levels were beginning to flag.

I stopped in a small square to study my map and try to get my bearings and directions to the hostel. Here I was very fortunate to run into the 'Spanish Ten' once again. It turned out that they were booked into the same hostel as me, so I tagged along with them as they seemed to know where they were going and I didn't. We arrived at the hostel at about 2.30pm, but a sign on the door said that it wouldn't open until 4pm. So we all headed to a little cafe across the square from the hostel to have a drink and a rest while we waited on the *hospitalero* to show up.

Registration at each hostel on the Camino generally followed a set pattern. First you surrendered your passport and your *credenciál* (pilgrim passport) to the *hospitalero*. He/she recorded the necessary details (name, nationality, last stop, etc.) in their ledger and then stamped your *credenciál* with the hostels unique *sello* (stamp). You may then be allocated a particular bed, but more often than not you are simply shown or directed to a dorm and left to choose your own – or settle for whatever's left. This being a private hostel, as opposed to a municipal *albergue*, we were each allocated a particular bunk and also had the luxury of being allocated a locker for personal use. Lockers were rarely provided in the municipal hostels, but as most pilgrims lived very minimally out of their rucksacks, this was generally not a problem. And in my experience security was never an issue on the

Camino, where everyone seemed to trust everyone else. Although this may not have always been the case.

I had recently learned about a pilgrim who had been caught thieving in Zarautz. He had been subsequently tortured and mutilated and then had his 'bits and pieces' put on display. I hasten to add that this particularly nasty incident actually happened around 430 years before my arrival in Zarautz. The unfortunate pilgrim in question, who had come from Genoa in Italy, had stolen a number of artefacts from the *Iglesia de Nuestra Señora la Real*, a church in the town. However, he had been captured before he could make good his escape and was subsequently put to death by being drawn and quartered. Thankfully nothing remains of the morbid site where the gruesome remains of the pilgrim were once exhibited, presumably as a warning to other pilgrims who might have had robbery on their minds. However, the *Iglesia de Nuestra Señora la Real* apparently contains the tomb of its 'pilgrim thief'. Well, they do say that a criminal always returns to the scene of the crime!

After being allocated a bunk in an eight-bed room, I patiently waited on the ten Spanish pilgrims to clear the washroom before performing my own washing duties. Regular washing on the Camino was of course essential, both of oneself and of one's clothes – not necessarily in that order and often together, saving time and water. Later, all freshened up and my washing hung out to dry, I entered the hostel's small common area only to meet up with Miguel and Rory once again. The three of us spent a bit of time chatting and sharing advice on dealing with blisters and aches and pains and the like – fairly standard Camino chat. Thankfully, I was faring well and not suffering any problems at this stage. Both Miguel and Rory had some minor issues, but nothing too serious – although you wouldn't have thought it to listen to Miguel. He really was a bit of a drama queen.

After our evening meals, Miguel headed to his bunk at about 9pm, while Rory and I sat chatting in the common area for about another hour. Like me, he had also encountered a few problems in the early stages. In addition to his mistaking Pasajes for the first stage end point the previous day, I also finally discovered why I had lost track of him at Biarritz Airport. Apparently, he had indeed followed a large group of pilgrims from the plane on to a train heading to Sant Jean Pied de Port, which is the starting point for the Camino Frances – a totally different route to the Camino del Norte. It was only when he noticed that everyone seemed to have a different guidebook from the one he was carrying that he realised his mistake, got off the train and made his way back to the airport and then on to Irún. Anyway, he had now managed to get to Zarautz despite the setbacks. He hoped to make it all the way to Santiago de Compostela, and possibly even Finisterre, but he was on a much tighter schedule than I was. He had two big advantages over me though. Firstly was his youth. And secondly, he was also pretty fluent in Spanish. He would have been a fairly useful guy to have had around – so long as you didn't let him lead the way, that is.

*****

It was with some regret that I awoke – or rather, was awoken by the noisy 'Spanish Ten' – at around 7.30am. Unfortunately, I had to say farewell to Rory and my Spanish crew, who were all getting ready to set off on another day's walk. Miguel had already left much earlier, although no one had heard him go – like Zorro, he had simply disappeared into the night like a phantom. My regret stayed with me for a time, as part of me felt like I should have been getting up to continue walking also, rather than spending a day by the beach. However, I had learned from my Ulster Way walk, and also from a friend's experience of walking the Camino del Norte, that it is best not to over stretch yourself too early on in the process. I had deliberately planned in rest days to build up my stamina gradually and I was going to stick to my plan as best I could. I would certainly miss my encounters with all the people I had become acquainted with over the last couple of days – it was surprising how attached you became to fellow pilgrims in such a short space of time. On the plus side, however, there was that two and a half kilometres of beach and the potential for a surf in the Bay of Biscay, so, if the truth be told, my regret was a bit half-hearted.

I stayed in the hostel until just before noon, using the WiFi to book a room in Guernica for two nights later in the week. Guernica is a fairly major tourist attraction and once again I didn't want to leave accommodation to chance, particularly as I would also be stopping there for a rest day. However, I decided that I was going to take my chances with the *albergue*s again for the next couple of nights. I had messaged a couple and, although they didn't take reservations, they were fairly confident that there would be bunks available. Feeling more relaxed about my accommodation for the foreseeable future, I spent a bit of time chatting with Josepa, the young guy running the hostel (the *hospitalero*). Josepa was learning English and was doing very well, while I was still struggling with the basics of Spanish. However, Josepa taught me probably one the most useful Spanish phrases I had learned to date, which was, *"Habla mas despacio, por favor"*, which simply meant "speak more slowly, please". The Spanish do speak at a terrible rate of knots – although they probably think the same about people from Ireland. I suspected that this useful phrase would be deployed a lot in the coming days and weeks, along with *"Una cerveza, por favor"*, of course.

After gathering up my belongings and walking the short distance from the hostel to check into the Hotel Zarauz (without the 't') for the night, I spent a few hours wandering around the lovely town of Zarautz, particularly along its wonderful beach front and promenade. Zarautz is known for its long beach breaks and the waves had looked super when I had arrived in town the previous day. I had therefore been hoping that I might have got in for a surf today. Howerer, as luck would have it, the swell had all but disappeared – nothing but small waves, little 'ankle slappers', lapping on the shore.

I had a nice lunch in a busy cafe on the sea front with beautiful views over the bay. *Bocadillos* are the big thing here for lunches – essentially a heated, filled baguette. With a glass of the local beer or *chacoli* to wash it down, it was a simple yet satisfying mid-day snack. My chosen lunch venue seemed perfectly idyllic, but no matter how sublime the setting, or how tasty the food, there was always something, or more precisely 'someone', missing. That was a fact that I couldn't escape, no matter how far I walked or how far I travelled from home. I certainly hoped that I could find some peace along the Camino. Perhaps it would come at Santiago, or perhaps Finisterre? There is a tradition of 'letting go' at Finisterre on the West Coast of Spain, which I hoped to reach at the end of June. This letting go is often expressed by pilgrims through the act of burning something symbolic. I certainly wanted to let go of the heartache, but I didn't want to let go of my memories of Jacqui. And therein lay the great dichotomy – at this stage I didn't believe it was possible to let go of one without the other.

I returned to the beachfront in the evening and suffered a disappointing *menu del dia*, 'menu of the day', at a cheap and cheerful café as I sat at a table outside watching life go by. It had started raining, but there were still lots of people out walking with their umbrellas – it was just like a Bank Holiday back home. I only hoped that my 'Weather Angels' had been permitted into Spanish air space. During my Ulster Way trek, I had started to think of Jacqui and a good friend, who had also died due to ovarian cancer, as my 'Weather Angels', who had helped ensure that the worst of the weather was held back until I had completed my day's walking. And, low and behold, as I was heading back to the Hotel Zarauz, the sky started to brighten to a dusky pink glow in the west, which of course was my direction of travel on my Camino. Then, to add to the spectacle, a rainbow appeared in the sky to the East, creating a splash of vibrant colour against a dark sky. Perhaps my angels had arrived after all.

*****

I was too early for breakfast when I was ready to leave the Hotel Zarauz at 7.15am and so I decided to walk around the coast to the next town of Getaria, which was just over six kilometres away, and have breakfast there. The ground was still wet from the night before as I made my way through a waking Zarautz. However the strip of early morning blue sky visible high above me, as I passed between the tall buildings lining the narrow streets, held out the promise of a lovely day ahead. On the western edge of the town I passed by the multi-belled Zarautz Tower, which stood next to the *Iglesia de Nuestra Señora la Real*, the resting place of the sixteenth century pilgrim thief.

The walk around the coast, following the roadside footpath, was very pleasant and peppered with sights of both local fishermen and cormorants perched on rocks, all waiting patiently to catch something tasty. The views back across the bay to Mount Talaimendi, which I had descended on my approach to Zarautz two days beforehand, and the sweep of the long beach fronting the town in the early morning sunshine, were absolutely glorious. Looking towards Getaria, the town appeared to be set on a low, narrow causeway between the mainland and a mouse-shaped islet, known as El Ratón, meaning 'mouse island'. I was also struck by the sight of a large farmhouse overlooking Getaria. It was bordered by tall, narrow fir trees and perched on top of a rolling hill that was lined with perfectly ordered rows of vines. Set as it was this morning, against a pale blue sky, it presented the most idyllic pastoral scene – I could easily imagine it as a beautiful painting by Van Gogh. Looking in the opposite direction, there was still some cloud cover out to sea and the escaping silver rays, spilling down onto the water's surface, created a divine sight. The wonderful views around me that morning made it feel so good to be alive. But then, the inevitable thoughts of loss crept in once again and cast a dark shadow over my landscape. There was no escaping such feelings. They would rush in suddenly and envelop me without warning, regardless of, or perhaps because of, the beauty around me. I suppose, I was never really totally free of such feelings – they were always there, like my own

Farmhouse on a hill overlooking Getaria

personal, dark cloud following closely overhead. And at any time, that cloud could come down around me and obscure the beauty of the world and leave me feeling trapped. At such times, I simply put my head down, focused on my next objective and marched on. Sometimes I felt that if I didn't keep moving forward, I would be trapped under the cloud for ever.

Thankfully Getaria offered a few welcome distractions from my early morning melancholy, including, by this stage, a much needed breakfast. I called into a small bakery and coffee shop for a croissant and a '*café con leche*', which was essentially a flat white and a popular morning beverage amongst pilgrims. Back home, I always preferred my coffee black, but I quickly took to this milky staple, which just seemed to perfectly complement the whole character of the Camino – warm, comforting and wholesome. Getaria was a picturesque town with neat cobbled streets winding their way from the substantive monument to its most famous sailing hero, Juan Sebastián Elcano, in the town centre, down towards its busy harbour. Wandering down one such street, hemmed in by four storey buildings either side. I was confronted by the imposing tower of the 15th century *Iglesia de San Salvador* looming above the surrounding shops and houses. It was located directly ahead, apparently bringing the street to a dead end. However, as I got closer I realised that the street dog-legged around the tower and passed under an archway to continue on towards the harbour. I stepped over Elcano's tomb, just inside the doorway to the church, and entered the dark interior to explore this oddly shaped building and wonder at its peculiarly sloped wooden floor. Curiosity satisfied, I headed back up to the centre of the town to pick up the Camino route once again.

I climbed a steep, cobbled laneway up and out of Getaria and then followed dirt roads and stone tracks through gentle rural hills for a couple of kilometres before arriving at the small hill-top hamlet of Azkizu. This was home to the rather austere looking *Iglesia de San Martin de Tours*. The current church here is built over a medieval acropolis and the remains of one of the oldest Christian churches in the region, dating back to the sixth century. Apparently, a key to the church could be obtained from a local resident, but when I saw the photographs of the ancient skeletons resting in their excavated tombs displayed on an external sign, I decided to keep on moving. Trying to rid my mind of images of death and decay, I was happy to enjoy the distraction offered by a little Jack Russell dog on the road out of town as it trotted along just ahead of me, carrying a half-baguette in its mouth as it went. After a time it turned into a farmhouse and disappeared round the back – quite a unique bread delivery service. Further on, I also encountered a number of Basque ponies in a field and I was amused to see that a few of them had large bells strapped around their necks, which clanked rather un-melodically as they moved around, leisurely grazing in their field of lush grass.

As I was approaching the beach town of Zumaia, and still trying to get the morbid images from the church sign out of my head, I started thinking about all the signs and symbols that are used to mark the

Camino. I had observed quite a variety already on my walk after only five days – yellow arrows, scallop shells, red and white stripes, wooden signs, ceramic signs, and even paint daubed on walls, lampposts and rocks. This led me on to further thinking about the meaning that other signs and symbols had to me and the importance they had played in helping me cope since Jacqui had passed away. I had my Weather Angels of course; and sunshine and rainbows had often suddenly appeared to lift my spirits when most needed. The humble blackbird had also become an important symbol for me and made me think of Jacqui every time I saw one, as it had always been her favourite garden bird. I even had a little blackbird badge attached to my rucksack. All of these thoughts about the importance of signs and symbols were going through my mind as I came round the final headland before Zumaia to be met with a superb view over the town and its beach. I suddenly stopped in my tracks. I couldn't quite believe it. I was astonished to see a tractor on the beach in the process of raking the sand. But it wasn't the sight of the tractor itself that astonished me. It was the fact that at the very moment that I had arrived upon the scene, it had just inscribed a huge 'J' in the sand. Call me a silly, sentimental fool if you want, but at that very moment my heart soared. It was surely a 'J' for Jacqui. I had come to learn that, when dealing with profound loss, there was an almost irresistible urge to look upon what are surely mere coincidences and elevate them to the status of signs from somewhere beyond this mortal life. There was little doubt that the 'writing in the sand' was man-made, but it was so easy for me to convince my vulnerable heart that there were other more heavenly forces at work. I therefore did not question the validity of my signs, but accepted them all too readily as messages from my loved one.

After taking time out to wonder at my latest revelation, I proceeded on into town, now with a bit more of a spring in my step. Zumaia was another beautiful coastal town, located on the River Urola and backed by the soft, green peaks of the Aizkorri Mountains in the distance. Crossing the footbridge over the river provided me with a clear view downstream towards the main part of the town, which was dominated

A 'sign' written in the sand at Zumaia

by the imposing and elevated edifice of the 15th century *Iglesia de San Pedro*. Upon reaching it, I wandered round the church and got a sore neck from continuously peering skyward to take in the gargoyles that protruded from the walls of the building, high up and seeming to defy gravity.

I left Zumaia behind and followed further dirt and gravel tracks through grass-covered hills for about three kilometres. Just beyond the small village of Elorriaga, I once again branched away from the official Camino route and opted instead for the alternative GR route, following the red and white markings along the coast towards Deba, my final destination for the day. This route zigzagged along the coastline for about seven and a half kilometres and it proved to be quite tough going in the afternoon heat. However, once again the visual rewards on offer made it all very worthwhile. One of the main benefits of taking this particular GR route was that it brought me to an incredible geological feature that the Camino route completely by-passes. This is the 'flysch', the longest set of continuous rock strata in the world. They date from the mid-cretaceous period to the present, a time period of over 100 million years, and stretch for a distance of about eight kilometres. But impressive statistics aside, the rock formations just simply looked spectacular, particularly when fully revealed at low tide, as they were when I happened upon them. It was almost as impressive as the Giant's Causeway rock formation on the north coast of Ireland and, indeed, in places it looked as if Finn McCool's Spanish cousin had used a giant rake to create an immense striated pattern across the shelf of rock as it stretched out from the cliffs for a hundred metres or more, before gradually disappearing into the pale blue waters in the Bay of Biscay.

The day became hotter and the terrain more challenging and it was late in the afternoon before I arrived into the pretty town square of Deba feeling very hot and sticky. I was looking forward to having a shower and getting freshened up properly. However, I discovered that the tourist office, where it was necessary to register for the local *albergue*, didn't open for another hour. So, I joined a couple from Canada, Diane and Mike, at a table outside a bar in the square and enjoyed a welcome cold beer.

The *albergue* in Deba, when we eventually got registered and settled in, was above a railway station, but very fresh and clean and surprisingly quiet. After showering, I relaxed in the common room for a time sorting through the day's photographs, writing my blog and responding to messages from home, before heading out to find somewhere to eat. By chance I met a German pilgrim, named Bernd, in a restaurant just off the main square and I joined him for the pilgrim *menu del dia*. We were served some pretty strange looking Basque dishes, but it all tasted surprisingly good; and at only €10 each, including a bottle of pretty acceptable red wine, it was fantastic value. A full bottle of wine each seemed a bit much, but, then again, there wasn't much of it left by the end of the night.

Bernd had been walking for about five weeks every year for the last three years. He had started his Camino in his home town of Stuttgart and had walked southwest through Germany and France and finally, this year, into Spain. He was also a keen photographer and like me he was always stopping along the way to photograph anything that caught his eye. He told me that he often took pictures of things that other people might pass right by, because they were in too much of a rush or didn't consider it worth photographing. He then searched his phone to show me an example. He had over 600 pictures of this year's trip stored on his phone and when he selected just one to show me, I was astounded. It was a photo of a street sign showing two walkers, a man followed by a woman. The thing was; someone had drawn angel wings onto the figure of the woman. I couldn't believe it. A pilgrim being followed by an angel. Out of all the photos he could have selected, that was the one he randomly chose to show me. I explained the significance of it to him and he was also amazed. Coming on the same day as I had witnessed my remarkable 'J' in the sand at Zumaia, it was another unexpected and very special moment. I had certainly hoped to experience something special on my Camino, but I had never dreamt that it would occur so early on. I wondered what other surprises might lay in store for me as I continued with my pilgrimage.

Year 44 AD

Hermogenes turned lugubriously and moved out of the dark shadows where he had been silently contemplating his next move. "If only that charlatan had stayed in Iberia, we could have ignored him", scowled the sorcerer. "By all accounts, he was having very little success there."

"Yes Master" Philetus agreed. "I understand that he had only managed to convert nine disciples to his so called 'Christianity' in all the time he was there. Hardly what anyone would call a resounding success."

"Certainly not. He was little threat to us while he was wasting his time trying to reach those pagan imbeciles in Galicia. But now the fool has seen fit to return to Judea with seven of his followers and seems intent on stirring things up among our very own people with his deceitful preaching. I really thought that Jesus Christ being crucified would have put an end to all this dangerous nonsense. We simply cannot allow such heresy to continue unchallenged Philetus."

Philetus knew only too well that his Master only used his given name when he was about to ask him to do something secretive. The tall, gangly figure of the sorcerer was now standing close, towering over him and staring down at his face, like a dark bird of prey ready to swoop.

"What do you wish me to do, Master?" asked Philetus.

"I want you to keep a very close eye on this apostle of Christ, known as James. I want you to follow his every move; listen to his every word and bring me back evidence of the falsehood that he preaches. And then we will crush him and his followers." Hermogenes closed his fist into a tight ball before Philetus' face as the word 'crush' escaped from his thin lips in a hiss moist with venom.

Over the coming days, Philetus did as he had been instructed and watched the apostle James closely. But the more he saw of the apostle and the miracles he performed, the more he came to believe in James' preaching and in the word of the Lord. Philetus returned to Hermogenes and told him that he was certain that the preaching of James was true and that he himself was going to become one of James' disciples. "Master, I saw him perform many wondrous miracles. There is no doubt in my mind that I must follow the Lord God Jesus Christ. I am going to become a Christian and, please Master, I urge you to do likewise."

On hearing this blasphemy, the sorcerer Hermogenes was enraged and, summoning his dark powers, he cast a spell over Philetus. The servant felt his limbs grow so weak that he slumped to the floor and found that he could no longer move, except to speak. "Please Master, I beg you to release me."

The sorcerer laughed down at Philetus and said "Now let's see how mighty your beloved apostle is. Now we shall see if your James can save you." He stormed off, calling behind him, "I will send word to your family to come and remove your traitorous carcass from my home."

Chapter Two: Buen Camino
(Days six to nine – Deba to Zamudio)

I awoke early in the Deba *albergue*. You don't really have much choice when you're sharing a room with four other *peregrinos*. It was about 8am though before I had gathered everything up and got myself organised to leave. I was almost the last to vacate the *albergue* – I was going to have to speed up my morning routine. I had a coffee and a neopolitana at a local café, bought some fruit in a local supermarket and then attempted to pick up the Camino route once again. After being helped by a local woman, I eventually found my way onto the footbridge that crossed the Río Deba. I then started to climb a track that took me both higher into the forested hills and further inland. It would be a few days before I sensed the taste of salt in the air once again.

The early part of today's walk was the most pleasant, with its cooler temperatures and the wonderful birdsong that accompanied me as I climbed up through the forest paths. These were not the dreary, boring commercial forests that I had often experienced on my Ulster Way walk the previous year, but lovely natural woodlands that had probably been here for centuries. It became much tougher though, as the heat of the day built into the high 20s. Lots of forest clearings started to appear along the path, leaving me more exposed to the full glare of the sun. The terrain became incredibly varied, with forest tracks, tarmac roads, concrete pathways, muddy lanes and rocky trails all combining to ensure that this section fully earned its maximum rating of five for difficulty in my guidebook. And I wasn't surprised to read that today's walk involved a total ascent of 915 metres.

After all the uphill climbing, the final 2km approach to Markina-Xemein was down a long, steep, rocky track. And it was while descending this track that I first met Ron from Holland. It was a very fortuitous encounter because, in addition to being great company, Ron was also an expert in the practice of 'Comanche running'. He was a big fan of the old style western movies and from these he had learned how to do what he called a 'Comanche run' when negotiating a steep slope. He showed me how to do it and it was actually very effective and I would come to use it many times during the rest of my Camino. It basically involved trying to keep everything above the knees steady and letting the lower legs do all the work, with feet turned out, letting momentum carry you forward and down. It may all sound very strange, but we had a great laugh careering down the dusty track, getting lots of bemused looks from other pilgrims as we hurried past them like two idiots who had been out in the sun for too long.

Before we knew it, we were at the bottom of the hill and entering the outskirts of Markina-Xemein. Here we came across a highly unusual church; the hexagonal Sanctuary of *San Miguel de Arrechinaga*. The church was founded in the eleventh century, but it was neither its age nor its shape that made it so unusual. As we stepped through the doorway to look inside, we were confronted with the sight of a church interior entirely dominated by three huge boulders. Bizarre was the word that immediately sprung to mind. The three giant, odd-shaped boulders, that appeared to support each other, are said to be millions of years old and are probably the naturally eroded remains of a huge rock outcrop from the hillside. At some point in the past, the boulders had gained some sort of religious association and, according to legend, a local hermit called Saint Pollonio came to live under them in the middle-ages. A medieval chapel was subsequently built around the stones, but it fell into ruin and then, in the eighteenth century, the present chapel was built over the ruins, again surrounding the giant boulders. A splendid figure of *San Miguel*, Saint Michael, sword in hand and standing over a serpent, stood against one wall of the chapel. Another local legend claims that Saint Michael killed and then buried the devil beneath the boulders long before a church was built on the site. And, in a site positively coming down with local legends, another one says that a young man must pass three times underneath the huge stones if he wishes to be married the following year. This strange ritual apparently still takes place. I had no desire to seek a new

Three huge boulders dominate the interior of the Sanctuary of San Miguel de Arrechinaga

wife, but even if I had, I'm afraid that I hadn't fitted the description of 'young man' for many years now.

Ron hung back in the church and I allowed him some personal space. Despite the history and legends surrounding this unique little church, I was to find no sanctuary here. I pushed on into the centre of town to join a small group of pilgrims waiting for the local *albergue* to open. Ron soon arrived and half an hour later we had all booked into the *albergue*, which was located inside the *Convento de los Padres Carmelitas*. It was a huge building, but apparently there were only three nuns in residence. I secured a bunk in a mixed dorm with nine other pilgrims, including Ron. He warned me about a group of snoring and farting Germans who were also in the dorm and that he had had the 'pleasure' of sharing a dorm with the previous night. I wondered if I might have to move my mattress into the reception area if things got too claustrophobic or aromatic. The volunteer *hospitalero* who looked after the *albergue* was called Jesus. He was a small, stocky man with a broad smiling face, accentuated by a thick, dark moustache and he made everyone feel very welcome. He had an Alsatian dog called Pride, which was recovering from a spinal operation, and it lay very patiently at its owners sandaled feet, as Jesus meticulously recorded all the details of each pilgrim; name, country, age, passport number, etc. I joked with Ron that it was lovely to meet Jesus on the Camino and that "dog" was "god" spelt backwards – he thought this was hilarious. I was just happy to have finally found someone who appreciated my corny jokes.

Later, Ron and I, along with a few others, enjoyed a few beers in an attractive square next to a public park, which was full of young children playing happily in the early evening sunshine. We then had a meal in the small but cheery Restaurante Pitis, close to the *albergue*, which turned out to be very good indeed. Back at the *albergue* and everyone was in bed by 9.30pm, except me. I still hadn't quite adjusted to the Camino routine of bedding down at such an early hour. I eventually turned in at around 11pm. I then discovered how difficult it was getting into a sleeping bag, on the top bunk, in the dark, while trying not to disturb everyone else in the room.

*****

Our dorm started to stir at about 6.30am. I hadn't slept particularly well, but not due to any snoring and farting Germans. My lack of sleep was mainly due to the loud creaking noises the door made every time the owner of a weak bladder headed out to the toilets. There must have been quite a few weak bladders as the disturbance seemed to go on throughout the night; either that or it was just one person with a very serious problem. Regardless, I must have got sufficient rest though, as I didn't feel tired at all when I climbed down from my bunk. Ron and I naturally fell in with each other again as we left the convent. Ron thought it strange that we hadn't seen a nun during all the time we were there. I then told Ron that when I was eating with Bernd in Deba two nights before, he had been trying to describe the convent in Markina-

Xemein to me. He had struggled to recall the English word for a convent and instead said, "You know, the place where the monks' wives live". At the time, the mouthful of wine I had just taken almost ended up being sprayed over the table.

Ron and I had walked all of 50 metres before we diverted into a little café to have breakfast. My guidebook warned that there may be no further opportunities for food before reaching Guernica, so we judged it best to eat before leaving town. We ordered coffees and filled croissants and while we were waiting, two South Korean women from the *albergue* came into the café and ordered coffees to go. They were stereotypically polite and deferential in their manner and they were both carrying quite substantial rucksacks for their petite frames. They collected their drinks and shuffled out again smiling and bowing graciously as they went. Ron and I sat on to have our breakfasts and probably left the café about 15 minutes later. So we were very surprised, after we had walked a kilometre out of Markina-Xemein, to meet the two South Korean women coming back again. They explained that they had left the café and forgotten to pay and were now heading back to put things right. It was certainly very honest of them to head all the way back, particularly to somewhere that would probably never see them again – and all for the sake of a couple of euros. After we waved them off once again, Ron and I pondered as to whether we would have been quite as honourable as the South Korean women if we had left without paying. I'm sorry to say that we weren't at all certain that we would have been.

We left the streets of Markina-Xemein to join a narrow dirt path that ran through some woods and alongside the Río Artibar. After about five kilometres we passed through the small town of Bolibar, ancestral home of Simón Bolívar, one of the greatest *'libertadores'* (liberators) of Spanish America, as acknowledged by the stone monument to him in the town's main square. We continued heading inland, mainly through wooded areas and rural farmland. The weather was perfect for walking most of the day and Ron was very good company. We were both the same age, in our mid-fifties, and had a fair bit in common. Our paces matched very well and we were both very happy to walk alongside each other for the whole day. He had a similar sense of humour to mine and he made me laugh quite a bit along the way, which helped pass the time nicely. Some of Ron's humour was intentional, but there was also some unintended humour arising out of his misunderstanding of some English words and phrases. His English was generally good, but understandably on occasions he appeared to struggle with some of the finer points. When I read from my guidebook that we would soon be joining a 'medieval' monks road, Ron quite seriously asked me if I knew what had made the monks so 'mad and evil'.

The 'mad and evil' monks road actually led to an oasis of peace and calm that was the *Monasterio de Zenarruza*. A striking stone carving above the monastery's entrance, of an eagle holding a human skull in its talons, depicted the legend that an eagle had brought a skull here from a nearby crypt and it was this that prompted the monastery's construction. I had come across similar stories in Ireland, where churches had been built in a particular location purely on the basis that a bird had carried something significant there – nothing as dramatic as an eagle with a skull though. It was simply wonderful to wander round the tranquil grounds of this fourteenth century monastery and to visit its beautifully serene cloister. However, the experience of serenity was only truly complete when I pressed my ear to the locked doors of the church and listened to the Cistercian monks evocative chanting as they performed their mass. Despite the solemnity of the moment, I couldn't help wondering if their wives were busy back in the monastery kitchens preparing lunch.

After resting in the grounds of the monastery for a short while, Ron and I returned to the Camino route and headed further into the hilly countryside, following a rocky path for a few kilometres before descending into the village of Munitibar. At one point along the way, we heard a very rapid "tat-tat-tat-tat…" in the woods, like someone was beating a couple of sticks repeatedly against a hollow wooden tube. Ron informed me that it was a woodpecker at work. Woodpeckers are a very rare visitor to Northern Ireland and, never having heard one before in real life, I wasn't convinced by Ron's explanation; not until I spotted a tree with a couple of neat, round holes bored into its trunk – a tell-tale sign of the presence of woodpeckers for sure. We didn't manage to spot any of the elusive birds though, but it was still a treat to hear their strange, almost eerie sound reverberate through the woods.

We decided to stop in Munitibar for a short break, as we still had another 14km to go to Guernica. We discovered a little place slightly off route where we could buy some supplies. It was a bizarre little establishment, with the shop in a back room where you could pick what you wanted and then head to the bar area to pay. Here you had to wait your turn to be dealt with by the one, dour, little dynamo of a man who was doing everything from making coffees, cooking food, serving drinks and handling the check-out till. He managed all these tasks with great ease and control, with his head down so as to avoid making eye contact with anyone, but at the same time seemingly fully aware of everything that was going on around him and who was next to be served. There was no point in trying to attract his attention – he would simply get to you when he was good and ready and not a second before. Once we had finally made our purchases, we sat outside on a bench against the wall in the bright afternoon sunshine and ate our lunches.

Then we were off again to follow a combination of minor roads and riverside footpaths. At one point we came across a group of three stone crosses standing together on a small hill. It wasn't the first trio of crosses we had encountered and Ron wondered what their significance was. On this occasion, I was able to supply an answer. I told him that I believed that they were the Three Crosses of Calvary, which represented Jesus' Cross in the centre and a cross on each side representing the two thieves who had been crucified with Jesus at Calvary. I remembered reading this somewhere and, although I wasn't

Ron reaches out to a nervous young foal on the outskirts of Guernica

entirely sure as to its authenticity, it sounded like a very plausible explanation. Anyway, I spoke with a suitable conviction that had Ron happily nodding in agreement.

We passed a field with a number of Basque ponies and foals. We both stopped at the fence and one brown and white mare immediately came over to us for some attention which we happily provided. Ron clearly loved horses just as much as I did. The mare's brown foal, which looked to be only a couple of weeks old, hung back for a long time, watching it's mother from a safe distance, before it very slowly and hesitantly made its way towards us. Although it finally stretched out it's nuzzle to sniff a hand, it remained very cautious and never came within petting distance, regardless of how far we stretched over the fence to try and reach it.

As Ron and I were entering Guernica we unfortunately had to part company, as he was going to an *albergue* and I had already booked into a pension for the next two nights. Tomorrow he would be heading to

Bilbao, while I would be having another day off as I wanted to see round some of Guernica. However, I once again experienced the mix of regret at parting company with a fellow pilgrim who I had enjoyed spending time with and relief at knowing my body was going to get a welcome rest. We shook hands and promised to stay in touch as best we could.

I made my way on alone through the streets of Guernica town to locate my pension. It was centrally located on a busy street, but my room was on the third floor and at the rear of the block and turned out to be very quiet and comfortable. I had crossed paths briefly with Bernd again earlier and we had agreed to meet at the Tourist Office at 6pm. So after getting settled into my pension and freshened up, I met with him as planned and we sat at one of the many bars with seating out on the paved pedestrian area of Pablo Picasso Kalea – *kalea* being Basque for street. It was another warm and sunny evening and after a few leisurely beers to whet our appetites, we went for something to eat. We bumped into Sue, another pilgrim who Bernd knew, and she was happy to join us. We didn't have to look too far to find our restaurant for the evening – there were plenty to choose from and they all looked pretty decent. Once we were seated, I discovered that although Sue was English, she had lived in Belize for many years. Prior to settling there, she appeared to have lived all over the world in her 70-plus years. She had led a very colourful life and she entertained Bernd and me with her tales from around the globe. We had a fantastic meal in the restaurant. It was so good that I planned to return the following night.

*****

I spent my day off exploring Guernica and the surrounding area. I first took a train out to the picturesque coastal town of Mundaka. I wandered round its narrow streets, the sheltered beach and the pretty harbour area and enjoyed the exterior grandeur of both the *Iglesia de Santa Maria* church and the *Basilica Santa Katalina*, before boarding the train again for the short journey back into Guernica.

I needed to buy an adaptor plug to replace the one I had left behind somewhere and I eventually found one in a little hardware store as I was making my way back into the centre of Guernica. My attempts at communicating with the store's proprietor reminded me of the Two Ronnies famous and very funny 'Four Candles/Fork Handles' sketch. Having looked up the Spanish word for plug and told him what I wanted, the elderly proprietor, complete with brown shop coat and stepladder, spent ages rummaging around in boxes on the top shelves and then proudly presented me with a rubber plug for a wash basin! After explaining a bit more and pointing to an electric socket behind the counter, he rolled his eyes and disappeared up the step ladder again and a few minutes later came back with the correct item.

I then set off for Calle Allende Salazar to find the sight that I had wanted to see ever since I realised I would be passing through Guernica. Although only a ceramic tile reproduction of the original painting by Picasso called "Guernica" (which is on display in Madrid), it is still a dramatic and powerful work of art. The painting was created by Pablo Picasso, following a brutal attack on Guernica in 1937, as a warning to the world of the savagery of fascist military regimes. During the Spanish Civil War, on 26 April 1937, the combined 'mad and evil' dictatorships of Franco, Mussolini and Hitler led to the saturation bombing of Guernica and the subsequent strafing of fleeing townspeople. It was market day in Guernica when the attack occurred and the town was packed with villagers. The attack resulted in the town being destroyed and hundreds, perhaps even thousands, killed. The painting captures the horror of the destruction in a typical Picasso style, with bodies all distorted and disjointed. I'm not a massive fan of Picasso's cubism, but it's a style that matches the subject matter perfectly on this occasion and manages to convey the nightmare and horror of war to great effect. After taking some time to consider the simple and powerful message behind the imagery, I visited the nearby Guernica peace museum, which was incredibly moving. I couldn't help but compare the horror and disbelief etched on the faces captured in the grainy black and white photos on display with similar images

Ceramic tile reproduction of the painting by Picasso called "Guernica"

captured over the years of atrocities in Northern Ireland, including in my home town of Omagh. Pain is pain; grief is grief; loss is loss; no matter where you happen to call home. Unfortunately, Picasso's warning continues to go unheeded, but the new town of Guernica serves as a testimony to the resilience of its people and their capacity to move on from tragedy and rebuild.

When I came out of the museum in the late afternoon, the rain was pouring down and the temperature had dropped to a cool 15 degrees. It was certainly appropriate weather for the sombre mood that inevitably followed me out onto the streets of Guernica as I left the museum. I dashed over the wet pavements back to my pension and got freshened up and then spent a bit of time catching up on my blogs. Later I headed back to the same restaurant as the night before. The food was just as good but the atmosphere just wasn't the same without the company of Bernd and Sue, who, unlike me, had re-joined the Camino that morning. The restaurant was much quieter than the night before – in fact, I was its only customer – and it was a rather sad and lonely dining experience.

As I sat alone, I once again wondered if I was doing the right thing by allowing my new friends to get ahead of me each time I stopped for a rest day. However, I was happy that I had taken the time to explore Mundaka and Guernica and I was content to not rush ahead. I had time on my side and I didn't want to be dragged along with the steady flow of pilgrims at the expense of missing out on valuable experiences along the way. I had learned that life can be extremely fragile and all too short and I didn't want to rush ahead towards the end without taking time to appreciate the journey – this applied both to the Camino and to life in general. A half remembered line from a song came to mind, "Time's always running out the door you're running in". No-one can stop time running out, but you can certainly take your time getting to the door. Besides, if I hadn't stopped in Guernica I might never have met Jane and that would have been a shame.

I had drained my glass of its last drop of red wine and was waiting for the bill, when a woman about my own age appeared at the door of the restaurant. She saw the place was empty, apart from me and a bored waitress, and seemed about to leave, when she caught my eye and smiled warmly.

"You look like a lonely pilgrim sitting there," she said.

"Yeah, it must have been something I said," I replied. "What makes you think I'm a pilgrim, by the way?"

"The dress sense and the empty bottle of wine kind of gives it away."

"It's that obvious is it? You look like you're off to the disco yourself."

She was wearing a rather unflattering mix of walking gear and had a green neckerchief tied loosely around her neck.

"Touché," she laughed, before explaining that she was looking for her friend that she was walking the Camino with. She had thought that he might have been at this restaurant as they had heard that it was good.

"It is," I said. "Why don't you come in and wait to see if he shows up. I'll buy you a coffee if you like. I was just about to leave, but I wouldn't mind a bit of company before heading back to my lonely pension for the night."

"You sure there's room?" she quipped. I liked her immediately. She had an easy, relaxed way about her. No airs and graces. She closed the door behind her and pulled up a chair at my table. "Dermot" I said, reaching out my hand.

"Hi Dermot, I'm Jane," she said as she shook my hand gently.

"Pleased to meet you," we both said in unison as the waitress approached the table with my bill.

"Sorry," I said to her "Would you mind bringing us two coffees instead please?" The waitress gave me a strange look, but then turned and headed back to the kitchen to place my order.

"So you've come from Markina-Xemein today," I said. "Did you stay at the *albergue* in the convent in the centre of town?" She nodded and I then asked, "You met Jesus and his dog Pride then?" I decided against risking my Jesus and God joke.

"Ah yeah, I sure did. He was an absolute dear and he really doted on that poor dog."

We talked about our experiences on the Camino and our coffees soon arrived. Jane had started out from Irún a couple of days after me, but she had not taken any days off as I had.

"Well you've caught up with me now, so I guess you can take things a bit easier from here on," I said.

She nearly choked on her coffee. "You're a quare laugh, you are."

"Ah, it's great to hear an expression from home," I said. "Whereabouts are you from anyway?" I knew from her accent that Jane was from somewhere in Northern Ireland, but beyond that I found it hard to pin her down.

"Oh, I used to live in Belfast, but I moved from there a while back," was her vague answer and, even before I had decided not to press her further on it, she asked. "So why are you walking the Camino?"

It was now my turn to be vague. I didn't feel like unburdening my soul to a stranger I had just met, even if she was from back home and very friendly. "Ah, I just felt I needed a bit of time and space to myself you know. Things back home have been rather difficult over the past year and I needed to escape for a bit. Sort myself out, you know."

"Ah, so you're here to find yourself? You and a hundred or so others. Jeez, with the number of people out here trying to find themselves, we should all get together and form a big search party," she laughed.

I laughed along, although I felt a little uneasy at her making light of my plight. Of course that was my own fault, as I hadn't exactly been straight with her.

"What about yourself," I asked before she could detect anything other than humour on my face, "why are you walking the Camino?"

"Hmm, well, I actually never planned to do the Camino. My friend wanted to do it and wanted someone to come with him. I was at a loose end and so here I am. We have a very flexible arrangement though and so we're not together all the time. We're not a couple or anything like that, but I like to keep an eye on him. He's quite capable of looking after himself, but he's also a little vulnerable."

Before she had time to elaborate further, the waitress approached our table again and said the restaurant was closing early. I couldn't blame them as it had been so quiet and it didn't look like things were going to pick up, even given the Spanish custom of dining late. Jane said it was time she was moving anyway to get back to her *albergue* before its doors were locked. So I settled the bill and we left the restaurant to go on our separate ways.

"*Buen Camino* Jane," I said, before we parted, "I hope we meet again."

"Oh, I'm sure we will," she said with a smile, before she turned and headed off for her *albergue*.

I watched her go until she disappeared around the corner at the end of the street. Turning to head back to my pension, I found that thoughts of the enigmatic Jane wouldn't leave my mind. I really hoped that I would meet her again.

*****

I woke up to rain and after a quick breakfast I gathered up my rucksack and stepped out once again onto the wet streets of Guernica. I soon picked up the Camino route heading out of town, which brought me past the slightly confused looking Gothic-Renaissance style *Iglesia de Santa María* and the *Casa de Juntas*, an important meeting place for the Basque government. In the grounds of the *Casa de Juntas*, enclosed in an elaborate rotunda, was the stump of a legendary oak tree known as the *Gernikako Arbola*, or the Tree of Guernica. By ancient tradition, Basques held assemblies under a tree, usually an oak, to discuss matters affecting their communities. Over the centuries, as Guernica became more prominent, the *Gernikako Arbola* acquired particular importance and it eventually became symbolic of the traditional rights of the Basque people. The trees are always renewed from their own acorns and the newest oak tree, the fifth, was planted in March 2015, while the tree stump in the rotunda is the remains of the "Old Tree" that lived until the 19th century.

I left the paved streets of Guernica behind and picked up a track heading through a heavily wooded area. It rained for most of the morning, but it was quite magical to see the mist blowing through the tree tops in the forests across the valley – what Jacqui would have called dragon's breath. With the rain, the reduced temperatures and the paths through leafy woods, I almost felt that I was back walking the Ulster Way again.

The persistent rain resulted in some very muddy, and very slippery, sections, particularly on the forest tracks. I literally grew a few inches taller at one point, as the sticky mud gradually built up under the soles of my boots. I eventually had to stop and find a stone to scrape off the layers of dirt from my boots as they were becoming so difficult to walk in. Then, a little later, I figuratively grew a few inches taller, when a lady suddenly called out *"Buen Camino"* to me from the upstairs window of her house as I passed by. *Buen Camino* is a traditional greeting for pilgrims that simply means 'good walk'. Many of the local people here appear to have a great respect for pilgrims, or *peregrinos*.

Back in the twelfth century, a French scholar, monk and pilgrim called Aymeric Picaud, is believed to have written the Codex Calixtinus. It was, essentially, one of the earliest known tourist guidebooks, giving background information for pilgrims travelling the Way of Saint James. One chapter is entitled 'How to treat Peregrinos' and offers the following advice:

"Pilgrims, poor or rich, whether coming or going to the place of St James, must be received charitably and respected by all peoples. Many have met with God's anger because they did not want to look after pilgrims to St James, and the needy.

"At Nantua, a town between Geneva and Lyon, a weaver, repeatedly denying bread to a beseeching pilgrim of St James, found the cloth on his loom suddenly ripped away and crashing down.

"At Villeneuve, a poor pilgrim of St James asked for alms from a woman who had bread under hot cinders, who replied that she did not have any. The pilgrim said to her, 'May the bread you have turn to stone.' When he left her house and was far away, the woman went to the cinders, thinking the bread was there, and found a round stone in place of the bread.

"At the city of Poitiers, two French veterans returning from Santiago without anything to call their own, looked for hospitality from the house of Joannis Gauterius all the way to St Porchaire, without finding it. In the very last house of the street, next to the basilica of St Porcarius, they were given hospitality at the home of a poor man, and by the working of divine vengeance, that night the swiftest fire burned the whole street, from the house where they had first asked for hospitality, all the way to the one which received them, and there were about 1,000 houses. And truly, by the grace of God, the home remained in which the servants of God were guests.

"Which is why it should be known, that peregrinos of Santiago, poor or wealthy, in justice should be taken in, and diligently attended to."

So perhaps the locals respect for modern day pilgrims walking the Camino de Santiago, came more from a deep seated fear or superstition that something nasty might befall them if they were not nice to the travellers, rather than out of any genuine reverence. However, I was happy to take any kindness shown to me in the spirit it was hopefully intended. I waved and called *"Gracias"* back to the woman at the window and continued on my way, feeling a few inches taller as a result.

The more I learned about Aymeric Picaud though, the more I doubted that the Spanish would have had much respect for him, regardless of whether he was a pilgrim or not. In his 'guidebook' he provides some descriptions of the places and peoples he met while on his pilgrimage and they are often very far from flattering. For example, Navarre is a region in northern Spain, which the Camino Frances passes through and which I came close to while walking between Irún and San Sebastian. Its capital and largest city is Pamplona, famous for its annual running of the bulls. Here's what good old Aymeric had to say about the locals of Navarre.

"Navarrese eating and drinking habits are disgusting. The entire family – servant, master, maid, mistress – feed with their hands from one pot in which all the food is mixed together, and swill from one cup, like pigs or dogs. And when they speak, their language sounds so raw, it's like hearing a dog bark. These are an undeveloped people, with different customs and characteristics than other races. They're malicious, dark, hostile-looking types, crooked, perverse, treacherous, corrupt and untrustworthy, obsessed with sex and booze, steeped in violence, wild, savage, condemned and rejected, sour, horrible, and squabbling. They are badness and nastiness personified, utterly lacking in any good qualities. In some places, when they get warmed up, the men and women show off their private parts to each other. The Navarrese also have sex with their farm animals. And it's said that they put a lock on the backsides of their mules and horses so that nobody except themselves can have at them."

Somehow, I couldn't see the Navarre Tourist Board wanting to use this description in their promotional material. However, maybe it goes some way to explaining why those bulls seem so angry when chasing through the crowds in Pamplona each year.

I took shelter from the rain for a short time under the extensive portico of the Church of Saints Emeterio and Celedonio in the small village of Goikolexea. It was a peaceful spot to rest for a while and to have a bite to eat. The church dates from the sixteenth century and is dedicated to the memory of two Roman legionnaires who were martyred for their Christian faith. I joined the road again and pushed on for another one and a half kilometres to Larrabezu, a pretty little town that displayed a number of notices at prominent locations declaring that the land I was now standing in was not Spain, or France, but Basque country. I had spotted a fair bit of graffiti on the way that, in common with these notices, called for the Basque right to self-determination and for the repatriation of all prisoners to Basque country. Although the violence and the armed struggle of the past had been brought to a permanent end, it appeared that there were still some difficult issues to be resolved. The similarities between this part of Spain and back home in Northern Ireland obviously did not stop at the weather and terrain.

Another three and a half kilometres brought me to Lezama. I had hoped to find accommodation here in the local *albergue* or, failing that, in a pension in Zamudio, which was a further three kilometres beyond Lezama. However, both *albergue* and pension were already full upon my arrival and I therefore had to rethink my plans. Fortunately, my friend Ron had emailed me the day before to say that he had also had trouble finding accommodation. He had eventually ended up in a hostel in Derio, which was off route and wasn't mentioned in any of the guides. I'm glad he had found it, because my guidebook had run out of options. So I headed for Derio and, after another two kilometres or so, I managed to get a single room. If I hadn't been so desperate though, I very much doubt that I would have taken Ron's advice, as his email had clearly said that the hostel was in an old cemetery and I really didn't fancy sleeping in a graveyard. However, it turned out that Ron had actually meant an old seminary. I'm not sure whether this was a translation or auto-correction issue, but once again Ron had inadvertently made me laugh.

Later, before turning in for the night, I visited the hostel's communal kitchen to get a drink of water. Here I got talking to a couple from Azerbaijan, who were making a cup of tea for themselves at the time. They offered me a cup also – it was a 'special' brew using black tea and a herb, which was vaguely familiar, but which I couldn't quite identify – I think it was safe enough. We sat together in the common room to drink our tea, which they had along with biscuits which they spooned condensed milk onto. We were soon joined by a couple from

Ukraine, including both couples' children. Both men spoke a little English and we were able to have a good, albeit rather stilted, conversation. They explained that they and their children were all 'political refugees' and that they had only arrived in Spain five days ago. They were very friendly and hospitable and really just wanted a better life for their four children (two each), who were all under ten and adorable. After finishing my tea, which was very refreshing, I wished them luck for the future and headed to bed. However, I continued to wonder at just how hard it must be to feel forced or coerced to leave the country you called home behind to seek a better life elsewhere in a strange country. It also dawned on me that I obviously wasn't the only one staying at the hostel who was seeking some sort of sanctuary.

After his family had brought him home and laid him in his bed, Philetus instructed his son Jeremiah to seek out the apostle James and inform him as to what had happened. When Jeremiah told James about the evil spell that Hermogenes had cast over his father, James gave him his handkerchief and said, "Give this to your father and tell him that our Lord heals those who are hurt and frees those who are trapped".

When Jeremiah gave his father the handkerchief and repeated what James had said, Philetus was released immediately from the spell. He rose up and went to join James as his disciple. When he learned of this, Hermogenes was furious. He was also greatly concerned that the rest of his disciples might turn away from him and follow James. So, he summoned many devils and commanded them to bring both James and Philetus to him bound, so he could exact his revenge on them.

James was awakened in the dead of night by a terrible unearthly wailing and howling that filled the darkness around him. He immediately sat up in bed, only to be confronted with the dreadful sight of four devilish figures swirling and twisting in the air before him and calling out his name. James was greatly unnerved, but he remained calm and asked the devils what they wanted. They cried out pitifully that the sorcerer Hermogenes had summoned them and demanded that they bring James and Philetus to him. "He has had us bound in chains of fire and he will torment us until we do as he says" they howled.

But James said, "The angel of God shall unbind you," and as he made the sign of the cross, the devils were immediately freed from their chains of fire. They were so relieved and thankful to be set free that they promised to serve James in any way he wished. James then said to them, "Go now and bring Hermogenes to me. Bind him, but do not hurt him". The devils obeyed and went and bound Hermogenes and brought him to James.

Chapter Three: Personal Guide
(Days 10 to 14 - Zamudio to Laredo)

Morning saw me back in the kitchen of the hostel in Derio at just after 6am for a quick breakfast. I then pulled my gear together, headed out of the hostel and made my way back to Zamudio to pick up the Camino route again. The next five or six kilometres of my walk were mainly through fairly pleasant rural and wooded areas. As I climbed the roads and tracks to Monte Avril, a hill overlooking Bilbao, I found myself doing something that I had never imagined myself doing. I recorded a video of myself 'singing' a modified version of the song 'It's a long way to Tipperary', with a view to posting it on Facebook later. My special version of the song went as follows:

It's a long way to Santiago
It's a long way to go
It's a long way to Santiago
For the sweetest girl I know.

Farewell San Sebastian
Goodbye to Irún
It's a long, long way to Santiago
It's one thousand Ks for you.

I of course dedicated it to Jacqui. It was a heartfelt rendition and I thought that it would make a bit of a change from my usual posts. I continued with my steady climb to the top of Monte Avril and, as I gradually descended its other side, I was rewarded with great views of the city of Bilbao below.

On entering Bilbao, I stopped at the hugely impressive structure of the *Basílica de Nuestra Señora de Begoña* (Basilica of Our Lady of Begoña), built on the slopes overlooking the city centre. The basilica is dedicated to the patron saint of Biscay, the Virgin Begoña, and tradition tells of an apparition of the Virgin Mary to the people of

Bilbao at the site in the early sixteenth century. The Basque Country has a long tradition of fishing and seafaring and in the past sailors believed that the Virgin Begoña helped sailors in distress. Indeed sailors traditionally offered thanks to her, on first catching sight of the basilica's steeple, when they returned safely to Bilbao. After taking in the magnificence of the external structure, I felt compelled to step inside, not out of any religious necessity, but simply because the natural appeal of the design seemed designed to draw one in. I passed through the huge portico and stepped into the cool darkness of the basilica, and almost felt embraced by the peace within. The interior was just as magnificent as the exterior and, as I stood in the central nave, taking in the monumental proportions of the building, I was in awe of the vision, the dedication, the architectural skill and the immense labour that must have gone into creating such a structure. My guidebook pointed out that the basilica had a bell tower containing 24 bells, one of which weighs a ton. When it comes to creating magnificence, there is little that inspires as completely as religion.

I returned to the daylight outside and followed a long series of steps down into the Plaza de Unamuno. At this point, I simply followed the pretty bronze scallop shell markers in the pavement, which led me through the city. It was actually quite enjoyable and I took my time wandering through the busy city streets for a couple of hours, stopping off at a small street café to have a coffee and pastry to help maintain energy levels. The crowded and colourful streets, the city centre cafés and the multitude of shops were a significantly different experience from the rural solitude of the previous few days and, indeed, I believe that it was this contrast that made it so enjoyable. However, the enjoyment quickly dissipated as I left the hustle and bustle of the city centre behind and began a very long route through the industrial outskirts of Bilbao and its neighbouring areas.

I trudged many kilometres through a tedious grey landscape and really saw very little of interest until I approached Portugalete. Here I watched in amazement as a large tram like carriage was transported above and across the surface of the River Nervión from one side to the other. As I drew closer, I could see that the carriage was suspended on a system of wire ropes coming from the huge metal gantry that spanned the entire width of the river. I later discovered that this was the Vizcaya Bridge, a transporter bridge, which carries both passengers and cars across the wide river.

I had earlier booked into a pension in Portugalete, which was about eleven kilometres from the centre of Bilbao. My feet had become quite sore from the prolonged walking on the hard, unforgiving pavements. Thankfully there were no blisters resulting, but I was never-the-less extremely grateful to the good people of Portugalete, who seemed to be very innovative when it came to ease of transport. For, not only had they created their unique transporter bridge, but they had also installed an amazing system of moving escalators on some of their steeper streets. It was such a joy to ride up the escalators rather than having to punish my throbbing feet further by climbing up Portugalete's hilly boulevards. In fact, I enjoyed riding on the escalators so much that I ended up missing my turn off and riding higher than I needed to. But, no worries – I just rode the neighbouring escalator down again until I reached my turn off and then followed my mobile's Satnav to the address of my pension for the night.

I got into my room, showered, did my laundry and charged whatever gadgets needed charging. This was becoming an almost automatic daily routine. I then headed into the centre of Portugalete to find somewhere to eat. The first restaurant I ventured into also happened to be the one chosen by Sasaki, a Japanese man I had met on the Camino a few times the previous day. As soon as Sasaki spotted me, he called me over and invited me to join him. Sasaki was a retired engineer/designer from outside Tokyo for Kawasaki. He was quite a comedian and it was hilarious to watch him interacting with the locals – he didn't have a word of Spanish and, of course, no one in the restaurant had a word of Japanese. So he used a lot of hand gestures and onomatopoeia sounds. When the waiter arrived to take our orders, Sasaki made his way down the menu and went through a repertoire of animal sounds to determine whether the dish was mainly comprised of chicken, beef, sheep or pig. Thankfully, the waiter was not perturbed in the slightest and in fact wholeheartedly entered into the spirit of it. It was like listening to a very bad rendition of 'Old McDonald Had A Farm' and it was certainly the most entertaining food ordering I had ever witnessed.

*****

The next morning I woke up to the sound of water gushing and, when I looked out of my window, there was a small river flowing down the street outside. In no rush to venture outside for a soaking, I was content to take my time getting ready. I only had a relatively short walk of about 12km today, so there was really no need for me to hurry. By the time I did eventually step outside about half an hour later, the rain had totally stopped, although the streets were still pretty wet. I was a bit concerned that I might have difficulty finding somewhere open so early on a Sunday morning to have breakfast. However, I needn't have worried. The hospitality of the Spaniards towards a lone pilgrim came into play once again and a local man, who was out walking his dog, led me to a fabulous café a few streets away. I had noticed that the local people in this part of Spain were very happy to lead you to the place you want to go to, so long as it's relatively nearby. Maybe they just found it easier, rather than trying to explain directions to a dumb foreigner like me, but I preferred to believe that they were just a very friendly and helpful people.

The café was a real feast for the eyes with its counters and display cabinets positively overflowing with an array of delicious pastries and pies. And the prices were so much cheaper than back home. I had a cheese and ham filled croissant, a *napolitana de chocolate* and a coffee all for the price I would have paid for a cup of coffee in Ireland. And the food and the coffee tasted every bit as good as it promised to be. Such simple pleasures undoubtedly reached new heights when you spent most of your time living the life of a humble pilgrim.

It was with some reluctance that I finished my tasty breakfast and tried to muster some enthusiasm for the next stage of my Camino. Once I was sure that not a single delicious crumb had escaped being dabbed and collected by a licked fingertip and safely transferred to my lips, I pulled on my rucksack, thanked the woman behind the counter and headed out the door. I almost immediately picked up the scallop shell markers. As I followed the streets out of Portugalete, an elderly woman stopped me in the street to wish me "Buen Camino". This underlying respect by locals for pilgrims had become more noticeable as I moved westwards. I received similar greetings from passing cyclists and other walkers on the route. It certainly helped to buoy me along.

A lot of today's walk was alongside cycle paths and was quite pleasant going with the grey skies hiding the heat of the sun for the early part of the day. I was certainly very glad to have completed the tedious stretch from Bilbao to Portugalete the day before and to have put the hard pavements of the industrial suburbs of Bilbao well behind me.

A few kilometres out of Portugalete, I caught up with two English guys and fell in with them for the rest of the way to Pobeña, my destination for the day. They were easy company and our paces were well matched. James was originally from Liverpool, but had just returned from a few years in Australia, and Fran was from Newcastle. They were both junior doctors and we had quite a lengthy discussion about the state of the National Health Service in the UK. Fran was also a singer/songwriter and lead singer with a group called Ajimal that had released their debut album the previous year. Fran's musical ability got me thinking and when we stopped in Pobeña for lunch, now in beautiful sunshine, I plucked up the courage to ask him and James if they would join me in a rendition of 'It's a long way to Santiago'. I filled them in on the background and was delighted that they immediately accepted my invitation. We headed back the short distance to the footbridge leading onto the beautiful sandy Playa de la Arena and recorded a video of the three of us belting out the song. I was

Fran and James on Playa de la Arena

grateful to Fran and James for agreeing to participate in my crazy idea and I later posted the video on Facebook to help raise awareness of my fundraising efforts.

For me, Pobeña was the end of my day's walk, but Fran and James had planned to walk on. Pobeña and the beach next to it, Playa de la Arena, were beautiful and it was so nice to be back on the coast again after the last few days of walking inland. I only felt slightly guilty as I waved the two English guys off on their next 17.5km leg to Castro-Urdiales, while I headed to find the local *albergue*. It wasn't hard to find as Pobena is such a small place. It was only around 1.30pm when I arrived and I joined a German man, Waldemar, to wait outside for the *albergue* to open, which would be at 3pm according to a sign on the door. Waldemar was from near Hanover and his English was as good as my German, which is to say "non-existent". So 'Google Translate' on our mobile phones came to the rescue. It really was a fantastic little app and was certainly a big improvement on how we might have been forced to communicate in its absence; by talking slowly and loudly and using exaggerated gestures, becoming increasingly frustrated until giving up and just smiling at one and other. The *hospitalero* arrived early and we were admitted by 2.30pm. I registered, got another stamp on my credential (the official log of my journey), picked my bunk, ditched my rucksack and then headed off down the street to book a room for the following night in a nearby apartment – it was a Camino 'rule' that you could only stay one night in each *albergue*.

I went for a stroll over the beautiful sandy beach at Playa de la Arena, which stretches between two green headlands at opposite ends that almost appear to mirror one and other. On the way back I took a pathway through the flat parklands behind the beach and crossed the footbridge into Pobeña again. I paused to watch a couple of dogs playing fetch in the lazy waters of the River Barbadún before moving on to relax in the sun on a park bench and watch life go by in this quiet corner of the Basque Country. The bench was situated in an area of salt marshes, bordered by a circular promenade, with only an occasional elderly local couple out for a slow stroll round the loop. I thought of Fran and James struggling on through the midday heat for another 17.5km as I soaked up the warmth and, for once, I felt no regret whatsoever at having let my fellow pilgrims go on ahead. I eventually dragged myself away from my sunny bench and headed back towards the *albergue*, pausing once again, this time to watch some ducks and geese waddling and splashing about in a small tributary to the river. The hours passed by easily in this beautiful oasis of calm.

When I eventually arrived back at the *albergue*, I found that the number of pilgrims booked in to stay had grown considerably. About another dozen people had arrived, including a couple from Dublin and a funny 'comedian' from Japan called Sasaki. I invited him to join me for tea, but he declined as he wanted to get to bed so he could get away early the next morning. I therefore headed round to the small restaurant tucked in behind the *albergue* and took a table for one. I tried to strike up a conversation with a young bearded Italian at the table next to me, but he didn't seem to want to converse much, even though I knew he could speak English from his exchanges with the waiter. I left him to continue his meal in sullen silence.

After dining, I was in no hurry to head back to the *albergue*. I called into a local bar which was very quiet – only a couple of local barflies propping up the bar and a foursome playing bridge at a table in the corner. However, there was a decent WiFi signal and so I took a stool at the bar and ordered a beer, which I sipped slowly as I composed my next blog for Facebook. As I looked around at the stoical locals in the bar, I thought sardonically to myself that I was really going to have to rein myself in and ease up on the wild nights, if I was going to stand a chance of completing my pilgrimage.

And when I arrived back at the *albergue* well after dark, my 'wild night' appeared to know no end. For there, lying on top of my bed I found a pair of lady's knickers. *Hola, hola*, I thought as I patted down my bed in the semi-darkness to see if I could locate the owner. But I discovered that my bed was of course empty and that the knickers had simply fallen from the bunk above, where they had been hung from a bed rail to dry. The owner was fast asleep in her own bed so I returned the knickers to the rail beside a matching bra and, with a sigh (more of relief, than of regret), I climbed into my bottom bunk alone. Mind you, the atmosphere in the dorm was anything but conducive to any thoughts of romance, as the snoring baton was passed from one bunk to the next throughout the night. Just as one snorer died down, another one started up. It was a bit like that Budweiser advert with the frogs except an awful lot louder. Every so often the racket quietened down sufficiently to allow sleep a chance, but, just as I was about to nod off, the noise started up again and the torture began anew. It was at times like this, I thought to myself, as I compressed my slim pillow against both ears, that really put the 'grim' into 'pilgrim'. To be honest, I can't be absolutely sure that I didn't join in the chorus myself at some stage during the night, but I doubt it – I really don't remember being asleep for long enough to get a good snore started. I was certainly looking forward to my single room in the Apartmentos Murrari the next night.

*****

The next morning, I was up early, but not too bright, with the rest of the *peregrinos*. There was simply no chance of having a sleep in when staying in a dorm full of eager pilgrims readying themselves for the day ahead. I gathered up my things, checking that all the underwear was my own, and headed round to the café behind the *albergue* for a leisurely breakfast. It was a nice feeling, knowing I could relax while my fellow pilgrims were setting off on the next leg of their journey. I bumped into Sasaki again and grabbed a quick photograph with him before he too joined the mass migration. I couldn't check in to my apartment for another few hours, so I wandered around Pobeña and Playa de la Arena again – this was not a hardship. It was still a little cool at first, but it soon warmed up to become another glorious day and it made for a very pleasant morning, walking across the almost deserted beach and exploring the hill at the east end of Playa de la Arena. I sought out the peacocks I heard calling while on the beach and I found several of them wandering around the grounds of what looked like a rather grand retirement home in La Arena. The male birds in particular strutted around looking like royalty, with their wonderful tail feathers trailing in the leaves and dust behind them. They really looked like they should have a small band of serfs following behind them in order to hold their beautiful, long trains off the ground as they proceeded.

Playa de la Arena is another well-known surf spot on the north coast of Spain, but yet again the conditions were not favourable for surfing, with only small messy waves lapping on shore. I left the sandy beach, crossed the footbridge once again into Pobeña and checked into to my very nice apartment, which I had all to myself. It may have cost more than three times the rate of most *albergues*, but I would have been happy to pay twice as much again for a decent night's sleep. Once I had settled in and had a bite of lunch in the cafeteria downstairs, I headed back to the beach where I chilled for the rest of the day until it was time to eat again and then I had an early night. It was a hard life, but somebody had to do it.

With Sasaki from Japan in Pobeña

*****

I was up bright and early the following morning. I'd enjoyed a much better rest in the apartment than I had experienced in the noisy *albergue* the night before. Okay, I had no women throwing their knickers at me; but you can't have everything. I had a nice coffee and a *napolitana de chocolate* in the cafeteria below the apartments before setting off for my destination for the day, Islares, which was a very respectable 25km away. It was a beautiful day for walking right from the outset and the scenery and sights along the route were just wonderful.

My route began in surreal fashion as I followed three ducks that waddled slowly across the park ahead of me. Just as I was wondering if I would be following them all the way to Islares, they waddled off towards the river to the right, while I veered off to the left and began a surprisingly long and tiring climb up a flight of steps that brought me up the side of the hill at the west end of Playa de la Arena. It was a much more strenuous start to the day than I had expected, but the reward on reaching the top, of a fabulous view across the beach in the soft early morning sunlight, made every step worthwhile.

I made my way along an elevated coastal path which followed the track-bed of a former railroad that was used to carry iron ore to ships waiting in the bay. I stopped frequently on the path to turn and gaze back at the impressive views, as the waking sun slowly rose from behind the hill opposite. A red-breasted robin kept me company as I went, hopping from one fence post to the next as if waiting on me to catch up each time, but more likely wishing to keep a safe distance ahead of this lumbering creature with a load on its back. My wonderful nature trail continued, as I encountered blackbirds catching early morning worms, a greenfinch flitting from branch to branch, a bumblebee already busy feasting on nectar and collecting pollen, in addition to a variety of colourful wildflowers. However, what stopped me in my tracks was the sight of a billy goat as I came around a bend in the coastal path. He was mainly jet black, but with a few small patches of tan on his belly and legs, and he was standing on his hind legs by the side of the path, with his front hoofs raised and resting against the trunk of a small tree. And there he was, 'happy as Larry', scratching the top of his head against the branch above him. He seemed to be in such a state of stupor that he was totally oblivious to my presence. I managed to get a few photographs in the can before his itch was totally satisfied and he moved on to join the rest of his small herd on the slopes beneath the path.

Shortly after my encounter with the goats, I passed through a tunnel in the rock face. It was shored up with a rickety lattice-work of wooden posts and planks, presumably to protect walkers from the risk of falling rocks. It looked like something left over from an Indiana Jones movie set; 'Indiana Jones and the Lost Pilgrim' perhaps. The path then curved inland and descended into a valley and the small village of Ontón. Here, I and other pilgrims were faced with a dilemma, as there were now two routes to choose from; either a trek further inland along what were described in my guidebook as quiet roads or a more direct coastal route. I favoured the coastal route as usual, but I experienced some difficulty finding the right path. I met a couple of Canadian pilgrims, Jesus and Christina, who appeared to be equally confused. They went one way and, unconvinced by their map reading skills, I opted to go the other. However, it soon became quite apparent to me that, on this occasion anyway, it was my map reading skills that were questionable. Fortunately, I hadn't gone too far before I met Philippe, a Spanish man from Castro-Urdiales. Philippe was out for a morning hike himself and was completing a loop from Castro-Urdiales to Ontón and back. Luckily I met him just as he was about to join the coastal route back to Castro-Urdiales and he was able to lead me to the correct path where I soon caught up with the Canadian pilgrims, who's directions I had ignored earlier. Of course, I should have known to follow Jesus. I suffered a little good-natured bantering at my expense, but I also had a comeback when I proudly announced that I had now managed to obtain the services of a local guide.

Philippe acted as my personal guide for the next 12km. He had no English and I had very little Spanish, but we got along just fine. He set quite a pace and it wasn't long before the Canadians fell far behind and eventually disappeared from sight. However, I was determined to keep up with Philippe, even though it was quite hard going as we encountered hill after hill. Philippe had probably walked this route many times before and he was only carrying a small back pack. It became quite clear to me that he was not going to reduce his pace for any pilgrim and, in my efforts to never fall too far behind, the sweat was soon dripping off my brow. He did glance behind occasionally to see if I was still there. Although I suspected that, if I were to fall too far behind, he would have simply marched on regardless. Thankfully, I never got to put this theory to the test as I arrived in Castro-Urdiales more or less at the same time as Philippe. Before he broke away to head for his home, Philippe pointed me in the right direction to continue with the Camino route. As we shook hands, I drew upon the few words of Spanish that I had been rehearsing for the last kilometre, and said *"Muchas gracias. Eres una muy buena guía."* – "Many

My 'personal guide' Philippe leading me into Castro-Urdiales

thanks. You are a very good guide." He laughed at this and said *"De nada"* – "You're welcome" – so I presumed he had understood my laboured pronunciation.

Castro-Urdiales was quite simply a beautiful coastal town, with beautiful beaches, a beautiful church and a beautiful marina. Before heading into the town for some lunch, I made my way down onto the beach at Playa de Brazomar, kicked off my boots and socks and thoroughly enjoyed the soothing cool waters as I paddled the length of the sandy shore. It was just what my hot feet needed after my 'route march' with Philippe. I sat on the sand for a while to let my feet dry and then I pulled on my socks and boots once again and continued into the town centre. And it was here that I met up with Jesus and Christina once more.

"Ah, hello again. We were wondering where you had gotten to," Jesus teased good naturedly. "Isn't it fortunate you had Philippe to show you the way or God knows where you might have ended up."

"Fair game", I replied, holding my hands up and taking it on the chin, "but I've been paddling in the sea and relaxing on the beach for the last hour. Have you just arrived?"

"Touché" Jesus replied and Christina laughed.

They were both sitting outside a small restaurant awaiting their orders and they invited me to join them, which I was only too happy to do. I hadn't had a proper conversation with anyone since meeting Fran and James two days earlier.

Jesus explained that he was originally from the Basque region of Spain, "but my family left to pursue a new life in Canada when I was about four years old, so I have no real memory of my country of birth."

Christina was a native Canadian. "We met and fell in love while we were both studying at the University of Toronto" she added "and we married shortly after graduating." Not dissimilar to my own path with Jacqui, but I let the thought pass unspoken. Instead I said "Well, with your names, it was sort of inevitable that you would get together."

They both laughed, perhaps just to humour me though, as I'm sure that it wasn't the first time that they had heard such a comment. Jesus continued, "This is my first time back in Spain since I left as a child. We stayed with some relatives near San Sebastian before embarking on the Camino de Santiago." It turned out that they hadn't actually come to Spain with any intension of walking the Camino. "Oh, we were aware of it, probably like many other people, through the movie 'The Way', starring Martin Sheen", he explained, "but we had come to Spain primarily to explore my roots and meet our relatives. Then we heard and learned more about the Camino while we were here. I have more relatives living in Galicia, you know, the region where Santiago is located, and it suddenly dawned on us both, almost simultaneously, that it would be nice to walk from San Sebastian to Santiago."

Christina added enthusiastically, "We literally both woke up one morning and I said to Jesus 'I know what you're thinking' and I was thinking exactly the same thing. It just seemed so appropriate, while we were here in this area, to follow in the footsteps of thousands of others and walk the Camino."

Both Jesus and Christina had retired from work recently and so, like me, they had no time constraints placed on them. It was therefore no problem for them to extend their stay in Spain to incorporate a few weeks walking.

The aromas filling the air, as waiters dashed past with plate after plate full of grilled sardines, prawns and octopus, heightened everyone's appetite. Our lunch at the little pavement café was quite sublime as we were gently warmed in the afternoon sun and surrounded by the happy sounds of satisfied diners at the tables around us. After we had finished our lunch, Jesus and Christina wanted to venture into town to look around the shops. I too was in no rush to leave this attractive town, but my particular desire was to get a closer look round the medieval quarter, overlooking the harbour area.

"Perhaps we'll meet later in Islares" I said as we stood up to go.

"Now, are you sure you'll be able to find your way there without Philippe?" was Jesus' cheeky response.

"*Buen Camino* to you too" I said laughing as I turned to leave.

I headed off along the promenade towards the stunning *Iglesia de Santa María de la Asunción*, which together with the lighthouse constructed on the ruins of the *Castillo de Santa Ana*, dominated the seafront of Castro-Urdiales. The Gothic-style church was both impressive in design and huge in stature. Its proportions and presence brought to mind more a cathedral than a church. By turns both gorgeous and grotesque, the combination of pinnacles, flying buttresses and bizarre gargoyles around the exterior of the church were a feast for the eyes. I found myself totally mesmerised as I slowly circumnavigated the church's perimeter, with my gaze drawn heavenwards. *"Perdón"* I spluttered to an elderly Spanish man, as I nearly tripped over the small dog he was walking. He just looked at me like I was a bit simple. And perhaps I had indeed become a bit simple, as I was confronted with the sheer genius of human endeavour on show before me.

Unfortunately the church doors were firmly bolted closed, denying me access to the undoubted treasures that lay within. So instead I wandered up to the lighthouse to enjoy fantastic views back across the town's extensive harbour and beyond to the headlands stretching eastwards along the coast for as far as the eye could see. The sky was blue, with just the occasional fluffy white cloud, and the sea a deep azure flecked with silver, as the breeze-groomed ripples caught the sunlight. It was truly glorious.

Despite the attractions on offer, time was marching on and I felt that I should really be doing the same. So I reluctantly left the medieval quarters and attempted to get back on the Camino route. The town stretched for quite a way to the west of the harbour area also and the long promenade embraced another couple of lovely sandy beaches. However, as I turned inland at the end of the second beach, the words Jesus had left ringing in my ears earlier came back to haunt me, as I encountered real difficulty in finding the correct route out of town. Perhaps I had become too used to following behind Philippe and relying on his local knowledge rather than my own navigational skills. However, I eventually managed to escape the many charms of Castro-Urdiales, though I do admit that I had to confer with a few locals along the way.

As with most of the coastal towns I had passed through, Castro-Urdiales was no exception in that my approach had involved a fairly steep descent and, as I was now finding out, my departure involved an equally steep ascent. On this occasion the climb was not made any more pleasant due to the fact it involved a fair bit of walking on pathways alongside busy roads. I was about 4km out of Castro-Urdiales before I finally and thankfully joined some very pleasant coastal paths and tracks. These took me on my final few kilometres to the pretty little coastal town of Islares.

Here I got a bed in the local *albergue* and discovered that Jesus and Christina had already booked in. I was also pleased to see a small band of assorted pilgrims I had met briefly in Pobeña at breakfast earlier. Jimmy was in his 70s and from Scotland and he had somehow teamed up with Maik from Germany and Hana (short for Hanischka) from the Czech Republic, who I estimated to be in their late-20s. There were three tier bunks in this *albergue*, with the bottom bunk being almost at floor level. I was fortunate to get a bunk, as some who arrived after me simply had to find a space on the floor to bed down.

That evening I headed to the nearby Bar Elisa for a meal in the company of Josephe, known as 'Peppe', a 33-year-old barman, musician and care-worker from Italy, and Jurgheim, a 60-year-old retired doctor from Germany. I recognised Peppe as the man I had tried, unsuccessfully, to strike up a conversation with in the restaurant in Pobeña a couple of nights previously. He seemed a little more friendly and sociable tonight. There were lots of others from the *albergue* in the bar also. Many of the small bars and cafes along the Camino route appeared to thrive on the pilgrim trade. The atmosphere in Bar Elisa was friendly, but most of the pilgrims didn't linger too long after they had finished their meals and instead headed back to the *albergue*. Pretty soon everyone else apart from me, the barman and a couple of locals had left. I decided to sit on for a little longer to compose and post my blog, making use of the bars WiFi, which the *albergue* was without. A notice in the *albergue* had read 'No WiFi – it's good to talk'– a very admirable sentiment, but I had my legion of Facebook followers to satisfy.

Unfortunately, I didn't notice the time passing in the bar and it wasn't until after I had posted my blog that I thought to check the time. It was 10.15pm. Damn. I had missed the 10pm curfew. I rushed back to the *albergue*, which was only a few minutes away, but all the lights were out and the doors locked. Shit. I couldn't believe it. At 55 years of age, I had been locked out for being home late. I knocked on the door for a few minutes, but this brought absolutely no response. So I moved round to the side of the building, to the window of one of the dorms. After a few discrete taps on the glass, a friendly face appeared at the window. It was Hana from the Czech Republic. She smiled when she recognised me and signalled that she would open the front door. A couple of moments later, Hana had the front door unlocked and I, like a naughty school boy, was sneaked into the *albergue* under the cover of darkness. I whispered my thanks to Hana and said goodnight, before heading to my bunk. I subsequently had the best sleep that I had had in any *albergue* so far. Perhaps I should stay out late more often, I thought.

*****

I was well rested and up feeling refreshed early the next morning. As I stepped outside the now unlocked front doors of the *albergue* to enjoy the fresh air, I was greeted with a beautiful sight. The whole of the sky was awash with the colour of peach and, as I watched the sun slowly rise from beyond the sea, a pathway of gold stretched across the water from horizon to shore. I was joined by a small number of other pilgrims and we stood in almost reverential silence as we witnessed this miraculous awakening of the day.

It was so tranquil walking through Islares and past the town's gorgeous beach in the early morning sunlight that bathed the surrounding slopes in a soft, warm glow. Unfortunately, upon arrival at the next village, the café we had all been depending upon for some breakfast was not yet open and wouldn't be for another hour. There were definite advantages to getting on the road early on the Camino, not least of which was being able to walk in the cooler part of the day. But there were distinct disadvantages also and finding somewhere open early enough to have breakfast was certainly one of them. The smarter pilgrims were well prepared and bought something for breakfast the day before. I wasn't one of them, but fortunately I still had half a doughnut left over from one that Waldemar had given me in Pobeña. I also had fresh water in my pack. It was meagre fare for sure, but certainly better than nothing at all. It would have to suffice until I found a café or shop that was open.

It was nearly 12km and some two and a half hours later before I finally happened upon somewhere that was open for business. It was in a town called Liendo, which was situated in a beautifully lush, green valley; the perfectly named Valle de la Villaverde. My delight at coming across the cafe was added to when I spotted a familiar face sitting at one of the tables outside with her dog. This was Sara from Northern Italy, who was travelling with her golden Labrador, Freccia. I had met them both briefly a couple of days before. I waved and said a quick hello, before diving into the café to obtain some much needed nourishment. Once I'd collected my order of coffee and filled croissant, I headed back outside and joined Sara and Freccia to catch up with them as I wolfed down my late breakfast. Sara had stayed in the local *albergue* in Liendo the night before and was now considering walking the short distance to Laredo, which was only another six kilometres away. She explained that the previous day's terrain had been very tough on Freccia and his two front paws had become grazed and sore; so they would not be able to go very far. She hoped that they would be able to make it to Laredo, which was a fairly large town, and that she would be able to find a vet there to have a look at Freccia.

Shortly after sitting down with Sara, more familiar faces from my *albergue* in Islares started to arrive – all gasping for *café con leche* and food. However, it was another 15 minutes before Peppe finally appeared. He was limping quite badly and appeared to be in quite a bit of pain. He flopped into the first available chair and explained that his right knee was quite swollen and very sore. Between Freccia and now

Peppe, this was fast becoming the 'café of the lame'. Fortunately, Jurgheim, the retired doctor from Germany, had also arrived. While I nipped back into the café to get Peppe a coffee and something to eat, Jurgheim examined Peppe's knee. When I returned to the table, Jurgheim's verdict was that Peppe needed to get a pair of walking poles as soon as possible to take the strain off his knee. I had a pair of walking poles strapped to my rucksack that I hadn't needed since getting over Mount Jaizkibel at the start of my Camino.

"No problem Peppe", I declared, as I unstrapped my walking poles and handed them to him, "take these and see how you manage. I can get them back when we get to Laredo."

His initial protests soon died down when I reassured him that I hadn't been using them for quite some time and that I certainly didn't need them for the final stretch of today's walk.

"Sorry old chap, but I'm afraid I don't have anything to help you," I said, as I ruffled the hair on Freccia's head. He looked up at me with a mournful expression, even though his tail was sweeping back and forth.

Possibly relishing getting back into his former role and not being too fussy about his patients, Jurgheim also had a look at Freccia's paws. After a few moments he declared with some authority that his paws were quite tender and that Sara should really get him to a vet. Sara and I just looked at each other and smiled.

Refuelled and refreshed, the café, come temporary doctors surgery, gradually emptied as pilgrims began to get on their way once again. However, both Peppe and Sara sat on and waved everyone else off, saying that they hoped to see us all again later in Laredo. I exchanged phone numbers with Peppe before going, so that I could meet up with him to recover my poles. I then also rejoined the Camino and walked for the remainder of the day largely on my own. The walk from Islares to Liendo had been a very pleasant hike through beautiful verdant hills and valleys, but the final six kilometres from Liendo to Laredo was less enjoyable as the whole route was along a roadside verge.

Despite the tedium of this stretch, the final approach into Laredo itself, with views over its long, crescent beach of Playa de Salvé, was beautiful and extremely rewarding. Although much of the town above the beach was made up of unattractive, modern buildings, the eastern end, where the Camino route entered, was the more pleasant old part of the town and dramatically situated on the slopes of La Atalaya hill. I descended a long flight of stone steps and passed through an archway in the old stone wall fortifications near the bottom and stepped onto cobbled streets. Here I bumped into fellow Irishman, Ray, and we both made our way to the *albergue* in the *Convento de San Francisco*. We were booked into the convent *albergue* by a very fastidious nun who sat very formally on one side of a bare wooden table while Ray and I took it in turn to sit in the single straight-backed wooden chair opposite and answer the list of questions about our name, nationality, age, starting point on the Camino, starting point today, mode of transport, etc. It pretty much covered the standard information requested at every *albergue* I had stayed at so far, but this was first time that the answers were transcribed in such a slow and meticulous manner. She was not unfriendly; it was just that she was so serious and diligent in her approach. When she ran through the list of rules governing our stay, there was little doubt that she meant what she said. So I took very careful note of the fact that the convent doors would be locked at 10pm and would stay locked until 6am the following morning.

After being shown to our four-bunk room and the usual showering and laundry routine, I walked the short distance to a privately run *albergue*, where I had arranged to meet Peppe. He told me that the walking poles had helped him immensely that afternoon and he was extremely grateful. However, he thought that he might not be able to purchase his own poles until he reached Santander, which was still at least two more days walk away. I considered for a moment the spirit of the Camino and the belief that many pilgrims carry with them – that the Camino will always provide. I had already experienced it for myself. On my first day, Gabriel showed up and gave me a lift to another hostel in Irún when his own was full. And only the previous night, Hana had got out of bed to let me into the *albergue* after I had been locked out. Surely one can't avail of such good spirit and not be prepared to contribute something back? And so I give Peppe my walking poles. I was very happy to be able to help a fellow pilgrim out. Quite simply, he needed them and I didn't. Peppe could now continue with walking his Camino and my backpack would be a little lighter into the bargain. He insisted on buying me a meal that night and I readily accepted his offer and agreed to meet him later.

In the meantime, I walked the Streets of Laredo, humming the tune of the song, made famous by Marty Robbins and Johnny Cash, as I went. I explored the cobbled streets of the historical quarter, Puebla Vieja, packed with busy bars and restaurants. I discovered that Laredo could be regarded as the original home of flower power. For here, on the last Friday of August each year, an event takes place known as *la batalla de los flores* (the battle of the flowers), during which large floats carrying fantastic figures entirely covered with vibrant flowers and petals are paraded along the central streets. This festival also includes a flower-throwing fight, similar to the legendary tomato fight in Buñol, but, one imagines, considerably less messy. The festival apparently concludes when a giant sardine is buried on the beach. It all sounded truly bizarre.

I met up with Peppe again at around 7.30pm at his *albergue* and we walked the short distance to a restaurant nearby. Not wishing to take unfair advantage of Peppe's offer to pay for the meal, I followed his lead and ordered a modest but satisfactory meal from the pilgrim menu. Peppe was quite an intense young man and I got the impression that, as well as struggling physically with his bad knee, he was also struggling mentally with something that he had left behind in Italy. He seemed dissatisfied with his life back home and, in common with many others, had come on the Camino to give himself the space needed to decide on his future direction. It seemed that many people who walked the Camino regarded it as taking time out, an opportunity to press the pause button on their normal lives, to allow themselves time to think about what they really wanted from life. They may feel stuck in a rut, whether it is a job, a relationship or a lifestyle that no longer feels right, but they are unsure of how to change. The Camino provides that break from the routine and a chance to get back to basics. It helps people decide what's really important in their lives. Peppe wasn't specific about his problems, but he said enough to make it clear that he had issues that needed sorting out. He quizzed me about my reasons for walking the Camino and, not wishing to add to this young man's burdens, I was just as vague as he was and simply said that I needed some time away from the pressures of everyday life.

Despite both of us dancing around the real issues, or perhaps because of it, the time passed by more quickly than expected. We were so engrossed in conversation that we lost track of time and when I finally glanced at my watch I was shocked to see that it was 9.50pm. I jumped to my feet, apologised to Peppe, leaving him to settle the bill and made a quick exit. I had to run the last few hundred metres in order to reach the doors of the convent *albergue* before the nuns locked them for the night. I made it just in time and met Ray on the way in. He had also rushed back to beat the pilgrim curfew. He was quite peeved at having had to leave a local bar where he had been enjoying a good football match on the big screen. We begrudgingly made our way to our dorm. Here we found that we had been joined by a Swiss man called Michael. His English was quite good and we chatted for a short time before turning in for the night. We all agreed that today's walk from Islares to Laredo was much further than the 23km cited our guidebooks. The final words on the subject went to Ray. "There is no feckin' way that today's walk was only 23 klics. It was at least 30. And that's not even counting the feckin' detour I made when I missed that feckin' turn off after leaving Islares this morning." Ray had lived and worked in Germany for many years, but was originally from Dublin and, as a consequence, he was very fluent in both German and cursing.

Hermogenes stood before James, bound in chains and watched over by his captures. The four devils turned and twisted menacingly in the air around his bowed head. James had sent for Philetus and his new disciple now stood beside him looking upon the cowering figure of the sorcerer who was once his Master.

Philetus was very fearful of the dark powers commanded by Hermogenes, and said "He is a great danger to us James. We should turn him over to the very devils that he himself conjured up. Let them deal with him and we can then be sure that he will be unable to cause us any harm."

But James said, "Philetus, this is your opportunity to show that you truly believe in the Lord. You must behave as Jesus Christ would have expected you to. You must therefore find it in your heart to forgive Hermogenes and set him free."

Philetus was at first very reluctant, but soon he understood and trusted in his new Master and his Lord. He approached Hermogenes and removed the chains that bound the sorcerer and allowed them to fall to the floor.

Hermogenes was completely confused by this act of forgiveness and said to James, "Why did you have me bound and brought here only to set me free again?"

James replied, "I wanted to show you the way of the Lord Jesus Christ and I also wanted you to understand that you have nothing to fear from me or my preaching. I have no desire to convert you or anyone else against their will. I merely show people the way. It is then up to them as to whether they wish to follow or not. You are free to go."

"But these devils will surely slay me as soon as I am out of your sight," Hermogenes wept.

James approached Hermogenes and handed him his staff, saying "Carry this with you and the devils will not harm you." James looked at the devils to make sure that they understood and they receded into the darkness, hissing in frustration as they went.

Hermogenes was so impressed by all that he had witnessed that he renounced his sorcery and brought all of his books of spells so that James could burn them. However, James was afraid that the 'odour of the burning might do evil or harm to some fools' and so instead he had Hermogenes cast the books into the sea. Hermogenes then gave himself over to the Lord and converted to Christianity.

Chapter Four: Beaches
(Days 15 to 21 – Laredo to San Vicente de la Barquera)

I woke from a sound sleep in the *Convento de San Francisco* in Laredo. I felt well rested and refreshed; ready for another day of walking. Breakfast was served at a huge communal wooden table by the same nun who had registered Ray and me the day before. She was the only nun I had seen in this convent and she appeared to do everything single-handedly, but I'm sure that there must have been a small army of colleagues in the background to keep things running smoothly. Breakfast consisted of coffee, biscuits and *Tarta de Santiago*, a Spanish almond cake – not the healthiest of breakfasts, but delicious and very welcome. At around 8am, I stepped out through the main doorway of the *albergue* and into the large vestibule area. Here I sat on the stone steps to pull on my boots and survey the wet morning beyond, as I waited for Ray to join me.

We tramped through the rain for a few kilometres along the town's promenade and soon caught up with Peppe, who was slowly, but steadily making his way in the same direction as the handful of other pilgrims already on the road. Everyone was heading towards the end of the peninsula to catch the ferry across the Bay of Santoña. Peppe had his left knee well strapped up and had his new walking poles proudly deployed. I apologised once again for the hasty departure the night before and he thanked me once again for the poles. We all continued at our own paces and we all arrived on the beach at the end of the peninsula in good time to await the ferry's arrival. It was a pretty dismal morning and we were all sporting our wet gear, but everyone was fairly cheerful as they boarded the small ferry and paid the small fee for the short crossing to the town of Santoña.

Upon disembarking, Ray and I continued together through the streets of Santoña, heading out of town and past the grey stone walls of Dueso Prison. "Hey, we might have been better staying in there last night. I bet they were able to watch the feckin' footie through to the end," said

Ray, obviously still smarting from having missed the end of the football match the night before. All seemed quiet as we passed the penitentiary, but little did we know that on that very day news was just breaking on a Guardia Civil manoeuvre called 'Operation Overbooking', which had smashed a drugs cartel operated by prisoners in Dueso. Of course, there was no indication of anything amiss as Ray and I casually continued on past the prison walls, but the inmates may very well not have been permitted to watch the 'feckin footie' at all the night before!

It wasn't much further before we escaped the pavements onto Playa de Berra and crossed the wet sands to the hill at the end of the beach. At this point we were faced with having to decide whether to take the easier and longer road option or the harder and shorter hill route. It would normally have been a 'no brainer' for me to opt for the hill route, but today's wet conditions gave me pause for thought. While Ray and I were considering the options, we were joined by a band of about another six pilgrims from the ferry, including Maik, Hana and Jimmy. After some discussion, we all opted for the hill route and we set off up a gently sloping sandy path to begin with. However, this soon gave way to a rather treacherous climb up some very rocky and muddy paths that took us over the hill and down the other side. Everyone found it quite challenging, although once again I felt that my Mourne Mountains training certainly helped. Jimmy, being the eldest of our group, found it the most difficult and Maik and Hana assisted him as best they could, even though he continued to protest to them for treating him like a pensioner (which of course he was). "I'm not over the hill yet" he claimed, failing to recognise the ambiguity of his statement. At one point, as Maik was reaching up to help Jimmy down a particularly steep section, Maik lost his balance and fell backwards, careering down the slope for a few metres before coming to rest in a clump of bushes. Fortunately he missed any of the rocks that he could so easily have contacted. He picked himself up again and brushed himself off – fortunately nothing injured but his pride. We all made the descent down the western side of the hill without further incident and finally stepped onto another long and sandy beach. This was Playa de Noja and it presented quite a striking landscape with its numerous large rocky outcrops protruding from the sand and the water beyond. We then followed the beach along its two kilometre length into the small town of Noja itself.

Most of us stopped in Noja for a coffee and something to eat at a busy little bar overlooking the beach. I had originally planned to stop here for a rest, but I was now reluctant to become separated from my fellow pilgrims, some of whom I had become quite friendly with. Most were heading for an almost legendary *albergue* in Guemes, which was another 15km away. It was still quite early in the day, and so I decided to abandon my planned stop in Noja and continue walking so that I could arrive at the Guemes *albergue* with people I knew. Ray gave me a slap on the back. "Good man yourself," he said, "Sure it looks like there's feck all to do here anyway."

The additional kilometres I had committed to walk proved to be quite tough and we were hot, tired and thirsty for a cold beer by the time we reached Guemes. However, after we registered and settled into the *albergue*, intriguingly called *La Cabana del Abuelo Peuto* (Grandpa Peuto's Cabin), the heat and exhaustion were quickly forgotten – the cold beer was another matter though. This *albergue* was a wonderful place, in a wonderful setting and run by wonderful people. It was established as a hostel in 1999 by Ernesto Bustio, grandson of Peuto, the owner of the original house, which was built in 1910. Ernesto, the 74-year-old *hospitalero*, was at the door to meet and greet everyone arriving to stay at his personally created Nirvana. With his shock of white hair, white beard and small wire framed glasses, Ernesto looked just like a stereotypical Father Christmas, but without the costume. And although he didn't have a sack of gifts slung across his back or resting at his feet, he did provide the most precious gift desired by pilgrims on their way to Santiago – a very comfortable and hospitable place to rest and eat.

Remarkably, this *albergue* was one of just a handful that operates on a 'donativo' basis, whereby each guest makes a donation of their own choosing to the *albergue*, rather than being charged a set fee. I was now so glad that I had made the decision to push on, because, although the additional 15km from Noja were quite tough, this was without doubt the best *albergue* I had encountered on my Camino so far. And I had arrived with my pal Ray as well as a number of other familiar faces, such as Jesus and Christina.

The only problem with the *albergue* was its remoteness. This of course added greatly to the feeling of peaccfulness and tranquillity, but there was no bar close by and both Ray and I still craved a cold beer. We stood outside the *albergue* debating whether it was worth walking the two kilometres to a bar in the village. It was now just before 7pm and dinner at the *albergue* was scheduled for 8pm, so we didn't really have time to walk there and back. We were more or less resigned to giving up on the bar, when Ray spotted two farmers returning to their car after dropping off a sheep in a field next to the *albergue*. "Come on" he said, as he took off in their direction, "We'll ask these guys for a lift." Once they understood that these two Irishmen weren't wishing to hijack their vehicle, the farmers agreed to give us a lift. So Ray and I piled into the back seat and were driven the two kilometres to Bar Luis. Both men appeared to be quite delighted to be helping two pilgrims find a bar, but they declined our offer to buy them a drink – they probably had their next passenger to pick up; probably one with a wool coat and four legs.

Ray and I were the only customers in Bar Luis, which was a quaint little pub that wouldn't have looked out of place in a small town back in Ireland. After a couple of glasses each of the cold and refreshing local beer, we headed back up the road on foot towards the *albergue* once again. We were surrounded by rural beauty as we strolled along casually; rolling green pastures and darker, forested hillsides and we watched a buzzard fly by, very close and low to the ground, gliding with silent intent. We made it back to the *albergue* just in time to join the rest of the pilgrims at a number of large, heavy, wooden tables for a communal meal of traditional and wholesome Spanish fare.

Unfortunately the tranquility of Guemes did not last. I was sharing a dormitory with eight other pilgrims, including Ray. It was very spacious and comfortable and I fell asleep quickly after such an exhausting and eventful day. However, it wasn't long before I was woken by a large German woman sleeping in the bunk opposite. She was without doubt the most consistent, long-distance snorer I had encountered on my travels so far. Even my earplugs provided little resistance to whatever particular frequency this woman was broadcasting at. I pushed them in as far as I could, pulled the pillow over my head and managed to get some intermittent sleep between her snoring episodes, which seemed to make the very room vibrate.

*****

I rose at dawn after a torturous night spent enjoying brief periods of sleep constantly interrupted by the jackhammer being operated by the German woman in the bunk opposite. As I lifted my head slowly up off the pillow, groaning feebly in the process, I looked over at her, fully expecting to see her in a hard hat and bent over her pneumatic tool, perhaps even displaying ample 'builder's bum'. But she was fast asleep and looked an absolute picture of tranquillity and innocence. She stirred as I was getting dressed and greeted everyone with a very pleasant *"Guten Morgen"*, totally oblivious to the nightly mayhem she had inflicted on her eight roommates. Of course no one said a word to her about her snoring, but simply responded to her greeting with a chorus of "good mornings" in a variety of languages – there seems to be an unwritten rule amongst pilgrims not to comment on others nocturnal habits; well not to their faces anyhow.

I was on my way to the shower block to try and freshen up when I was met by Ray who was rushing back towards the dorm to fetch me. "Have you got your camera?" he asked excitedly. I held out my wash bag and towel and just looked at him, as if to say "What do you think, Sherlock?" He ignored my gesture and persisted, "Quick, go get your camera. You won't believe the sunrise out front." I looked in that general direction, but the view was mostly blocked by buildings and all I could see was a slight peachy glow fringing the outline of the original house. Nevertheless, I dutifully returned to the dorm, fetched my camera and headed round to the front of the *albergue* with Ray. And wow. It was absolutely stunning. Before me was simply one of the most wonderful sunrises I had ever witnessed. The light clouds in the sky were on fire as they were lit from below by the warm light of the sun, as the distant horizon ever so slowly dipped with the earth's rotation to herald a new day. The scene before me was made all the more magical by the layer of 'dragon's breath' mist that had settled in the valley below. It was another beautiful, life enhancing moment and I was so grateful to Ray for having come back to find me. I could almost forgive him for 'adding' to the moment by playing Michael Buble's version of 'Feeling Good' on his phone and singing along as the sun came up, about it being a new dawn and a new day and feeling good. Actually, it was a highly appropriate song choice and Ray could certainly hold a tune, so after my initial bristling at this slight intrusion to the mood, I relaxed and enjoyed the moment. More people started to appear to enjoy nature's display for the ten minutes or so that it lasted. We all then began to move inside to enjoy the communal breakfast and everyone did indeed appear to be feeling good.

Later, as I was leaving *La Cabana del Abuelo Peuto*, I paused to study a large framed painting of Peuto and his wife, Vicenta that adorned an exterior wall of the *albergue*. Peuto and Vicenta were depicted in monotone, as if the picture had been painted from an old photograph. They were perhaps in their seventies, standing beside one and other, close but unsmiling, rather grim and austere looking. Peuto had his hands in his pockets and Vicenta had her left arm draped over his shoulders – a picture of solidarity with a hint of affection. In the bottom right hand corner of the painting was a message in Spanish that translated to read "To Vicenta and Peuto who in 1910 built this house

Sunrise at Guemes

for their family. And to Ernesto who extended it so that we all could enter." Grandpa Peuto's Cabin and Ernesto certainly provided a truly remarkable and unforgettable experience.

I waited out front of the *albergue* for Ray, petting the huge resident Golden Great Pyrenees dog that was lying basking in the early morning sun. It was the family pet and looked like a Golden Retriever on steroids. Once Ray joined me, we set off on the road together once again. We were both happy to be in each other's company for the day and we soon fell into our respective rolls once again – Ray talking and me listening. Ray could talk for Ireland and Germany both. Today's walk was quite stunning. The weather was gorgeous throughout and the scenery along this part of the Camino was simply beautiful. The route took us through more rural solitude out towards the sea once again and then along high cliff top paths. We enjoyed incredible views along the coastline in both directions and over stunning beaches, such as Playa de Langre.

It was on one of these coastal paths that we met two middle-aged Austrian ladies who, like us, had stopped to take a few photographs of the wonderful land and seascapes. They noticed Ray's rucksack and expressed concern that the straps were not adjusted properly. They felt that it was putting a strain on his back that would lead to problems later on if not corrected. It was quite amusing to watch these two women set to work on Ray's rucksack, one in front and one behind, tugging and pulling at various straps, while Ray stood there quite helpless with his hands in the air. Ray thanked them and assured them that his rucksack was now much more comfortable. But as we set off again, leaving the Austrians behind to take more photographs, Ray whispered to me "I can hardly feckin' breathe. As soon as we get out of sight of those two busybodies, I'm putting this back the way it was."

Later, the route dropped us down from the cliffs and onto a long beach that stretched for a few kilometres into Somo. We threw off our boots and socks and were soon joined by other pilgrims who followed suit and we all paddled happily along the shoreline, enjoying the cool water on our liberated feet. The surf was pretty good here and again I looked on enviously as the local surfers caught wave after wave. But I remained with the group and we walked on towards Somo to catch the ferry across the Bay of Santander to the city of Santander itself.

On disembarking in Santander, Ray and I were joined by Anne-Aimee, a French woman we had met at the *albergue* in Guemes, and together we went in search of somewhere to have lunch and a place to stay for the night. After a very nice *menu del dia* lunch, and armed with some information from the local Tourist Office, we tried a couple of pensions without any luck and ended up checking into the pilgrim *albergue*, *Santos Mártires* (Holy Martyrs). It was adequate but extremely basic, although we had certainly been spoiled by Ernesto's wonderful 'Nirvana' like *albergue* near Guemes the night before. The contrast between the two *albergues* could not have been more stark, but that's all part of the rich and varied tapestry experienced on the Camino, as one weaves from place to place and from *albergue* to *albergue*.

Ray, Peppe, Anne-Aimee and I enjoying our evening out in Santander

After drooling over the surf at Somo earlier in the day, I decided to check out the local beaches around Santander to see if there was any prospect of getting on a surfboard. However, there was nothing doing. It seemed that Somo beach on the other side of the Bay of Santander was picking up all the swell that was going. Nevertheless, it was a beautiful, sunny afternoon and my walk along and between the beaches was quite a pleasant way to spend the hours before tea.

Later, back at the Holy Martyrs *albergue*, Ray, Anne-Aimee and I were joined by Peppe, who had also checked in. The four of us headed out to a restaurant where we sat at a table out on the pavement in a busy square and enjoyed another great meal, a few drinks and great craic. There was rarely a dull moment when Ray was about. Even Peppe was in jubilant mood. He was finding the walking much easier now that he was equipped with walking poles to take some of the weight of his weak knee and he was clearly a much happier person as a result. Anne-Aimee was in a great mood also, but it was tinged with sadness as she disclosed that today had in fact been the last day of her walk. She had only come to Spain for a week to see if she liked the Camino experience and her time was now up. Tomorrow she had to return to Brittany, where she lived and worked as a GP. She hadn't really enjoyed the Camino at first as she had found it quite a lonely experience to begin with, but when she had encountered us friendly Irish guys at Guemes and now also Peppe in Santander, she was much happier and sorry to be leaving. We were all very relaxed and jovial as the evening wore on, but at one point Ray looked at his watch and exclaimed, "Holy Feckin' Martyrs, they'll be locking the doors in ten feckin' minutes."

Once again the *albergue* had a 10pm closing time. It was now 9.50pm and we were a good 25 minutes walk from the *albergue*. I offered to run back and let the rest of them in. I set off running through the busy streets of Santander, drawing puzzled looks from many pedestrians as I dodged and weaved my way through the crowds. I made it back to the *albergue* just in time – out of breath but happy to have made it. However, I then found out that the elderly lady *hospitalero* actually locked the door with a key at 10pm and pocketed the key so that no one else could open the door either from the outside or the inside. So I spent the next 15 minutes persuading her to keep the door open to allow my friends back in. However, at a quarter past her patience was running out and she was just about to lock up when Ray, Anne-Aimee and Peppe finally arrived. She duly gave them a good 'telling off' for being late and breaking the rules. At least that's what I assume she was doing, because I didn't understand a word as it was delivered in rapid fire Spanish. She couldn't maintain her sternness though when Ray, Anne-Aimee and Peppe all displayed their chastened children looks – they must have been practicing them on the way back to the *albergue* – and she ended up trying to suppress laughter as she continued to wag her finger at them and scold. She 'chased' us all to bed, holding a finger to her lips to tell us to be quiet as we went.

*****

Ray, Anne-Aimee and I left the Holy Martyrs *albergue* in Santander at around 7.30am and went in search of a café serving breakfast. Peppe had left earlier as he preferred to get on the road early to make up for his slower pace. We found a café open near the bus station where Anne-Aimee was intending to catch a bus at 10am to Handaye, near Irún. From there she hoped to get a train back to Brittany. She was still very sad to be leaving and said she had cried earlier. But she was very glad that she had met Ray and I and very pleased that we had joined her for her final Camino breakfast. She was on the point of tears again as we hugged and said our farewells.

Ray and I headed out the door and gave Anne-Aimee a final wave through the café window before turning to make our way through the city streets to pick up the Camino route once again. We were about two kilometres away before we realised that we had both left the café without paying and that poor Anne-Aimee had been left with the bill for all three of us. Such gentlemen. Now, if we had been from South Korea, we would have turned around and walked all the way back to settle our dues. But we were from Ireland, so we shrugged our shoulders and kept on going. We did send Anne-Aimee an email to apologise though. Truth be told, she had totally disarmed us both with her emotional farewell.

The route out of Santander was long and fairly uninteresting, so it was great to have Ray's company once again. We ran into some torrential downpours along the way, sometimes accompanied by thunder and lightning, but we soon dried off again when it cleared up later and the sun finally made an appearance. The route crossed over railway tracks on a number of occasions, which was fine as they were legitimate crossing points. However about 14km out of Santander, at Boo de Pielagos, we were required to cross a railway bridge between Boo and nearby Mogro. The guidebook recommended getting on the train at Boo and travelling to the next stop at Mogro, although it also suggested that locals simply recommended walking alongside the line and crossing the bridge on foot. Neither Ray nor I were prepared to risk that for the sake of the few Euros required to take the train. "I'd rather end up on the feckin' train than feckin' under it", was the way in which Ray so eloquently expressed it. So we made our way to the platform at Boo de Pielagos and waited for the next train. We stopped for lunch in Mogro when we got off and then pushed on for the next 18km to Santillana del Mar. My guidebook actually described this whole section from Santander to Santillana del Mar as one of the dreariest legs of the Camino del Norte. I would have to agree.

By contrast, however, Santillana del Mar itself was quite an amazing place and made the long, boring trek beforehand feel entirely worthwhile. It was a beautifully kept medieval town; all stone buildings and cobbled streets. Entering the town really was like stepping back in time. The place was most definitely a tourist magnet and it was filled with quaint cafés, restaurants, bars and shops. There is an old saying that Santillana del Mar is 'the town of three lies', since it is neither holy *(Santi)*, flat *(llana)*, nor by the sea *(Mar)*, as implied by its name. The name actually derives from Saint Juliana (or *Santa Illana*), whose remains are kept in the town's Romanesque church and former Benedictine monastery. And although it's not actually by the sea, it's only just over three kilometres away from the coast, so I suppose it's relatively close given the overall size of Spain.

While wandering through the busy streets looking for the *albergue*, we met some other pilgrims who told us it was already full. This felt very disappointing at first, but actually turned out to be a blessing in disguise. Ray and I made our way to the local Tourist Information Office and the very helpful lady there equipped us with a town map and marked the location of a few hotels on it. Being careful not to recommend one particular hotel over another, she nevertheless happened to mention that one did in fact offer a few of its rooms to pilgrims at special rates. Ray and I immediately made our way to the *Casona Solar de Hidalgos*, the particular establishment in question. We couldn't believe our good fortune when we got to the reception of this three-star hotel to learn that we could have a shared room in the hotel for only €15 each. The hotel was a renovated, 16th century palace and a treasure trove of antique sculptures and artwork, suits of armour, dark stone flooring and exposed wooden beams. And when we opened the door to our twin room on the second floor we were gobsmacked. It was luxury compared to any of the *albergues* we'd stayed in, and that included Grandpa Peuto's Cabin in Guemes. Our room contained two actual beds, as opposed to bunks, and the floor to ceiling windows at one end of our room opened to look out over the picturesque terracotta rooftops and gardens of neighbouring houses behind the hotel.

After getting freshened up after the long day's walk and relaxing for a bit, Ray and I met up with Leticia, a young Spanish pilgrim, and her mother, Aurora, for a meal and a few drinks. Ray had met Leticia earlier on the Camino and they had got on very well together and had subsequently kept in touch, meeting up from time to time. Leticia's mother lived in the region and had joined her daughter to walk with her over the weekend. It turned out that they had also got a room in the same hotel and when we got back later, Ray, Leticia and her mum stayed downstairs for drinks, while I was the boring (sensible) one who headed straight to bed. I was determined to make the most of the comfort and quiet on offer at the *Casona Solar de Hidalgos*.

*****

Despite being the earliest to bed, I was the last one to rise; although none of us were up particularly early. After breakfast, we were waved off from the door of the hotel by our jovial host, Andrés, at just before 10am – rather late by pilgrim standards. We joined the Camino route once again, following the cobbled streets out of Santillana del Mar, and gradually working our way past a large contingent of French day-hikers in the process. On the outskirts of the town we passed a sign pointing towards Santiago de Compostela and declaring the distance as 534km. It was a sobering thought to realise that I had to date covered less than a third of the total distance I was intending to walk.

Ray, Leticia and Aurora on the road after leaving Santillana del Mar

The route was mainly along minor roadways through gently undulating and grassy fields, with the snow-capped peaks of the Picos de Europa occasionally visible in the far distance. The banter between the four of us was good along the way, with Ray doing most of the talking and me attempting to explain to the Spanish mother and daughter what he was going on about. At one point, after Ray had been on a particularly long roll, I asked Leticia what the Spanish for "zip it" was, pretending to close a zip across my mouth to indicate what I meant. The Spanish word she gave me, *"ciérralo"* was repeated a number of times throughout the day's journey at Ray's expense – all in the best of humour of course.

It was a pretty pleasant and largely uneventful journey, but, as always, there was plenty for me to photograph, including a fair quotient of striking church buildings. The first of these that we encountered was the 18th century *Iglesia de San Martín de Cigüenza*, about 9km out of Santillana del Mar. The marvellous Baroque facade of the church, which was comprised of two huge symmetrical towers either side of an imposing archway, was very impressive. I took time to admire the church's detail, including a beautiful little metal plaque of Saint James on horseback, before hurrying on to catch up with the others.

We stopped for some lunch in the village of Cóbreces, about four kilometres beyond Cigüenza, and admired the views of the two large pastel-coloured buildings through the restaurant window – the red *Iglesia de St Peter ad Vincula* and the sky-blue Cistercian Abbey of Viaceli. The Neo-Gothic style *Iglesia de St Peter ad Vincula* (Church of Saint Peter in Chains) was particularly impressive with its octagonal dome and two strikingly ornate towers either side, both sporting tall arched windows and soaring up into the blue sky above.

After another six and a half kilometres, we all stopped at a small church at a crossroads in the village of Pando, where it was possible to self-stamp our credentials. The interior of this small church was so serene and peaceful that, without communicating, we all understood each other's needs and were happy to take a bit of time out to enjoy the spiritual calm engendered by the stone walls, high timbered ceiling and vibrantly coloured stained glass windows. After we had replenished our souls we gathered together once again outside the little church and nodded silently to each other to signify that we were ready to leave.

The weather had been pretty nice for the most part, but we ran into some rain about an hour out of Comillas, our destination for the day. It also got extremely windy at times, no doubt due to the storm fronts we could clearly see sweeping inland ahead of us. However, although we pulled on our rain jackets and covered our rucksacks with their rain covers, we were very fortunate to escape the worst of the weather. As we were approaching Comillas, Leticia and I found that we had put quite a bit of distance between ourselves and the other two. We therefore stopped at a bus shelter on the outskirts of the town to wait for Ray and Aurora to catch up. There was a fork in the road at this point and Leticia and I watched with some amusement as Ray, with his head down and hood up, continued along the wrong road – he obviously hadn't spotted us in the bus shelter as he passed. Leticia was about to call to him, but I drew my fingers across my lips and whispered *"ciérralo"*. We let him wander on totally oblivious for a little while longer before we took pity on him and I then whistled to him to get him back on track. "I was just following my feet there," he said, adding "I'm feckin' knackered. And I could really murder a cold beer." Aurora arrived shortly after and the four of us then headed on into town, arriving at around 6pm. We made our way along the cobbled streets to the first bar we encountered and, with the weather now improved once again, sat outside on a couple of wooden benches and enjoyed our well-earned refreshments in the early evening sunshine.

I finished my beer and, while the others ordered another round, I went to check out the local *albergue*. However, on the way I ran into a German woman, Magdalena, who told me that the *albergue* was full. She walked back to the bar with me and we all had another beer outside in the sun, before our group of four went in search of a pension. We found one close by and later, after the showering and laundry duties we walked the short distance into the centre of Comillas and enjoyed a great *menu del dia* with a few beers and glasses of wine. Ray and I then moved on to sample some of the local brandy, which was very good and very cheap – always an excellent combination. A football match between Barcelona and Seville was on a big screen in the restaurant and this added to the atmosphere, with a group of Spanish men at the table next to us becoming very animated at times. Leticia and her mother left early, but Ray and I sat on and watched the rest of the game with a few more drinks. At one stage one of the Spaniards got up to head to the gents. Ray and I waited a couple of seconds and then let out an almighty roar as if Barcelona had just scored. The poor chap came rushing back to see what all the commotion was and his mates fell about laughing. As they say in Ireland, "the craic was good." More drink was ordered and thoughts of an early night were quickly forgotten.

*****

Following the late night session with Ray, we were both up at a surprisingly reasonable hour. We met up with Leticia and her mum for breakfast in a local café near the centre of Comillas. Unfortunately we had to say farewell to Ray. He was going to continue with his Camino this morning, but I had decided to have a long overdue rest day and Leticia was staying behind with her mum who was waiting on a friend to give her a lift back home later in the day. Naturally, I was very sad to be parting company with Ray, who had been a great mate over the last few days. It had certainly been superb fun. But two Irishmen on the Camino, with a plentiful supply of cheap wine and beer, is a good or bad mix, depending on which way you look at it. I had certainly enjoyed it while it had lasted, but I was now ready to slow down and take a bit of time out to reflect on why I was really on this Camino.

So after much hugging and backslapping, Ray headed off out the door to rejoin the Camino and I left Leticia and Aurora to have another coffee. I went to explore the town a bit more and took many photographs of the beautiful architecture on display, including works by Antoní Gaudí of Barcelona fame – the most outstanding of which was *El Capricho*, a summerhouse constructed from an unusual combination of iron, brick and pottery. However, the piece that I personally found to be the most striking and symbolic was Josep Llimona's fabulous marble statue of the Guardian Angel that stood high above the entrance to the town's hill-top cemetery. It made for a truly stunning sight; this powerful figure carved in white marble, standing defiantly atop the corner of a weathered stone wall, was simply dazzling against the deep blue sky over Comillas. I noticed that the figure was holding a sword in his right hand and I was immediately reminded of the fact that the Way of Saint James is also known as 'The Way of the Sword' where you fight your demons and find your strength. Thoughts of my own guardian angel came flooding in and I hoped that she would continue to watch over me just as this statue watched over this beautiful Spanish town.

*****

Josep Llimona's Guardian Angel standing above the entrance to Comillas' hill-top cemetery

The following morning, I set off for San Vicente de la Barquera. However, rather than taking the official Camino route, which was more direct and followed the main roads, I decided once again to hug the coastline as much as possible, which was longer but much more rewarding. I had met an Australian couple in the café where I had had breakfast before leaving Comillas, and they had recommended it over the official route. So off-route it was and it was definitely the best decision of the day. This alternative way took me round rugged headlands and over beautiful beaches, but the best bit was the fact that it took me through the little village of Trasvía. This pretty place was sufficiently elevated to provide superb views of the snow-covered Picos de Europa in the distance. These fantastic mountains were as stunning as I had hoped they would be when I had first learned that the Camino del Norte route passed within sight of them. The residents of Trasvía probably don't realise how lucky they are to be living where they do, but the scenes I experienced were pure 'chocolate-box' picture perfect.

From Trasvía I followed the quiet rural roads down towards the road bridge crossing the Ría de La Rabia (River of Rage), watching a small herd of goats grazing among the eucalyptus trees on the western bank as I went. The water in the river was very low and pond still when I was there and I could only speculate that this estuary fills quite quickly and gains a bit of life, rage even, whenever the tide comes in. From here I continued to eschew the official Camino route inland and instead followed the roads out towards the long, sandy beach at Playa de Oyambre. On the way, I crossed a tributary to the Rabia that resembled a eucalyptus graveyard, as it was littered with dead tree trunks protruding from the shallow riverbed, as if the arms of ghouls were reaching up out of their watery graves. It was an incongruous sight amongst so much natural beauty and served to remind me, as if I needed any reminding, that nature can have its dark side also and that death and decay is unfortunately part and parcel of all life. Normal service was soon restored, however, as I stepped onto the beach at Oyambre and walked across the firm sands for almost three kilometres. I then left the beach to pick up a lane that looked like it might take me in the right direction. This led me up and through some lush, green pastures, herds of very docile and contented looking brown cows and a number of gorgeous looking farm buildings and villas. With the white Picos de Europa once again visible in the distance, the combination of all these elements created yet more 'chocolate-box' scenes.

I picked up a narrow road out of a small hamlet that may have been Oyambre itself and followed this close to the coast until I was finally able to descend onto another wonderfully long beach at *Peña del Zapato*. I knew that *peña* translated as 'pain' and *zapato* as 'shoe', so *Peña del Zapato* literally translates as 'pain of the shoe'. How appropriate I thought, as I slipped off my boots and socks again and enjoyed the sublime feel of the cool water around my hot feet. I paddled my way towards the end of the beach, where San Vicente lay, still 4km away. My thoughts turned to the beach walks that Jacqui and I had enjoyed so much together in Ireland and elsewhere over the years. One of our favourite walks was across Curran Strand at Portrush on the

North Coast of Ireland where we had a holiday home that we had frequented as often as possible. Curran Strand stretches for three kilometres from the east side of Portrush to the limestone cliffs and arches at Whiterocks. There are also wonderful views out to the Skerries, a small line of rocky islands about one and a half kilometres offshore, and, on clear days, views of Donegal to the west, Dunluce Castle and the Giant's Causeway to the east and even the Scottish isle of Islay to the north-east. Memories flooded back to our last walk together along that beach. It was a short one, as Jacqui's energy levels were low as the cancer began to take its toll on her body.

"Hold up love," she said, squeezing my hand gently, just sufficiently to get my attention, "I think I've gone far enough." "Hey, that's my line" I replied. And it was true. It was invariably me who suggested that it was time to turn around and head back. I wasn't much of a walker back then. "I know love," she said, "but I'm starting to get a little tired. I'm just not up to it anymore. This bloody cancer has me drained." I nodded slowly in acknowledgement, as she continued. "I've something to ask you." She now had my full attention, but I wasn't sure that I wanted to hear what she was about to say. "We both know where this is going love. There is no getting away from it. I've been thinking about my ashes." The words hit me like a punch. There it was, out in the open for the first time. We had by this stage both reluctantly accepted the inevitability of Jacqui's death looming ahead, but we hadn't, until now, spoken about what would happen after her death. My mind just hadn't dared to go there. It could just about comprehend the end of the road, but beyond that there was nothing. Just a full stop – for both of us. The mention of her ashes suddenly pushed me beyond where I had feared to tread before. All I could do at that point was let out a low groan and turn away, still not wishing to face reality. Then she embraced me and I turned to her and melted into that embrace. She was the strong one. "I'm so sorry dear," I muttered between the tears, "I wish there was something more I could do." One's sense of helplessness in such an impossible situation is simply overwhelming. I had always been the fixer, the one who could put things right, the one who could repair and restore things. But not this time. "You really have nothing to be sorry for, my dear," she said, "It's not you that has done this to me. You have been here for me right from the start of this. I couldn't have got through all the treatment and hospital visits if it hadn't been for you. But there is something more I need you to do. You can help me plan for my funeral." Another body blow, and another groan. "And I want it to be a celebration. I don't want people with long faces, all dressed in black. I want people to wear something bright and to look back on the wonderful life I have had and to smile, not cry." After a time we agreed to contact a funeral director when we returned to our home in Belfast the following week. Damn it, she already had one in mind. "What about your ashes?" I managed through my sobs, "you said you'd been thinking about your ashes," at the same time realising that this was the first time that Jacqui had clearly indicated her intention to be cremated. "Here," she said, "I would like some of my ashes to be sprinkled here on this beautiful beach, where I hope you will continue to walk and surf. And then when you do, you will know that I will always be close to you."

I'm not ashamed to say that I added a few more drops to the salt water of the ocean as I walked with my painful memories towards the town of San Vicente de la Barquera. However my spirits lifted as I drew closer to this beautiful town and thought about the many other beach walks that Jacqui and I had enjoyed together over the years. The town was approached via the long stone Maza Bridge, which had 28 arches and was over half a kilometre long. The views from the bridge in all directions were simply stunning – the wide Maza estuary, backed by gently undulating pastures and the dramatic Picos de Europa to the south; the picturesque port and golden beaches to the north; and the historical town, with its castle, sanctuary and churches straight ahead to the west. Ray had sent me a message earlier to say that the *albergue* in San Vicente should be avoided. So I instead went in search of alternative accommodation online. I found a good hotel a relatively short walk away for a reasonable price. I booked myself in for two nights, as I planned to meet friends from back home here in two days'

The Maza estuary and multi-arched bridge at San Vicente de la Barquera

time. I hadn't particularly wanted to interrupt my Camino for another day, particularly only after having had a day off in Comillas. But I was looking forward to meeting familiar faces from home and, to be honest, I could not think of a nicer place than San Vicente de la Barquera to park the boots and rucksack for a bit.

My hotel was on the north side of the town and was clean, quiet and comfortable and provided a great base from which to explore this picturesque town. It was over another short bridge, and looked across a stretch of estuary water to both the ruins of the eighteenth century castle and the thirteenth century Gothic *Iglesia de Santa María de los Angeles*, Church of St Maria of the Angels.

*****

The following day I took the long walk back across the Maza Bridge to reach the beach once again and finally got the elusive surf I had been hoping for since I had first arrived in Spain. I was able to hire a surfboard and wetsuit from a local surf school and I eagerly headed for the sea. The waves were pretty small, but I didn't mind that much. It was just so nice to be in the water again and I have to say that surfing against the backdrop of San Vicente de la Barquera and the Picos de Europa was really something very special – just incredible. After a few hours in the water I felt totally satisfied – my mind and body completely refreshed in a way that only surfing can achieve. I returned my equipment to the guys at the surf school and wandered back to town in my shorts and sandals, watching the numerous lizards dive for cover off the pavement as soon as they sensed my appproach.

At the Maza Bridge, I spotted a small crowd gathered close to the start of the bridge. It became clear, as I neared the commotion, that an old cruiser had become lodged against the bridge and a number of locals and small tugs were trying to extricate it, with much encouragement or ridicule (I couldn't tell which) being offered by the onlookers on the bridge. I wondered at first if the old boat was worth saving, as it looked pretty ancient. The owners had either been trying to cultivate an on-board garden or the weeds had simply taken a firm hold – unlike the anchor it has to be said. The tide was still coming in and the rush of water towards the arches of the bridge was forcing the hapless boat up against the bridge sideways. There was no way that the two small boats deployed in an attempt to tow the boat off the bridge were going to be able to win against the strong current holding the older, bigger boat in place. I glanced at my watch and having checked the tide times earlier for surfing purposes, I knew that the tide would turn in less than half an hour and that the flow of water would then push the boat off the bridge instead of against it. I attempted to communicate this to a gruff old sailor on the stricken boat. He reminded me of the character Quint, the shark-hunter played by Robert Shaw in Jaws. He either didn't understand my broken Spanish or simply wasn't going to take advice from some meddling foreigner. He dismissed me with a derisive wave. I decided to leave them to it and watched the engine of one of the smaller boats start to smoke as I made my way over the rest of the bridge's 28 arches.

I stopped at a harbour side café in town for a coffee before going back to my hotel. I had a good view across the main estuary to the bridge and couldn't resist smiling to myself as I watched the previously stricken boat gently ease itself off the bridge as the tide turned. Sometimes, it's just so much easier to go with the flow instead of trying to fight against it. A metaphor for my journey perhaps. Not the physical journey I was on, but the much longer and much more difficult emotional one. Just as the flow of water had been pushing the boat against the bridge, so had the current of my grief been pushing me against the buffers of my life. I was stuck. I couldn't go forward and I couldn't go back. And I would remain trapped in the same position until something fundamental changed. Just as the stricken boat wasn't able to move away from the bridge until the tide turned, I could now see that my situation also needed a major change if I was ever to float free from my crushing pain and be released from the clutches of bereavement. No matter how hard the captain of the boat had tried, and in spite of the gallant help he was receiving from others, he was ultimately fighting against a force that was much too powerful. He simply had to wait until the tide turned before he could make any progress. So perhaps I also had to just wait on the tide of grief to turn. That was something that I had no control over and, in spite of the fantastic help I had received from friends, it was not something that could be influenced by others. I would just have to be patient and wait for the right time. Until then, I would just have to go with the flow and try not to fight against it. Grief was much too powerful a force to fight against. Needless to say, I truly yearned for the day when I would feel my grief easing and I could eventually lift myself off the buffers and return to some sort of normality. As I sat with my coffee, going with the flow of my thoughts, as it were, a wry smile came to my lips. For just as the old boat would now need a bit of attention, weeds and rust removed and any holes or damage patched up, so I would probably also be in need a good spruce up at some point in the future – although there's a limit to what can be achieved with an old wreck.

Sunset in San Vicente de la Barquera

With the estuary now full, San Vicente looked at its stunning best. Dozens of small, colourful fishing boats and yachts rested, alongside their reflections, in calm waters bathed in warm, early evening sunshine. Later that evening, as the sun was going down, I enjoyed some beautiful scenes as the sky turned a dusky pink above the Picos de Europa and bathed the town, castle, church and estuary in its soft, heavenly glow. All in all, the last three days had been absolutely amazing. They involved a day walking across the most beautiful of coastlines, with unbelievably long sandy beaches and with striking, snow covered mountains often in the background, sandwiched between two days resting in two of the most beautiful towns, Comillas and San Vicente. Despite my constant companions, of sorrow and loss, I felt truly blessed.

When the Pharisees realised that their sorcerer, Hermogenes, had been converted, they were not pleased. They blamed James and his preaching about Christ's crucifixion and ascension and feared that he would win many others over to believe in his Lord. A bishop, named Abiathar, rallied the people against James. A lynch mob was formed and they hunted down James who they found preaching with his disciples. The ringleaders of the mob put a rope round James' neck and dragged him off and brought him before the King of Judea, Herod Agrippa. King Herod saw James very much as a trouble-maker and agitator and, after listening to the testimony of Bishop Abiathar, he quickly commanded that James be taken away and executed by beheading.

As James was being dragged off to his execution, he passed a man with paralysis who was begging in the street. The man recognised James and, having heard of his miracles, cried out to him and beseeched James to help him. James caused his captors to stop in front of the man. Those leading him to his execution were intrigued to see what would happen next. Someone called out, "Well, come on then, follower of Christ. Let's see you work some of your magic now."

Others laughed and jeered at this, but James spoke to the man and said, "In the name of Jesus Christ, for whom I am to be beheaded, arise and be healed and bless the Lord your Maker". And the paralysed man was healed and rose to his feet.

The crowd was initially stunned by this seemingly miraculous event, but then calls of "Trickery", "Fake" and "Death to the heretic" started to ring out. However, a scribe, named Josias, who was leading James to his execution, saw the miracle and believed it to be the work of the Lord. He fell down at James' feet and begged forgiveness and asked to be christened. When the bishop Abiathar saw this, he had Josias taken and beaten and then gained consent from King Herod that Josias should also be beheaded along with James. While they were awaiting execution, James requested a potful of water and he used this to baptise Josias.

Chapter Five: Fragile
(Days 22 to 26 - San Vicente de la Barquera to Villaviciosa)

I checked out of my small but comfortable hotel in San Vicente de la Barquera just before 9am and took the short walk around to the Cafe El Manantial near the harbour, where I had arranged to meet my friends from Ireland. John and Aideen were over in Spain to visit their daughter in Madrid and then spend a few days on the North Coast. They were on their way to San Sebastián and I was delighted that they were able to take a slight detour to meet me for breakfast in San Vicente. It was great to see them and to exchange our Spanish experiences over coffee and croissants, as well as catching up with news from back home. One of their other daughters had walked the Camino Frances the previous year and so they were fairly familiar with the trials and tribulations of pilgrimages and *albergues* and all that that entailed. After breakfast, John and Aideen headed back to their car to continue their onward journey to San Sebastián. I sat on in the cafe for a few minutes to scribble a quick postcard to my dad. He didn't use Facebook and so I had promised to send him the odd postcard to keep him up to date with my progress. After posting it, I walked back to the end of the Maza Bridge and re-joined the Camino route.

My walking day started with a long, gradual climb out of the town and I fell into step with Gabriel along this stretch and walked with him for a good few kilometres. Originally from Bogota in Colombia, Gabriel had lived and worked in New York for the last number of years. However, he had lost his job recently and also got divorced and had ended up on the Camino on a spur of the moment decision after learning about it from friends. He was enjoying taking 'time out' from normal life and had no real plan or expectations from the Camino other than it giving him a bit of time for himself. He was hoping to get a phone call any day now inviting him to a new job in his area of expertise – nanotechnology – and if that happened, he was simply prepared to call a halt to his Camino and start a new life. It wasn't every day that I encountered a nanotechnologist from Colombia. It also turned out that his grandmother was originally from Ireland and he had just come from visiting cousins in Dublin and Galway. He told me about the political unrest and terrorism in Colombia and the efforts to reach a peaceful solution – the similarities to Northern Ireland's journey in recent years were quite striking. We caught up with a girl that Gabriel had met before and he fell into step with her while I moved ahead. The Camino is like that, in that you join people for a time and then you, or they, move on – and you may encounter them again or you may not.

And, as it happened, a few kilometres after leaving Gabriel and his friend behind, I caught up once again with Sara and her dog, Freccia, who I hadn't seen for over a week. The last time was at the 'café of the lame' in Liendo, where Freccia had been experiencing paw problems and Peppe knee problems. Thankfully, Freccia's paws had improved a lot after some treatment and rest and they were now very happy to be back on the road again. I may have 'lost' some of my pilgrim buddies through my stopping for rest days, but on this occasion it had fortuitously resulted in me meeting Sara again. Sara explained to me that she had acquired Freccia from his previous owners in Italy, who had no longer wanted him. He had also come to her already named Freccia. Interestingly, Freccia, is actually an Italian word for 'arrow' and being a golden Labrador, he was sort of yellow also. Yellow arrows, or *flecha amarilla* as they are called in Spanish, are of course frequently used to mark the Camino route. So you might say it was Freccia's destiny to walk the Camino or, perhaps, Sara's destiny to follow her 'four pawed yellow arrow'. Sara and I got on great together and I subsequently walked with her and Freccia for most of the remainder of the day – in fact all the way to La Franca, where Sara planned to stop at a campsite. It was difficult for her to find *albergue*s or pensions that would permit dogs, but campsites usually presented no problem.

We stopped at a café in the small town of Unquera for a break. Over coffee and snacks, I was greatly amused to learn that Sara, who worked in a kindergarten in Berlin, used Italian when talking casually with Freccia or giving him praise, but always used German to give her dog commands. Her German commands became quite obvious later when we came across a small herd of goats on a path a few kilometres beyond Unquera. Most of the goats scattered into fields well before we got anywhere near them, but one bold beast stood proudly on top of a low stone wall at the side of the path and just stared at Freccia as he approached. However, when Freccia started barking up at the goat, it suddenly leapt down onto the path again and dashed past us and through a gap in the wall into a field – all the time being pursued by Freccia. He hadn't a chance of catching the incredibly fast and nibble goat, but that didn't deter him from his pursuit. Sara thought this was hysterical at first and was in a fit of giggles at the antics of Freccia and the goat, but then started to panic as she quickly realised that it wasn't a great idea for her dog to be running amok through a field of farm animals. Her giggles then ceased and she shouted at Freccia in German, *"Freccia hör auf. Hör auf. Komm jetzt her"* and *"Böser Hund"* – "Freccia stop. Stop. Come here now" and "Bad dog." Freccia did return and Sara put his lead on for the rest of the day. She normally only used the lead when walking through busy towns as Freccia was usually such a docile creature and had never bothered with other animals before. She had been very surprised at Freccia giving chase to the goat. In Freccia's defence, I did suggest that the particular goat in question had appeared to me to goad Freccia into the chase and had also seemed to enjoy the sport.

When we reached La Franca, I reluctantly said farewell to Sara and Freccia and walked on alone for another five kilometres to reach the Santa Marina Albergue in Buelna. My trusty scout, Ray, who was now a few days ahead of me, had sent me a message earlier, recommending this particular *albergue*. And it was certainly a great place to stop. I was allocated a bunk in a six-bed dorm and was very fortunate to have the whole dorm, with ensuite facilities, all to myself. After the usual washing routine, I headed out to the grassy area at the front of the *albergue* to hang out my wet clothes. Here I was surprised to find Sara busy pitching her tent, while Freccia sat waiting patiently to one side. Sara explained that she always felt kind of isolated when she stayed in the campsites away from the rest of the pilgrims. So she had phoned ahead and was delighted to discover that this *albergue* was happy to accommodate her dog, so long as it stayed outside. And Maik, Hana and Jimmy were staying here also. I thought that they would have been days ahead like Ray, but poor Hana's legs and feet were suffering a bit and this had slowed her down and they had all decided to stick together. I duly christened them 'The Three Musketeers'. "One for all and all for one" we toasted as we sat at the picnic tables outside in the early evening sun, enjoying our first cold beers of the day. "Well if we are the Three Musketeers, then you must become our d'Artagnan" declared Hana and we all drank to that. It was great to be amongst such good company again.

*****

I was up for breakfast at a leisurely 8am in the lovely Santa Marina Albergue in Buelna. Most of the pilgrims staying were at various stages of having breakfast also and it seemed that no-one was in any particular hurry to get on the road this morning. However, after breakfast, even though many pilgrims were setting off around the same time, I still set off alone. I had decided not to take the official Camino route favoured by the rest of the pilgrims, which on this occasion simply followed the main road out of Buelna towards Pendueles. Instead I opted for the alternative coastal route once again – longer, but more scenic and away from the traffic. Unfortunately it also meant separating from Sara and Freccia again, as Sara sensibly preferred to follow the more travelled route, which she knew was suitable for Freccia, rather than taking a risk with a lesser known and possibly rougher route. And while my chosen route started off pretty straightforward with good, clear paths, after a couple of kilometres I began to think that perhaps on this occasion it might have been better to have followed the crowd. For the track I was on just suddenly stopped at a fence and there was nothing before me but field after field with no clearly discernible route through.

I could see roughly where I needed to get to about a kilometre ahead, but it was not clear how I was going to get there. Other than backtracking for miles, I had no option other than to simply climb over the fence into the first field and trek through the long grass and cows in the general direction I wanted to go. Some of the cows had pretty formidable looking horns and it was with much relief that I eventually climbed over a wall and dropped down safely into the grounds of a campsite.

I noticed on the way through that the campsite had two flags fluttering from a single flagpole in a central position. Under the red and yellow national flag of Spain, there was a flag displaying a yellow cross, the *Cruz de la Victoria* (Victory Cross), on a sky-blue background. This was the flag of Asturias and it reminded me that I had recently entered the region of Asturias, when I had crossed the River Deva in Unquera the day before. The Camino del Norte passes through four of Spain's autonomous communities – starting with the Basque Country, then Cantabria, Asturias and finally Galicia, where Santiago de Compostela is located. From the campsite, I joined the official Camino route once again and started to encounter other pilgrims along the way. Despite forecasts for rain, the sky remained as blue as the background of the Asturian flag and the coast once again avoided the showers, with any rain falling further inland over the mountains. However, the beauty of the various coastal coves along the way did compensate for the lack of views inland – the water was almost turquoise in places and many of the little sandy coves were completely deserted and their sands completely unspoiled by footprints.

I caught up with Gabriel from Colombia/New York and Justine from Georgia as I was climbing the road out of a little valley that cradled the pretty village of Andrin. The elevated roadway we were on provided superb views over a verdant coastline that appeared all the more luxuriant against the blue of the sea. Gabriel gradually slipped behind, as his feet were giving him trouble, and, having been waved on, Justine and I gradually pulled away from him. We both opted for the GR alternative route, which on this occasion led us away from the coast. However, it also got us off the main road and took us higher, providing great views of the coast and Llandes, the town we were destined for. The GR route actually followed an old 'royal road' into Llandes and passed by the *Ermita del Cristo del Camino*, a pretty solid looking stone building sitting alone in a clearing amongst the beech trees. The road alongside the *ermita* (hermitage) was quite striking as it passed through a very deep cutting between the beech trees, the walls of which appeared to be supported by the very roots of the trees themselves. It conjured up a medieval scene in my mind and, for a moment, I could almost imagine myself transported back in time. It was only Justine making her way down the road ahead of me with her modern rucksack and walking poles, that prevented the illusion from being complete.

Justine and I continued together for the next two kilometres into the town of Llandes. At the first bar/restaurant on the way into the town centre we came across Maik and Jimmy enjoying a beer. We joined them and various other pilgrims that we knew either passed us or joined us for a drink, including Gabriel, Hana and Sara and Freccia. My thoughts of walking on for another five kilometres to Celorio, my loosely planned finishing point for the day, soon evaporated. The company was just too good. Unfortunately, Sara and Freccia had to continue on out of town for a few more kilometres in order to find a campsite, but the rest of us booked into the municipal *albergue* beside the train station.

After attending to all my washing, I headed out to explore the sights of Llanes. It was a busy fishing port, which also attracted a lot of tourists due to its coastal location, its three sandy beaches and its spectacular cliff-top walk, the Paseo de San Pedro. And of course, these were all backed by the picturesque Picos de Europa mountains. The weather had changed from earlier and the sky now looked quite threatening, with dark clouds the colour of bruises closing in. I therefore decided against taking the cliff-top walk in favour of a stroll round the industrial harbour area and the pretty marina. The harbour of Llanes is famed for its 'Cubes of Memory', a bold work of public art created by Basque artist Augustín Ibarrola. Here, the large concrete blocks surrounding the end of the pier to act as a breakwater, had been painted by Ibarrola with images representing the history and nature of the region. Any pictures I had seen of this work had shown a highly colourful, vibrant and striking piece of public art that spoke of the artist's genius and daring. However, at the time of my visit, the cubes had become rather weathered and faded and I'm afraid they didn't have the impact perhaps intended. I estimated that the artist was now in his late 80's, and so I very much doubted that he would be back to give the cubes a fresh coat of paint. Perhaps he wouldn't wish for it to be freshened up anyway. Maybe he realised from the outset that his work would be temporary in nature and that it would eventually fade and disappear over the years as a comment on the ravages of time and the power of the ocean.

I headed back into town but was unable to find any of my fellow pilgrims and I ended up dining alone at a little restaurant near the marina. The meal was fine, but a rather sad and lonely experience and it left me with too much time to think about things lost. I was therefore feeling rather down as I plodded back to the *albergue* to get in before it shut its doors at 10pm. However, I met a group of three Frenchmen, Paul, Jean-Pierre and Gerard, along with Richard from Kansas in the common area. I shared my unfinished bottle of red wine from the restaurant with them and they shared chocolate and an infusion of Tila with me. They were very friendly and good fun to be with and, thanks to them, I finished the day in a better frame of mind.

✳✳✳✳✳

I was up early the next morning, as I had planned to walk 30km to Ribadesellas to make up for stopping early in Llanes. Shortly after leaving, I was joined by Stephen, who caught up with me when I stopped to take some photographs. Stephen was another Frenchman, who I had met briefly at the *albergue* during breakfast, and we subsequently walked together for the next 6km.

Stephen revealed that he was a Roman Catholic priest and that this was the third Camino he had been on. He was disappointed to find that so many of the churches on the Camino del Norte route were closed, which had not been the case on the Camino Frances route he had previously walked. He had hoped to meet more priests along the way and offer to say mass. So far he had only had two opportunities to do so and they had been on the first two days of his walk, over two weeks ago. However, he hoped to have better luck in Cuerres, which was where he planned to walk to today. Stephen was very easy company and the six kilometres I walked with him passed quickly. He spoke very good English, but with a strong French accent, which reminded me of Rene from the TV sitcom 'Allo Allo'. He told me about his community work back in his parish in France, much of which involved him in helping young people find their way in life. I had to suppress a laugh when he talked rather earnestly about his time with the scouts, which he repeatedly pronounced as "scoots".

It was another beautiful morning, as we wound our way along wide stony tracks that cut through fields green with tall grass, the blue sea often visible to our right and the mountains to our left divided top from bottom by a long band of white mist that the morning sun had yet to burn off. As we followed a road skirting around the small estuary of Barro, the *Iglesia de Nuestra Señora de los Dolores* (Church of Our Lady of Sorrows) came into view on the west bank. The church alone is exceptionally picturesque, but we came upon it at an opportune time, as the tide was in and the estuary was filled full with beautifully calm seawater that acted as nature's mirror. The image of the beautiful church was almost perfectly reflected in the estuary's still water and it made for a stunning scene that I was delighted to capture on camera. Whilst I was more than content to appreciate the exterior of the church and its surroundings, Stephen wanted to walk the extra few hundred yards off route to go inside, if indeed it was open. In truth, I wouldn't

*The Iglesia de Nuestra Señora de los
Dolores reflected in the estuary of Barro*

have minded visiting it also, but I sensed that Stephen wanted a bit of time on his own for quiet reflection and so we said goodbye at that point and I kept to the route while Stephen set off towards the church for some peace and prayer.

A little later I was walking past another church, which was right by the roadside. I was concentrating on my guidebook to see how far it was to the next town, when suddenly the church bell rang out the half hour very loudly and just a matter of metres from where I was walking. I nearly jumped out of my skin because it was so loud and so unexpected. I let out an equally loud and totally involuntary "F**k." It was just as well that I had separated from Father Stephen earlier, as I don't think he would have been too impressed. Possibly as punishment for my cursing outside a church, I managed to take a wrong turn shortly after this. I ended up going along a lane that eventually petered out. I attempted to go across some fields again for a time, but I couldn't see a way of linking up with the official route again. There were also a lot of obstacles in the way, such as thick hedges and barbed wire fencing. I doubled back to the point where I felt I had gone wrong and took the other path instead in the hope that I would have more luck with it. Although it didn't seem too promising to start with, a Camino scallop sign eventually came into view.

While approaching the town of Nueva, I was passed by two young girls on bicycles and they called out *"Buen Camino"* to me and I responded in kind, as they whizzed past. "Cheats," I thought to myself jokingly. There are actually three modes of transport that are officially accepted as valid for undertaking the Camino de Santiago pilgrimage – on foot, which is by far the most common; by bicycle; or on horseback. I had encountered a few cyclists since setting off on my Camino, but I had yet to witness anyone on horseback.

On entering the town of Nueva a short while later, I was surprised to see the streets filled with market stalls. I had arrived on market day. Feelings of loss once again crowded in. Jacqui had loved wandering around these sorts of markets and a holiday together wasn't complete without a visit to the local market. I have to admit that I wasn't always the most eager of partners to be dragged around the stalls, but God, how I wished I could take Jacqui by the hand now and casually stroll around this colourful and busy town market. I was tempted to hurry through and put the marketplace, and the painful memories it had raked up, behind me. But then I saw the two cyclists who had passed me earlier sitting on a bench in the town's small plaza and they waved and smiled at me. So, I smiled back and went over to say hello. They had just bought some pastries from a market stall and they offered me one. They were delicious, but we all agreed that they would taste even better with a cup of coffee. We headed to a café just around the corner and I treated them to coffees and we enjoyed these with the pastries outside at a pavement table.

Hannah and Julie were both students from Canada and were planning to cycle all the way to Santiago on the bicycles that they had brought over with them. They were young and enthusiastic and it was lovely to spend some time with them and exchange information about our respective countries and backgrounds. I made no mention of it, but these two bright young things had certainly saved me from my earlier melancholy and had prevented me from free-falling into self-pity. After we had finished our coffees and pastries, we wished each other well and I left them to explore more of the market, while I set off on foot once again. However, about a kilometre later, they passed me again and they stopped to ask if they could take a photo with me. I initially felt very privileged, but they then burst my bubble by explaining that they liked to get a photo with every pilgrim they met on the Camino. So it wasn't my dashing good looks that had caused them to stop. How my fortunes had changed. Less than a fortnight ago, women had been throwing their knickers at me! Anyway, I was very happy to pose for a photo with the girls, before they mounted their bicycles once more and rode off to eventually disappear over the brow of the next hill, little realising the joy they had brought to this fragile pilgrim.

From the outset today, the weather had been wonderful, but I'm afraid that that all changed suddenly at around 2pm when I ran into some heavy downpours accompanied by thunder and lightning. Although I donned my wet gear right away, I arrived in Ribadesellas over an hour later, soaked through to the underpants. I squelched my way to the hostel that Ray had recommended from his stay in this seaside town a couple of days earlier. It was certainly proving to be very handy having a 'scoot' to suss out the best places to stay in advance. And it really was a super *albergue* in a wonderful location. It was an extremely well maintained old colonial style building, with wonderful fish-scale roof tiles, that sat just in from the promenade overlooking the long but narrow beach of Playa de Santa Marina. Even though it wasn't looking its best in the wet, grey weather when I first arrived, it was still a most impressive *albergue*. It was fantastic to get inside and out of my wet clothes and have a nice hot shower. As luck would have it, I ended up with a bed in a four-bed room with the three Frenchmen from last night's *albergue* in Llanes, Paul, Jean-Pierre and Gerard. Jean-Pierre carried a tin whistle in his rucksack and was an accomplished player and he treated us all to a little tune or two before dinner. Because it was so wet outside, I decided, like most other resident pilgrims, to dine in the communal dining area of the *albergue* itself, where a decent selection of food and drink was on offer. There was a friendly atmosphere over dinner, although everyone seemed a little jaded and retired to their rooms soon after the meal was finished. I did likewise. I was certainly looking forward to a good rest after the day's long trek.

*****

The three Frenchmen woke me early the next morning. I was tired and could easily have stayed on in bed, but there was little point as the others moved around the room pulling their things together. I think they were trying their best to be quiet, but there are limits as to how quiet three fully grown men can be on bare wooden floors. So I got up as well and joined them and other early risers for breakfast downstairs in the *albergue*, before returning to the dorm to repack my rucksack. The sea view out the dorm window was wonderful. The previous day's rain had now cleared and it was a gorgeous morning and I captured a lovely image of the sand, sea and sky, all nicely framed by the tall dorm window. Unfortunately, my boots were still very wet from the previous day's soaking. So I tied the boots to my rucksack and opted to walk in my socks and sandals instead.

I left the *albergue* and enjoyed a very pleasant start to my walk along the promenade of Ribadesellas. I had the sea to my right and a number of very grand old-colonial style houses to my left. These had mostly been built in the nineteenth century by locals who had made their fortunes dealing in the Cuban tobacco trade. The scenery beyond Ribadesellas was beautiful, with stunning sea views to one side and striking pastoral and mountain views to the other constantly vying for my attention. Once again I was struck by the similarities of the coastline to the North Coast back home in Ireland, but, in addition, today I was also struck by the similarities of the rocky mountain ridges and peaks to the Mourne Mountains in County Down. Imagine both of those vistas coming together in the one place – it was just wonderful. The route was incredibly varied today and also took me through rolling, grass-covered pastures and forests of eucalyptus, but never straying too far from the Mediterranean-like sea and a coast fringed with numerous long, sandy beaches. I also passed through the delightful old village of La Vega, steeped in rustic charm, and for the first time I started to see some hórreos, which are traditional grain stores common in the Asturias and Galicia regions of Spain. They are typically built of wood or stone and consist of a hut or shed type construction, raised off the ground by pillars, which are topped with flat, overhanging stones to prevent rodents gaining access to the store.

After a section of paved medieval road cutting between trees and rocks, I passed through the village of Berbes and then joined a path over the cliff tops for about five kilometres before dropping down to reach the lovely Playa de la Espasa. My guidebook then directed that I should follow the N-632 away from the beach for the final 2km stretch into

The view out the dorm window as I prepared to leave the albergue in Ribadesellas

La Isla. But I was having none of that – why follow a boring paved road when there's a gorgeous beach to stroll along instead? I followed the beach and stopped off at a little picnic area about a kilometre out of La Isla. Here I had a short break and thoroughly enjoyed resting in the hot afternoon sun. I was intrigued to find that nearly every wooden post and tree trunk here was covered in a multitude of intricately patterned snail shells, the reason for which completely eluded me, but it provided another nice photographic image.

I met Paul, Jean-Pierre and Gerard once again, sitting outside a bar/café on the way into town and I stopped to have a coffee with them. They told me that the *albergue* would not be opening for another hour, so I decided to stop for a while longer and have a beer and pizza for lunch. The Frenchmen moved on and I moved inside to have my lunch, as I was getting slowly roasted at the table outside in the full glare of the sun. As I was enjoying my pizza and cold beer I watched a waiter go through the elaborate performance of pouring small glasses of cider for a table nearby. This involved him standing in the middle of the floor, holding the glass low in one hand over a small metal bin placed in front of him, raising the bottle of cider above his head and then tipping it so that the liquid poured from a great height to be caught in the glass below. The waiter was obviously well practised, as none of the cider missed the glass. This was obviously a common sight in the café, as I think I was the only one watching him intently with my mouth open! I later discovered that this is a traditional way to serve cider in this part of Spain as it helps to aerate the cider, thus giving it a delicate sparkling taste.

A lot of other familiar faces started to arrive in the café and, by the time we were ready to leave for registration at the *albergue*, there were about 15 of us. Registration for the *albergue* in La Isla was at the *hospitalero*'s own house and after she had taken everyone's details, etc. she led us all en masse to the *albergue* itself, which was about five minutes' walk away. She was an elderly *señora*, but she was certainly no pushover and kept everyone in check. Whilst registering us on the porch outside the front door of her house, a young, female pilgrim must have assumed that that her home was the *albergue*. But when she moved to enter, the elderly *hospitalero* made it abundantly clear that if she set foot over the threshold of her home she would have severe trouble walking the rest of the Camino. Of course, I am merely guessing at what she actually said, as her warning was delivered in a rapid fire Spanish dialect that I hadn't a mission of understanding, but the general gist of it was nevertheless quite clear. The young pilgrim hastily stepped away from the door, as the *señora* continued to mutter under her breath, possibly about how stupid and rude some pilgrims were. When we finally reached the actual *albergue*, I discovered that my Three Musketeers, Maik, Hana and Jimmy, were also booked in. There were 24 beds in the *albergue*, all in the one dorm, which, I thought, would make for an interesting night.

*****

Despite sharing a dorm in La Isla with 23 other pilgrims of mixed age, sex and snoring abilities, I actually had a pretty decent sleep. People started shifting at around 6am and I rose also to join my fellow boarders in an early morning silent 'pilgrim dance', as we moved around each other gathering our things together and waited for an opportunity to use the limited bathroom facilities. Once outside, I removed the newspaper I had stuffed into my still wet boots the night before – they were still a bit damp but okay to wear. I set off, following the Camino route, which now headed inland – it wouldn't be until the end of the next day that I would return to the ocean, when I arrived at the city of Gijón.

I was delighted to receive a message from my daughter Hannah, along with a beautiful song called 'Santiago' that she had composed and recorded especially for me. It brought tears to my eyes as I headed down the road early on the 26th day of my pilgrimage. She had been following my progress closely on Facebook and the words of her song clearly reflected that. She is a very talented young lady and thankfully she takes after her mum, and not her dad, when it comes to her singing abilities.

I know your heart is full of lead
I know it doesn't make any sense
I know it doesn't get easier with every step
I know you do and don't want to forget

I know it's harder than anything
To want nothing more than to see her again
To reach out to hold her hand
And close your fist around nothing

Just keep following the yellow arrows
Keep following the blackbirds
Keep on following the long winding road
To Santiago
To Santiago

In the flowers in the dancing rain
In the sand in the water
In the music in the wind
You can feel her

Faces of new and old friends
Help to ease the pain
Every bright new day
Makes the world a little warmer

Just keep following the yellow arrows
Keep following the blackbirds
Keep on following the long winding road
To Santiago
To Santiago

I know sometimes you just want to scream
And curse and kick and cry on your knees
Sometimes that's the way it has to be
Before you can pick up and keep pushing

Against the darkness in your eyeline
Against the clouds blotting out the light
Because you know that although it's so hard
You've come this far, you have to fight

Just keep following the yellow arrows
Keep following the blackbirds
Keep on following the long winding road
To Santiago
To Santiago
See you in Santiago

And I would see her in Santiago; both her and her brother, Matt. They were planning to join me for a week and walk into Santiago with me. I was so looking forward to seeing them.

I encountered some new faces on the Camino today, such as Markus from Germany and Laurie from Arizona. However, I only fell in with these folk for short periods, preferring to mainly walk alone today – I needed a break from people sometimes, particularly after sharing a dorm with 23 other pilgrims. There were some long, steady uphill gradients to deal with today. Of course, for every uphill there was a downhill and today certainly brought its fair share. If I ever regretted having given my walking poles to Peppe at all, it was on the steep downhill sections, as they could place quite a strain on the knees. However, the 'Comanche run', that I had learned from Ron, continued to be deployed to very good effect and made going down steep slopes a lot easier, even if it didn't look particularly elegant. I just had to be careful not to get too carried away, as I rushed downhill, as a careless tumble could have brought my Camino to an abrupt end.

The scenery wasn't too spectacular compared to previous days, but it was a pleasant walk nonetheless and, despite the day starting out very grey, the threatened rain never materialised. I arrived into my destination for the day, Villaviciosa, just after noon and just behind Maik. We stopped at a bar in the town's centre for the customary reward of a cold beer and a snack. Others drifted in as we sat and, while discussing accommodation options, I learned from Maik about a good pension nearby. Gert from Holland and I went off to check it out. There were no single rooms left, but there was one double with bunks available for €15 each including breakfast. Gert and I both jumped at it – moving from a 24-bed dorm to a room for two sounded like luxury.

After getting settled in and freshened up, I headed out for a little walk round the town, admiring the splendid City Hall and other grand colonial style buildings and learning that Villaviciosa is the most important municipality in Asturias for the production of cider. In fact, the town is often described as the 'apple capital' of Spain. That evening, as I was returning to the pension, which overlooked the gardens at the rear of the City Hall, I noticed a little 'fledgling' flapping around in the middle of the street. I ran out to scoop it up, before it was run over by a car, and brought it over to the gardens, where I gently set it down on the grass. It might have been a goldfinch chick, as it had a little splash of bright yellow on each of its wings, and it had probably fallen out of its nest in a nearby tree. I think that it was too young to have properly fledged and it just floundered around on the grass, constantly cheeping. I felt so powerless to help this vulnerable little creature. I picked it up again. It was so small and light in my palm and, as soon as it felt the warmth of my hand, it tucked its head under its wing and snuggled in like it was settling in for the night. However, I couldn't carry a chick around with me all night and its best chance of survival was probably to be left where its parents might find it and keep feeding it. So I reluctantly placed it on the ground again, close to a hedge so that it wouldn't be trampled on by unsuspecting walkers cutting through the park. I then walked away, hoping that it would survive.

A little chick snuggles into the palm of my hand for warmth in Villaviciosa

Later that night, after a meal out with Gert and a friend of his, a young Polish lad called Matthew, I checked back on the little chick. With the help of the torch on my mobile phone, I found it a short distance away from where I had placed it. Unfortunately it hadn't survived as I had forlornly hoped it might. It was at this point that some rather unexpected emotions suddenly came to the fore. I know that there was really no comparison, but I nevertheless couldn't help thinking about the last time I had felt so totally helpless when it came to caring for a fragile life, hoping against hope that death could be somehow evaded. Feeling defeated, I slumped down onto one of the garden benches and surrendered to my raw emotions. Tears welled up, not for the pathetic little bundle of feathers under the hedge, but for the memory of my dear wife, who sixteen months earlier I had been utterly powerless to help as she was torn away from me by cancer. The door to my dark room, where I tried to shut away my pain and loss, had been forced open once again and I felt myself drawn deeper into the darkness. I had to acknowledge that, although I was upset that the chick had died, in some ways it was also a relief that I no longer had to care for it. To be honest, if it had still been alive when I had returned to the gardens, I really don't know what I had planned to do with it. I didn't want to consider if this thought had any parallels with any of the maelstrom of thoughts that had coursed through my mind when I had lost Jacqui. However, before I could completely slam the door closed on such a consideration, I glimpsed enough to see that there probably were. I recalled Jacqui's words from a few days before she passed. "Dermot, I really don't want to go on like this. This is no life. It's just existing. There's only discomfort and pain. If I should start to slip away, please just let me go. I don't want to be resuscitated. Please, I don't want to be brought back to this." Although it pained me more than I can say, having witnessed what Jacqui had suffered through, it wasn't difficult to agree to her request. That often repeated phrase, one that was understandably offered again and again following Jacqui's death, intruded, unbidden and unwelcome – "at least she is at peace now". It was true of course and, in the end, it was what she had desired. And, God forgive me, but it was what I had desired also when we were beyond the point of no return. My feelings turned to anger. Anger that she and I had both been left with no choice other than to accept the inevitable. Anger that she had been taken away from me. Anger that I was powerless to help her. I headed for bed, cursing a poor little, helpless chick for having had the impudence to fall out of its nest in front of me and inadvertently stir up such emotions.

James was first to be brought before the executioner. His place of execution was simply an open square in the centre of town; an area that was routinely used for markets and celebrations. James did not resist, but simply allowed himself to be brought forward to his executioner and then knelt before him as he was requested to do so. He knew that there was no escape and that there was no point in resisting the inevitable. He thought about his Master, Jesus Christ, and only now did he fully appreciate the immensity of the sacrifice he had made in martyrdom. At least my end will be swift, he thought. Thankfully, he wouldn't be forced to endure the torture and agony that his Master had suffered in his final hours. He now prayed with all his might that he would soon join his beloved Master in heaven.

As he felt the sharp edge of the cold steel on the nape of his neck, James called out "Father, forgive them, for they know not what they do", emulating the very words his Master had used at his crucifixion. The executioner raised his sword from his aiming spot on the back of James' neck, the blade glinting in the sunlight as it moved upwards in an almost perfect arc. It then stopped for an almost imperceptible moment at the top of its sweep, before it swiftly descended and sliced through flesh, tendon and cartilage as if it was no different to the air before it. The crowd let out a unified gasp, which quickly turned to cheers as the executioner lifted James' now lifeless head from the dusty ground and held it aloft by its hair for all to see.

Josias, who had been forced to watch all this, was then dragged kicking and pleading for mercy to meet his executioner. The executioner growled in his ear, "Keep still and I promise it will go better for both of us." Moments later Josias' head was also held aloft and the crowd cheered once more. The spectacle now over and the mob's bloodlust satisfied, people started to drift away from the square as the life blood of the two decapitated bodies seeped into the dirt beneath them and James and Josias entered into martyrdom.

Chapter Six: Design for Life
(Days 27 to 30 – Villaviciosa to Muros de Nalón)

Gert had set his alarm for 6am. I silently cursed under my breath at being disturbed so early after finally managing to get to sleep at God knows what hour, as I wrestled with my dark thoughts from the night before. At least I had plenty of time to get freshened up and pack my rucksack before heading to the café next door for an early breakfast. After breakfast with Gert and Matthew, the three of us headed off together out of Villaviciosa, enjoying the architecture of the various municipal buildings as we went, including the Peon Palace, the Riera Theatre and the thirteenth century *Iglesia de Santa María de la Oliva*. About a kilometre out of town, we came across what looked like the smallest church in Spain, *Capilla de San Juan de Amandi*. It reminded me of the diminutive St Gobbin's Church in Portbraddan on the north coast of Ireland, although the setting here was no match for the beauty of Portbraddan, which nestles against the cliffs at one end of the stunning Whitepark Bay. This particular church sat rather incongruously in the middle of a rather nondescript and dusty junction in a small hamlet. We were pleased to find a fountain at the rear of the chapel, which had a small sign fixed to it giving the impression that the tap actually dispensed cider. However, we were disappointed to discover that it only flowed with water, although it was fresh and cool and probably a better option for pilgrims at this hour of the morning.

Another kilometre beyond here, we came to a fork in the road that presented a dilemma for some pilgrims. And that was whether to continue straight ahead on the Camino del Norte route or to take the left fork and join the Camino Primitivo. The Camino Primitivo, or Original Way, was the first major pilgrimage route to Santiago and is reputed to be one of the most beautiful, challenging and rewarding of the Camino routes. However, I had planned to walk the Camino del Norte and I wasn't going to change those plans at this late stage – if it's a toss-up between the mountains and the coast, the coast is always going to win in my book – it was the very reason I had chosen the Northern route in the first place. Gert and Matthew were both of a similar frame of mind, although I think Matthew was the most tempted of the three of us to switch allegiance. I think if it wasn't for the fact that he had fallen in with Gert, he might have taken the more challenging route.

Anyway, we all stayed on the road leading straight ahead. However, we soon began to wonder if we had indeed chosen the less challenging way, as it wasn't long before we were faced with a very steep climb up through forest tracks to an elevation of 425m. This was followed by a descent and then another climb of over 200m. I welcomed the effort required though, as it helped assuage the gloom that still pervaded my thoughts from the night before. It also helped that I had the company of Gert and Matthew, although I tended to pull away from them on the steep ascents. Thankfully, the weather was ideal for walking – overcast and cool. The three of us met up again at Peón, which was about the halfway point for the day's walk. After a break, I set off with Gert and Matthew again, but once again I left them behind on another long hill and unfortunately that was the last I saw of them.

However, about 6km out of Gijón, I met up with a young couple, Nicolas and Nelly, from Agde, near Montpellier in southern France, where they both worked as private nurses. Nelly had little English, but Nicolas spoke English well and so he acted as our interpreter. We chatted briefly and then gradually separated, but we kept coming together again at various junctions to collectively scratch our heads and examine the directions and maps in our guidebooks. Nicolas turned out to be an excellent guide and after a while I put my own guidebook away and just followed him and Nelly – a short distance behind at first, but the gap closing gradually until we all comfortably fell into step together. We entered the coastal city of Gijón together and decided to leave the official route and walk the extra kilometre or so alongside the River Piles, so that we could enjoy a stroll along the promenade above the city's main beach, Playa de San Lorenzo.

View across the beach at Gijón to the old town with the Iglesia de San Pedro visible at the end of the promenade

The sun had emerged from the clouds by this stage and the beach and the city looked wonderful in the afternoon sunshine. The long expanse of golden sand stretched ahead to touch the eastern side of the city's old town of Cimadevilla in the distance. This historic quarter sits on the hill of Santa Catalina, a peninsula jutting out into the Cantabrian Sea, and was dominated by the magnificent *Iglesia de San Pedro*, perched commandingly by the water's edge and resplendent against the clear blue sky. However, despite the undoubted historical and visual attractions that lay ahead, we had other more urgent needs on our minds. We were tired and hungry and also needed to find somewhere to stay. Surprisingly, there were no pilgrim *albergue*s in the city of Gijón, so we went in search of the local Tourist Office to enquire about accommodation options. The tourist official there was extremely helpful and he recommended that we stay in the city's student accommodation, phoning ahead on our behalf to reserve a double room for Nicolas and Nelly and a single room for me. We thanked him and made our way into the old part of the city where the Cimadevilla Cultural and University Residence was located. It was basic, but bright and cheerful, and after registering and getting our credentials stamped, we threw our gear into our respective rooms, showered quickly and headed out to find somewhere to eat.

Thankfully we didn't have far to go as just around the corner was a small restaurant where a lot of Spanish people were dining, which was always a good sign. The food was excellent and once again unbelievable value. We had a great chat over our late lunch. Nicolas explained that he was walking the Camino in honour of his grandfather, who had raised him until he was ten years old. He then asked me about the reason for my pilgrimage and, for the first time, I felt comfortable sharing my story with fellow pilgrims. So I told him and Nelly about Jacqui and showed him some family photos. I could tell that Nicholas was visibly moved and it was strange to watch as he translated my story for Nelly's benefit and to see her face mirroring Nicholas' expressions of sympathy, only a few moments later. Although I was relieved to share my story, I also regretted inflicting my sorrow upon this young couple. I apologised but they were having none of it, which was very gracious of them. I felt the warmth of their humanity and it felt so good. After lunch we went our separate ways, hoping to meet up in the hostel at some stage before Nicolas and Nelly joined the Camino again the following day.

I was two days ahead of my rough schedule and I therefore decided to keep my room for a second night and have a much needed rest day in Gijón. My body had been coping pretty well with the daily demands of walking relatively long distances, but I was beginning to feel like I was being pulled along with the never ending current of pilgrims rushing towards Santiago. I had skipped a planned rest day as a result and had also walked further than planned on some days – that's why I was now two days ahead. I was uneasy with this and decided to get off the pilgrim conveyor for a day and relax and explore some of Gijón rather than rushing through to the next stop. I didn't want to be part of the race and, after all, I had plenty of time to play with.

Having lunch with Nicolas and Nelly in Gijón

＊＊＊＊＊

I enjoyed the best sleep in a long time in my student accommodation and, even though I was taking a break from the Camino, I decided to get up early to join the other pilgrims for breakfast. I particularly wanted to catch Nicolas and Nelly before they left so that I could say farewell and wish them the best for the rest of their journey. And I was so glad I did. At breakfast, Nicolas produced a beautiful drawing that he had sketched the previous evening to commemorate both my Ulster Way and Camino pilgrimages. The drawing depicted a landscape scene, with a pathway weaving through forests and mountains, all encapsulated within the outline of a scallop shell and with 'K4J' and a *fleche* (arrow) beneath containing '1000-2000', shorthand for the kilometres walked in memory of Jacqui. I was totally flabbergasted. Not only that Nicolas had gone to the trouble to produce the sketch, but that he had also managed to encapsulate the essence of my walks so successfully. Nicolas was at pains to point out that his drawing was not yet complete and that he would send me the finished version when he returned to France. Although incomplete, it still looked wonderful and it was a truly remarkable gesture by someone who I had only met the day before. It turned out that Nicolas, in addition to being a nurse, was also a budding tattoo artist and had plans to open a tattoo parlour in his home town of Agde. I joked with him that I might just have to have his artwork tattooed somewhere on my body. I couldn't wait to see the finished artwork and I wasn't entirely joking about the tattoo.

After an emotional farewell to Nicolas and Nelly, I spent an hour or so exploring around Cimadevilla, the old historic quarter of Gijón, starting with a closer look around the exterior of the striking *Iglesia de San Pedro*. I then made my way up onto the steep hill of Santa Catalina, behind the old town, and was pleasantly surprised to find a large and grassy public park at the top of the peninsula, providing superb views out to sea and along the coastline. As well as the extensive remnants of a military battery dating back to 1902, the park was also home to a more modern structure – the *Elogio del Horizonte* (Eulogy to the Horizon) sculpture, designed by Eduardo Chillida in 1990. It stands large and imposing on the very edge of the headland and it is said that if you stand inside the sculpture you can hear the sound of the sea echoing from its concrete walls. However, the sea was too calm today and all I heard was the plaintive cry of a seagull circling in the blue sky overhead. On descending the hill on the other side of town I enjoyed elevated views over the large marina before dropping down into the heart of the historic quarter again and soaking up the culture on display, such as the Revillagigedo Palace, the monument to Pelayo (an eighth century king of Asturias), and the City Hall in Plaza Mayor. There was also the rather bizarre sight of the *Arbol de la Sidra*, a 'tree' sculpture made from 3,200 empty green cider bottles.

And that was enough culture for one day. It was now time for a surf. I found a surf shop just one street back from the main beach and hired a board and wetsuit and hit the small but fun surf that had started to roll in on San Lorenzo beach. After a couple of hours in the water I felt that it was time to return to shore. However, I almost left it too late. The tide had come in and the wide strip of sand that I had crossed earlier had all but disappeared while I was in the water. I suddenly remembered that I had left my sandals on the sand up against the promenade wall. As I rushed to collect them, a wave suddenly crashed in against the base of the wall and I watched with dismay as my sandals were washed away in the tide. There was a fair bit of splashing and cursing, as well as hoots from the promenade above, as I frantically chased after the only footwear I had apart from my hiking boots. I was still carrying my surfboard and I don't know exactly how I managed it but I was able to scoop up both sandals before they set off on their own independent adventures. As I held them aloft, cheers erupted from the small crowd on the promenade above who had stopped to witness the drama. Grinning from ear to ear, I took a bow and then I hurried towards the steps before the rising tide created any further problems.

After returning my board and wetsuit, I enjoyed a leisurely lunch in a lovely little café on a street corner with views out over the Plaza del Instituto where I was content to sit for a long while over a coffee and engage in some people watching, between catching up on my blogs. After having spent so long in rural locations and small towns, I hadn't felt terribly at ease coming into this big and very busy city yesterday. But today I was really enjoying it and I was happy to sit back and soak up the atmosphere and the architecture. From my window seat in the café, I could get a tantalising glimpse of a striking figure of Christ high above the roofs of the surrounding buildings and, after lunch, I was drawn up Calle Jovellanos to have a closer look. I soon discovered that the statue crowned the magnificent façade of the *Basílica-Santuario del Sagrado Corazón de Jesús* (Basilica-Sanctuary of the Sacred Heart of Jesus). The Basilica was closed, but that didn't really bother me, as I was content to stand outside for ages, just staring up at the truly glorious stonework together with the amazing wrought iron-work covering a huge round window above the entrance. The elaborate façade was topped with a stone platform supported on columns and it was this platform on which the statue of Christ then stood. I am not a religious person, but I could not fail to be both transfixed and moved

The magnificent façade of the Basílica-Santuario (left) and a close-up view of the figure of Christ atop the Basilica del Sagrado Corazón de Jesús

at the same time by the sight before me, as the white statue of Christ, with His right hand raised in blessing, soared into the clear blue heavens above.

I continued to stroll randomly through the city, happy to be surprised as I accidentally encountered one beautiful building after another, enjoying the freedom of walking aimlessly with no rucksack to weigh me down. I eventually found my way back to Plaza Mayor and from there it was only a short walk to my hostel, where I was happy to relax in the common room for a few hours, out of the heat of the midday sun.

All my city exploration had certainly worked up a good appetite and I ventured out again at around 7.30pm to find somewhere to eat. However, all the restaurants I came across were closed. The Spanish, certainly in Northern Spain anyway, tend to dine very late in the evening, typically after 9.30pm and often much later. I asked a couple of local men where I might find a restaurant and, after they talked animatedly for a minute, they both took off and indicated that I should follow – I was becoming quite used to this courteous behaviour by the Spaniards now. They led me through a few streets to a restaurant in Plaza Mayor, the main plaza of the old town, and suggested I try there. I thanked them and went in to check it out. I thought it would be outrageously expensive, given its prime location in a city thronging with tourists, but it wasn't at all and the food was absolutely superb. I enjoyed a mouth-wateringly good dish of *pulpo* (octopus), a speciality in this region of Spain, on a bed of potatoes, drizzled with paprika infused olive oil, all with a glass or two of local red wine – it was heavenly. I had a table looking out onto the grand square of Plaza Mayor and it was entertaining watching a local man sitting outside the window pour his *sidra* (cider) in the traditional way, while he relaxed with his evening paper. I was also amused by an elderly gentleman who seemed to spend the evening roaming from bar to bar to help himself to the free bar snacks, or *pinchos* – a cheap night out for sure.

*****

The following morning, I pulled my rucksack and hiking boots on again and followed the brass scallop shells in the pavements, heading west out of Gijón, under a slightly overcast sky. It was a bit of a slog for most of today's 24.5km, as most of it was on pavements and roads through industrial and residential areas, both on the way out of Gijón and on the way into Avilés, my destination for the day. This didn't come as a surprise to me though, as my guidebook quite pointedly cautioned that this was probably the least enjoyable stage of walking on the Camino del Norte. It even suggested that those pilgrims, not committed to walking every step of the way, might consider taking a bus from Gijón to a stop beyond the industrial district. However, I was not one of 'those pilgrims'. If I skipped walking kilometres here, I was only going to have to make them up at some other point in order to achieve my desired 1,000 kilometres for Jacqui.

As I was heading out of Gijón, alongside the marina, I was surprised to see the Three Musketeers, Maik, Hana and Jimmy, waiting at a bus stop ahead. I had had a few conversations with Maik over the previous days and, up until to now, I would have described him as a 'Camino purist'. He would become quite dismissive if he learned of anyone skipping ahead or taking shortcuts and was of the view that everything had to be done by the book and every kilometre had to be walked. So it was, as I say, with some surprise that I watched him board the bus with his two fellow Musketeers. I quickened my step to try and get an incriminating photograph, but they had boarded by the time I reached the stop and, unfortunately, the windows of the bus were of darkened glass and my camera couldn't pick Maik out. I did wave to him though as the bus pulled away from the kerb to let him know that I had seen him and I laughed as he tried to hide his face as I nevertheless pretended to take his picture. The thought of Maik being caught out kept me amused for a time. However, as I continued with my tedious trudge through the industrial belt of Gijón, I have to admit that it wasn't too much longer before I began to wish that I had joined the Musketeers on the bus also.

This certainly wasn't the prettiest part of the Camino that I had experienced so far. In contrast to the beauty and comparative serenity of Gijón, particularly its historic quarter where I had been based, this was all grim warehouses, fuming factories and loud, belching lorries roaring past. There were also a number of railway crossings encountered along this industrial zone and at one I became quite worried when I spotted six pilgrims actually heading along the train track itself. The signs were certainly a bit ambiguous here, but I instinctively knew that going down a railroad track could not be right. Dan, a pilgrim from Pennsylvania, caught up with me at this point and after a bit of searching we spotted a yellow arrow across a road junction leading away from the rail tracks. I shouted to the others, but they seemed intent on pushing on down the railway line. Dan and I left them to it and just hoped that we wouldn't be reading headlines the following day about six pilgrims meeting Saint Peter before they met Saint James.

We crossed over the tracks and Dan and I fell into step for a time. A little later, as we were going round a hairpin bend in the road, as it slowly climbed out of Gijón, we were relieved to see that, although far behind, the six pilgrims had finally gotten off the railway tracks and were now back on the proper, much safer route.

As the road continued to climb away from the city and we gradually left the noise and smoke behind, Dan stopped for rest. I pushed onwards and upwards to reach the Monte Areo Park, which is famous for its necropolis and is home to around 30 Neolithic burial mounds. Despite the purpose underlying this mountain, this section certainly provided a much more agreeable walking experience than what had gone before, as it cut through fairly pleasant rural areas. Some of the locals had even erected a little roadside refreshment point, with bottled water set out especially for pilgrims who might be running short. A makeshift sign at the water point kindly informed weary pilgrims that they 'only' had another 320 kilometres to go to reach Santiago. The next eight kilometres of the journey were interspersed with colourful hórreos, farm animals, quaint rural churches, fields being worked by hand and simple country dwellings.

I met up with a couple from Sweden, Peter and Enge, and walked and chatted with them for quite a while. They were an easy going couple and Peter was a good laugh. After the respite of the countryside, the final 8km of today's stage was a return to a hot and dusty industrial landscape, as the route approached Avilés. The bleats of goats and the clanking of cowbells were replaced once again by the clatter of steel and the revving of trucks. We came upon a little roadside bar in a layby that was little more than a few wooden picnic tables set outside the window of a house from which the enterprising elderly *señora* served a limited selection of beverages and sandwiches. And who was sitting at one of the tables? None other than Maik, Hana and Jimmy. "Hi guys. Are you waiting here on the next bus?" was the greeting I called to them as we arrived at their table. I took great delight in introducing the threesome to Peter and Enge and explaining that, when I had last seen them, they had been boarding a bus in Gijón. To be honest, I really didn't care how people undertook their Camino. It was an intensely personal journey for each pilgrim and each person had to do it in whatever way they could or decided they wanted to. However, it did irk me a little that Maik, who had previously been so outspoken about what he saw as pilgrims 'cheating', was obviously quite prepared to do so himself when it suited. I hoped that this might put an end to his 'holier than thou' pontificating. When our drinks arrived, I couldn't help proposing a toast to 'the Three Bus-keteers'. Thankfully, they all, Maik included, took it in the spirit it was intended and laughed good naturedly.

After our break, we all set off together and endured seemingly endless pavements alongside very busy roads before finally reaching the *albergue* on the edge of Avilés. After securing a bunk in the cavernous 48-bed dorm, and the usual showering and laundry duties, we had an hour or so to relax before dinner. I joined Peter at one of the tables in the courtyard at the front of the *albergue* and we chatted amicably as I watched him peel €20 notes from a damp wad of cash and spread them out on the table to dry. "I decided to do some money laundering today" he quipped, before adding "Always check your pockets before washing your trousers". Advice I could well relate to, as I had destroyed a pair of earphones a few days earlier doing the very same thing.

I was delighted to meet Dan from Pennsylvania again, who had also checked into the same *albergue*. Later he and I joined Peter, Enge and the Three Musketeers and we all headed into the pretty town centre for a few drinks and an evening meal. Avilés had been a prominent seafaring town in the Middle Ages, situated as it was along the wide estuary of the Rio de Avilés, but it's now a modern city and a major iron and steel centre. It must have been affluent in its day, and probably still was, as evidenced by the gorgeous pedestrianised streets running into the Plaza de España, where the monumental Town Hall sat alongside other architectural delights. As we approached the Plaza, we were corralled by the wonderful columns and arches of the shops and businesses on either side of streets paved with grey, terracotta and cream marble paving and bordered with neat rows of cobblestones. We eventually found the restaurant recommended to us by the *albergue*'s *hospitalero*, which was just off the Plaza de España. Its grandeur complemented the opulence of the town, but thankfully it didn't have prices to match. The drink, food, service and company were all great and we had an enjoyable evening before hurrying back to 'jail' before 10pm lockup.

*****

Despite the "aircraft hanger" of a dorm, with its 48 beds, I had a pretty decent sleep in the *albergue*. I was either getting used to sharing a sleeping space with lots of other pilgrims or I was getting the quantity of alcohol before bedtime just right. I was up shortly after 7am and, in addition to my usual preparations, I decided to sterilize my water reservoir. A good friend back home had given me a miniature bottle of gin before I had left for Spain for this express purpose. As I was half way into my walk, and having been reminded by a sign for Casablanca the previous day ("of all the gin joints..."), I thought that it was high time to break open the bottle. I poured the contents into the reservoir and swished the gin round for a few minutes and then discarded the remnants, thinking "what a waste." I then filled the reservoir with enough water for the rest of the day. I have to say that the first few sips of water that morning were much better than usual.

Once ready, I joined Maik, Hana and Jimmy for breakfast in a café just up the street from the *albergue*. We then set off together, through the pretty columned and paved streets of Avilés, passing by the large open space of the Plaza de España once again, the Romanesque-style *La iglesia de los Padres Franciscanos* and the rather bizarre statue of *"La Monstrua"* (The Monster) on the way. Behind this statue lies an abject tale of how not to treat a fat kid – sorry, a child showing a tendency towards obesity.

Jimmy, Hana and Maik, aka The Three Musketeers, on their way through the streets of Avilés

Apparently, when Eugenia Martínez Vallejo was six years old, her parents were troubled by her 'monstrous appearance' and they decided to present her to King Carlos II, as the Asturians had a fascination with 'dwarfs, buffoons and morons'. The king was impressed with Eugenia and had her attend parties in the palace for the amusement of his guests. The chronicler of the time, Juan Cabezas, wrote the following about her (with my corrections): *"The head, face, neck and other features of her are the size of two heads of a man, her belly is as huge as that of the world's greatest woman about to give birth. The thighs are so thick and crowded with meats that they become confused and imperceptible to the sight of their shameful nature. The legs are little less than the thigh of a man, so full of threads that they and thighs fall on top of each other, with astonishing monstrosity. And although the feet are in proportion to the building of flesh that they sustain, since they are almost like those of a man, she moves and walks with work, because of the greatness of her body."*

So, here we had, in the middle of a modern European town, a statue celebrating an obese child who was once paraded in front of Spanish nobility and called a monster. I pointed out to the others that the rotund figure in the statue was actually holding an apple in each hand. "By the look of her, I don't think she ate too many of those", was Jimmy's swift denouncement.

The walk through Avilés was followed by a climb out of town for a few kilometres, after which we took a sharp turn and zigzagged our way down a slope towards the coastal town of Salinas. On the way down, we separated out and, by the time I reached the town at the bottom, Jimmy had forged ahead, while Maik and Hana had fallen well behind. So I was now walking on my own again and as I wound my way through the streets of Salinas, I gave myself a little cheer to mark reaching the halfway point of my 1000K4J Camino. Over the last 29 days, I had clocked up 500km. I stopped and had a few celebratory sips of my gin flavoured water. That would have to do by way of celebrations for now I thought. I set off to find a cement track that marked the start of another steep ascent, this time climbing out of Salinas.

I caught up with Jimmy again later on and enjoyed his company for the second half of the day's walk, which took us through El Castillo de San Martin and Soto del Barco and on to our final destination for the day at Muros de Nalón. The route was both up and down and snaking – like a roller coaster and slalom combined, but obviously a lot slower. A lot of the route was through wooded areas and there wasn't a lot to see along the way, so we had ample opportunity to chat. Jimmy explained that he and Maik had been walking together since meeting each other in France and that they had taken Hana under their wings from the first day of her Camino in Bilbao. The three of them had been walking together ever since and got on really well together.

"Poor Hana has struggled with the journey at times," Jimmy said. "Her knees and feet have become quite sore. So Maik and I have had to slow down to keep her company and help her along. I really don't mind though".

However, he then disclosed that their little group would be coming to an end very soon. "Hana finishes today and will be starting back to the Czech Republic tomorrow" he said, before adding with a sigh, "I'll be very sorry to see her go. She's a good kid. Heart of gold." I had to agree.

It turns out that Hana's discomfort was also the reason why Maik and Jimmy had taken the bus along with her out of Gijón the previous morning. On learning of Maik's chivalrous intentions, I have to admit that I had felt a little guilty for ribbing him earlier about his 'cheating' on the Camino.

The weather remained overcast, but thankfully we didn't see any rainfall. So walking conditions were generally quite pleasant, although it did get a bit close and sticky in the last hour or so before we reached Muros de Nalón. However, we were rewarded with a great *albergue* at the end, with great facilities and it was such a treat to get under a hot shower and freshen up again – such simple pleasures meant so much when on the Camino.

We met Alan and Janette from New Zealand at the *albergue*. It was their unusual footwear that first caught our attention. Instead of the robust hiking boots favoured by most pilgrims, Alan and Janette wore what they called 'barefoot shoes' – they were like gloves for the feet, with individual toes, and quite flimsy looking. But their choice of footwear was perhaps the least remarkable thing about this couple, who were proud to let us that they were both grandparents. They described themselves as 'Raw Vegan Veteran Endurance Runners', looked super fit and seemed to be surviving the Camino entirely on fruit – they ate a lot of bananas. They were committed vegans and were pretty famous 'down under' where they were well known for their extreme exploits, including running an unbelievable 366 consecutive daily marathons in

Australia. When I asked them why they were doing the Camino, they explained that they had needed to escape all the publicity and media hype back in New Zealand and Australia following the release of 'RAW the documentary' about their lifestyle and endurance exploits. Most other people might have taken themselves off to an island in the sun or set off on a Mediterranean cruise, but not Alan and Janette. To have said that they liked to keep active would have been the understatement of the year. Despite all their achievements and undoubted fame, they were a quiet and humble pair and were certainly great advertisements for their lifestyle. A truly remarkable couple.

Exhausted by simply hearing of the New Zealanders' exploits, Jimmy and I took a seat in the large garden out behind the *albergue* and had a beer. Here, we watched a couple of locals starting to erect a large teepee in the middle of the lawn. The individual components were all laid out on the grass like a huge self-assembly kit from Ikea and the two guys were scratching their heads and wondering what to do next. It looked awfully complicated and provided us and a small group of other pilgrims with some amusement as we sat sipping our cold drinks and offering the odd unhelpful comment as if we were all suddenly experts in teepee erection. The teepee was going to provide extra sleeping space for up to ten pilgrims over the summer months for those who didn't mind sleeping outside. It would have been ideal for Sara and Freccia, I thought, but I had no idea where they were at this stage. Beyond the garden we could see the town of Muros de Nalón rising up on the hill ahead, nicely peaked with the spire of the *Iglesia de Santa María*. Jimmy and I decided to leave the teepee builders to it and we strolled up the hill to the centre of Muros.

The town was a strange, lifeless sort of place when we arrived, but we found a bar that was open and enjoyed a few beers at one of the tables outside, overlooking a small tree lined plaza. There was an elderly Spanish man sitting alone a few tables away, who was intently reading a document spread out on the table before him. He looked very like a Spanish version of Uncle Albert from the TV sitcom 'Only Fools and

Horses', but dressed in tee-shirt and shorts as opposed to a duffle coat and cap. "Oh Jesus, don't look now. I think he's coming over," whispered Jimmy under his breath and, right enough, a few seconds later José, who we later discovered was his name, was standing at our table and entering into an animated conversation with Jimmy about the document he had carried over with him. Jimmy indicated that he didn't understand, but this didn't deter José, who pulled a chair in from another table and sat down beside Jimmy and proceeded to show him the document more closely. I looked on and, although the A4 printed and bound document was written in Spanish and full of calculations, we were able to determine that it looked very much like a thesis he had completed on the subject of astronomy. We made the appropriate appreciative noises to José and offered to buy him a drink, which he politely declined. He was really taken with Jimmy, possibly due to Jimmy being closer to his own age. As he stood to leave, he pulled out another thinner document, which looked like a summary of his thesis, and he signed this and presented it to Jimmy, before returning to his original table. There he sat down, spread open his thesis and began reading through it very intently once again. He was obviously very proud of his work. We later learned from staff at the *albergue* that José was 92 years old.

After James had been beheaded, his disciples gathered together to decide what to do. They were distraught at the execution of their Master and were fearful that the Pharisees would come for them next.

"We are not safe here," cried one of the disciples, "We need to leave as soon as possible. Before Abiathar discovers where we are hiding and has us all executed also." They all looked to Joshua, who they now regarded as their natural leader, now that James was gone.

Joshua spoke, "You are right. We cannot stay here in Judea. We need to leave these shores tonight. But we are not leaving without James. Heaven knows what Abiathar and his followers will do to his remains come morning."

"But where will we go?" the other disciples wanted to know.

"Of that I am not sure," replied James, "We will have to put our trust in the Lord who will guide us to safety, if it is his will."

The disciples stayed hidden until nightfall and then, under the cover of darkness, crept back to the square where James had been executed and wrapped his remains in a shroud. They then carried his body to the town's harbour, keeping close to the walls of buildings as they went to avoid being seen by anyone who might cause them harm. In the harbour, Joshua left the others in the shadows with James' body and he went to see if he could find some means of transport. He found an old ship that was tied up against the harbour wall, but it had seen better days and had neither a sail nor a rudder. There were other better ships in the harbour, but they were all either secured or showed signs of life and Joshua didn't want to risk approaching anyone for fear of being betrayed. Left with little option, he went back for the others and led them to the old ship. They all climbed on board, carefully lifting James' remains onto the ship also. They then slipped the mooring ropes and pushed the ship away from the harbour wall as quietly as possible.

When the other disciples realised that the ship had no sail or rudder, they turned to Joshua and said, "How are we supposed to sail this ship anywhere with no sail to catch the wind and no rudder to steer us?"

Joshua answered, "Our faith will be our sail and the Lord will guide us."

The disciples were initially sceptical, but they soon all joined Joshua in silent prayer and entrusted their fate to divine providence. And an angel of the Lord duly appeared and guided the ship over calm seas until they arrived at a little inland port in Galicia, now known as Padrón. The disciples took James' body off the ship and laid it upon a great marble stone. They then watched in wonder as the body began to sink into the stone, as if the stone under James had become like molten wax. The liquid rock gradually closed around and over James' body and soon it was totally encased inside the stone, as if in a sarcophagus.

Chapter Seven: Telling Tales
(Days 31 to 34 – Muros de Nalón to La Caridad)

We had all enjoyed the hospitality and facilities at the excellent *albergue* in Muros de Nalón, but the morning was tinged with sadness. One of the Three Musketeers, Hana, had to begin her trip home to the Czech Republic today. I had grown very fond of Hana ever since she had rescued me from a night under the stars when I arrived back late to a locked *albergue* in Islares. "Goodbye, my d'Artagnan" she joked as we said our farewells. She would dearly have loved to have continued with her Camino, but unfortunately she had to return home to her work. She vowed to return to the Camino again though, as, in common with many others, the experience had really awakened something deep inside her that was not easily ignored. After lots of goodbye hugs, we left Hana to await her transport back to Bilbao, while Maik, Jimmy and I headed up the hill towards Muros de Nalón town centre.

At the small plaza in Muros de Nalón, I also bade a temporary farewell to Maik and Jimmy, as they continued along the official Camino route. I had decided to go off route today and take a longer, but hopefully much nicer route out to the coast and then cut back in to join the official route at El Pito. It would be about three kilometres longer, but I felt that I needed to escape the pilgrim route for a while – to go my own way and slow right down and enjoy the natural world around me. Despite my best efforts, I had still felt my competitive spirit coming to the fore on the Camino. If I sensed another pilgrim approaching behind, I would automatically quicken my step to try and prevent them overtaking. And when walking with others, it was hard to stop to look at the views or take a photograph, without feeling like you were holding them back. So, the early morning trek out to the two beautiful beaches about two kilometres from Muros de Nalón was simply sublime – it was so peaceful and the range of lovely flowers along the way was a real bonus. It had rained a little overnight and the blooms and leaves and cobwebs were still bejewelled with water droplets, which just added to the beauty and tranquillity. Everything looked refreshed and the ground gave off that earthy scent known as 'petrichor', which comes from the Greek *petra*, meaning 'stone', and *īchōr*, referring to the fluid that flowed in the veins of the gods in Greek mythology. And that very scent seemed to be setting me up for what lay ahead.

The road brought me first to the smaller of the two beaches, Xilo and then to the much larger Aguilar. The beaches were separated by a rocky headland known as the Castiello Tip. Both beaches appeared deserted and the sense of isolation and closeness to nature that I felt in this place was quite magical, even mystical. I have always been entranced by mythology and folktales, which of course abound in my home country of Ireland. I had really acquired my love of them to a large extent from Jacqui, who had always had a childlike fascination with such tales and legends and I had bought her many wonderfully illustrated books of folktales and fairytales over the years. It was therefore with great interest that I read about a legend associated with this very place.

A long time ago there was an enchanted fairy trapped by a spell in a cave inside the Castiello Tip. The fairy could only be released from the cave by a knight capable of carrying her down to the beach without stopping on the way or dropping her from his arms. Years went by and the fairy played on her own around her 'prison' without anyone saving her. Until one day a knight came and listening to her story, decided to save her. He took her in his arms and started to run towards the beach but, as he ran, the fairy became more disenchanted and heavier. Even so he kept running, closer and closer to the beach. But when he was almost there, a storm suddenly blew up with incredible thunder and lightning. It scared the knight so much that he dropped the fairy on the ground before reaching the beach and this was the last time anyone ever saw her.

I couldn't help but think of the many times I had carried my poor Jacqui in my arms in her final weeks, wishing desperately that I could save her from the evil cancer that had imprisoned her. There were no

Rocks reflected in the water at Aguilar Beach

dramatic storms with thunder and lightning, but dark clouds did gather around us, as the realisation that rescue was impossible became clear. In the end I had to set her down, I had to let her go, and I never saw her again. I left the road to cross the sands of Aguilar, leaving a single set of footprints as I went, my vision blurred once again with tears. I sat for a long time on the beach, until my vision cleared and my mood lifted a little.

The tide was well out, but it had left some shallow lagoons of sea water trapped in the sand and one of them in particular provided a nice photo opportunity, as the water's surface acted as an almost perfect mirror to reflect the cragged shape of one of the larger rocks thrusting skywards from the sand. As I was taking this and other photos, I spotted someone sitting alone near the top of the beach, who appeared to be watching me. As I drew nearer, I was surprised and delighted to see that it was Jane, who I hadn't seen since Guernica.

"Hello there Jane," I called, as I approached "I thought I had the beach all to myself this morning."

"So did I, until I spotted you swanning around with your camera down there," she responded, before asking with a smile, "Who do you think you are anyway? David Bailey?"

"Now, you're showing your age with that one. No, I'm Dermot. You might remember. We met in Guernica a few weeks ago"

"Oh, I remember okay. You were sitting alone in that nice restaurant when I was searching the streets for my friend. What brings you here? It's a bit off the Camino route."

"That's the very reason I'm here actually" I replied. "I just felt that I needed to get off the pilgrim treadmill for a bit."

"Well you've come to the right place. It's so beautiful and peaceful here," she said, before asking, "Have you heard about the Legend of Aguilar?" When I replied that I had just been reading about it, she asked "Well what do you make of it?"

I thought for a bit before answering, "Well, I think it could be seen as a parable about married life."

"Oh," she said.

"Yes, the man, the knight if you will, meets a charming little waif of a woman, the enchanted fairy, and takes her to be his wife. But as time and the struggles of married life go on – the journey from the cave to the beach – the woman becomes bored with her man, puts on weight and starts nagging him."

"That's the thunder and lightning, I suppose?" she chipped in.

"Correct. Then when they've almost reached their goal in life, the mortgage is paid off, the kids grown up and left home, and happy retirement beckons – the promise of the beach – she suddenly vanishes, ups and leaves him for a younger man, and he's left sobbing into the sand."

"My God, you have a very jaundiced view of marriage," she laughed, "You must have had a very bad experience."

"Well yes…..and no. I mean I had a very bad experience, but it wasn't my marriage. My marriage was wonderful actually. Sorry, I was really putting that spin on the story in an attempt to avoid what I really feel." And I then gradually told Jane my story – of how I had loved and lost Jacqui and how my world had fallen apart and why I had ended up on this remote beach in Spain, while on my Camino de Santiago.

"I'm sorry," she said quietly when I had finished.

"Please don't be sorry. You have nothing to be sorry for," I replied, our exchange echoing the words that had repeatedly passed between Jacqui and I when all hope had been lost. Me sorry for not being able to save her and her sorry for abandoning me, and neither of us able to do a blind thing about it.

"You know, I'm also here for similar reasons. I lost my husband, Joe, around the same time as you lost your Jacqui," she whispered.

Not for the first time, my selfish, self-centred, 'I'm the only one hurting here' attitude was laid bare before me. "God, I'm so sorry, I didn't know."

"How could you have?"

"What happened? To Joe I mean. How did he die?"

"Oh God, no, sorry, he didn't die. He just upped and left me for a younger woman."

It must have been a look of absolute horror on my face, as I realised how inappropriate and insensitive my earlier story about marriage must have seemed to Jane, that sent her into a fit of hysterical laughter. I didn't know how to react, but as Jane continued to be wracked with laughter, I couldn't help laughing too and soon we were both cackling with absolute abandon.

"Actually, that's not true at all," Jane managed as our laughter eased a little, "I just couldn't resist saying it after your take on the local legend. And it was worth it just to see your face. I did lose Joe, but not to a younger woman."

Well that just set us both off again on another fit of laughter. We were like two giggling teenagers who didn't know when or how to stop.

"Oh God, I haven't laughed so much in ages" she said, as she wiped the tears of laughter from her face.

"Me neither," I managed between my own fits of laughter. Eventually, we did settle down and things turned a little more serious again.

"I'm afraid I have a habit of being insensitive," I said and I told Jane about the book I had bought Jacqui for her last Christmas. "It was the sequel to a book we had both read and loved, called The Unlikely Pilgrimage of Harold Fry."

"Oh, I've read that. It's a beautiful book. One of my favourites actually."

"Yes, well, I didn't know it, but unfortunately the sequel is set almost entirely in a hospice and the central character is dying from cancer."

"No."

"I'm afraid so. Jacqui read the first few pages and then set it aside. Little did I know then that less than three weeks later Jacqui would be going into a hospice to spend the final few days of her life. I felt like a right idiot...but thankfully I had redeemed myself somewhat by writing a special message inside the cover of the book, which Jacqui loved. It said 'I would walk even further than Harold Fry if I thought it could save you. All my love forever. Dermot'. And I've been walking ever since. Of course, I knew I couldn't save Jacqui then and I know I can't bring her back now. God, how I know that. But I can try to save others. My walks are both in Jacqui's memory and to raise money for cancer research. It's just something I need to do."

"Yeah, I can understand that. It's lovely what you're doing. I'm sure Jacqui would be very proud of you. Since I lost Joe, I'm afraid I've been at a bit of a loss. I was therefore delighted when a good friend invited me to join him on his Camino."

"I don't suppose there's any chance of you and Joe ever getting back together again is there?" I ventured.

"Ha, not a chance. No, he'll have to manage without me now. Neither of us really wanted it to end the way it did and I do still miss him terribly, but it is what it is. And I want him to be happy. I really do."

"What about your friend. How's he getting on? And where is he anyway? I thought you were supposed to be keeping an eye on him?" This was the second time I had met Jane and I still hadn't seen her mysterious friend.

"Oh, he's doing great. He was actually finding that I was cramping his style a bit," she said laughing, but without any trace of malice. "We came to a mutual understanding early on. We check in on each other every so often just to make sure we're both okay and we walk together sometimes when we both feel like it. But at other times, we're happy to do our own thing. It's good for him to mix with others and make new friends and I'm more than happy to give him the space he needs to do that. But I'm always here if he needs me. I really think that this Camino will be very good for him. He's had a tough time of it recently."

"Sounds like you have also."

"Yeah, I've a few issues I need to address myself"

"Well you've come to the right place. Join the queue of the lost, broken, damaged, bereaved, screwed-up pilgrims making their way to the Holy Grail that is Santiago."

"Oh, I plan to go on out to Finisterre. I want to see the end of the world...and then decide if I want to come back."

We both smiled at that.

"Yeah, I plan to go there also. In fact I intend to walk from Santiago out to Muxía, then down to Finisterre and back to Santiago."

"God, you're a real gluten for punishment. Are you going to be wearing sack cloth and ashes also?"

"Nah, I think the walk will be enough of a challenge on its own. I need to do that loop you see in order to make my 1,000 kilometre target – my 1000K4J."

"Well, good luck with that." There was something about the way Jane said this that suggested she wanted to bring our conversation to a close.

"Thanks. Do you want to head on?"

"No, I want to take a bit more time here on my own, if you don't mind. Wrestle with my thoughts, you know. But, you head on, please. Don't let me keep you back." It was my cue to move.

"Yeah, okay, I suppose I can't sit here chatting all day. Better get back on the road. I've still a good few kilometres to go yet before I reach Soto de Luiña. Where are you planning to stop tonight yourself?" I was hoping that we might meet up again later. I hadn't felt as relaxed and as comfortable talking with someone since...well, since Jacqui had gone from my life.

"Oh, I haven't really decided yet. I'll just see how the spirit moves me" she added, smiling.

"Ok" I said, getting to my feet and shrugging my rucksack back on, "It's been lovely talking with you. I hope our paths cross again."

"Oh, I'm sure they will. I'll be looking out for you."

"That sounds like a threat," I said laughing, as I headed across the sand towards the steps that would take me back up onto the road again. *"Adios,"* I shouted back as I climbed the steps.

"Buen Camino," sailed in on the air, but when I turned to look back, Jane had already disappeared behind the rocks.

From Aguilar Beach, the road cut back inland for about three kilometres to El Pito. There were some very fine buildings in this small, but rich looking town, including the nineteenth century Italian Renaissance style Quinta de Seglas palace and the Romanesque Church of Jesus of Nazareth. The rest of the journey was pleasant enough if rather unremarkable, except perhaps for the huge highways in the sky that I passed under as I neared my destination for the day, Soto de Luiña. These amazing concrcte forms snaked high above the valley floor, leaping from one massive concrete pillar to the next, spanning incredible distances between hills in an absurd display of engineering brilliance. However, whilst the barely heard traffic high above me enjoyed almost level transit between one hill and the next, lowly pilgrims such as me were forced to follow the natural terrain of the

One of the 'highways in the sky' snaking high above the valley floor on the way to Soto de Luiña

Asturian landscape. And once again there were lots of steep ascents and equally steep descents along the route. It was hard going and although the weather remained overcast, it once again got very warm in the afternoon and this only added to the effort required. By the time I reached Soto de Luiña, I certainly felt that I had walked much further than the 18km I had actually covered.

Soto de Luiña itself was a one street town with a bar, hotel, restaurant and *albergue*, all seemingly run by the same man, who just kept popping up everywhere. The *albergue* was in a very old and rather rundown former school building. The kindest thing one could say about the facilities was that they were basic – but then you don't expect too much for €5. Instead of the usual *menu del dia*, I went to the local supermarket to get some food to eat at the tables outside the *albergue*. Maik and Jimmy, who had arrived earlier, did the same and the three of us joined a table at which two young German students, Angela and Lea, were working their way through a six-pack of beers. We all shared the beer and the two bottles of wine and food from the supermarket and probably sat up longer than we should have. However, we obviously didn't drink enough as none of us could sleep due to the snoring of two large German men in the packed dorm. Even my earplugs were of little use as the whole room seemed to resonate to the sound of their snoring and grunting. So far on this Camino Germany was way ahead in the snoring stakes.

*****

The following morning, I joined Maik and Jimmy and a guy from Holland, called Paul, in the *hospitalero's* restaurant for breakfast. Paul's rucksack was quite unique. He had injured his right knee when walking the Camino with a conventional rucksack a few months before and had had to abandon his walk and return home to convalesce. But he had returned recently to pick up from where he had left off. However, his knee had been so weakened that carrying the weight of a rucksack on his back just wasn't an option. So he had sourced a rucksack that he was able to pull behind him. It had a rigid handle and ran on two bicycle sized wheels on either side. I admired Paul's determination not to let injury deter him from completing his Camino – and the Camino Del Norte at that, not the easiest of Camino routes. Like myself, Paul was a keen photographer, but unfortunately he had recently lost his camera, along with three days' worth of photos. I really felt for him and hoped that he would somehow be reunited with it again. He was a really nice guy, but didn't appear to be having a lot of luck on his Caminos.

Maik and Jimmy left before I had finished breakfast and Paul was going to take the easier road route today, so I left Soto de Luiña alone in the early morning sunshine, taking the off-road route. It was quite pleasant going to start with, but the day gradually got hotter as I travelled on towards Cadavedo, my destination for the day. It probably only got into the very low 20's, but it made all the difference when you were walking with all your essentials on your back, particularly when there are lots of ascents and descents, as there were once again today.

It was definitely the hottest day I had experienced so far and it was the first time that my sun-hat had been required for quite some time. The route came tantalisingly close to a lovely stony beach at Ballota and so, rather than pass it by, I decided to make the short diversion down onto it so I could enjoy the sea view and have a short break. It was very calm and peaceful at the beach, but I was startled by a man in a wetsuit who suddenly appeared from behind a rocky outcrop, carrying about half a dozen large fish and a spear gun. He had obviously had a very successful morning fishing. Shortly after this a young German girl also appeared round the rocks. We said hello, but she quickly moved on. I had seen her on the Camino a number of times and at some of the *albergue*s, but she had always appeared a bit aloof and seemed to prefer to be alone. Each to their own, I thought.

I reached the small town of Cadavero in the early afternoon and stopped at a bar/restaurant where two other middle-aged pilgrims that I recognised were having a beer. I joined them and bought them another beer each and learned that they were Arnold from Denmark and Alejandro from Bilbao in Spain. They had met the previous year on the Camino Frances and had become very good friends, despite the fact that neither spoke the others language. This year, Arnold had flown to Bilbao and stayed with Alejandro's family for a few days before they had set off on the Camino del Norte. Arnold said that they had already booked into the pilgrim apartments about a kilometre outside of town. Alejandro very kindly offered to phone ahead on my behalf and he soon had me sorted with a room in the apartment that he and Arnold had already secured. We decided to eat at the restaurant, before heading on out to the apartment. Alejandro advised on the menu and I began to realise that it was very handy having a Spaniard for company on the Camino. Although Arnold had learned some Spanish since meeting Alejandro the previous year, it was interesting to see that they still relied to some extent on their first means of communication – Google Translate.

After lunch I stopped to buy some food supplies in the small shop next door and then followed Arnold and Alejandro out to the apartments.

*****

Our apartment outside Cadavedo was superb, so much so that I didn't waken until around 8.30am. Arnold and Alejandro had already left. I hadn't even heard them going, but I now had the whole apartment to myself for a very leisurely breakfast. I finally got on the road at just after 10am, but I wasn't worried about my late start as today's walk was relatively short – just 15.5km to the fishing port of Luarca. It had started raining overnight and it continued with a persistent drizzle for the first half of my journey, so it was on with the fetching 'pilgrim black' cape again. I must have resembled a rather unkempt black crow flapping along the highway in the wind and rain. However, I continued to follow the meandering route taken by the Camino, rather than going 'as the crow flies'.

The ground was pretty muddy in places, but passable with care – there were certainly some sections of the Camino that I wouldn't fancy having to negotiate after very heavy rainfall. However, today the sky cleared in the early afternoon and by the time I reached my destination for the day, I was feeling quite warm and tired. My journey today had been rather unremarkable for the most part. However, my arrival in Luarca somewhat made up for the dreary kilometres endured along the way. Luarca was a stunning little town with a very attractive harbour that nestled in a natural fjord like inlet surrounded by steep sided hillsides and cliffs. My first view into the town, from the high level of my approach route, was superb and the subsequent descent down through the streets of neat terraces and along the river to the harbour was very pleasant indeed. The water in the river was so transparent and clear that I paused frequently to watch the huge fish swimming lazily in the shallow waters, seemingly untroubled by the fact that they were in a town full of fishermen. Having sampled a little of the delightful ambience of this charming town, I decided to seek out the pilgrim

View down into the harbour at Luarca

albergue. It fell firmly into the basic but adequate category, but it was certainly good to get freshened up after another sweaty day of walking.

While later relaxing in the small common area of the *albergue*, I met a Spanish man, called Andrés, who had slipped and bruised his ribs very badly during the day. He was clearly in quite a bit of pain and he was waiting on a taxi to take him to the local hospital. He was hoping that after some treatment and perhaps a little rest, he would be able to continue with his Camino. I also saw a few familiar faces at the *albergue*, including the two German students, Angela and Lea, who I had met at in Soto de Luiña. They were keen to experience a *sideria* and invited me to join them later, after they had seen around some of the town.

I also bumped into the young German girl who I had last encountered briefly the day before on the stony beach near Ballota. I had seen her a few times before, but, as I had found at the beach, she had always appeared a bit wary of me, or perhaps just men in general. On this occasion, however, she seemed more approachable and so I offered her a cup of coffee, as I was making one for myself, and she accepted and she was quite happy to sit and chat with me for a while. Her name was Lena and she was walking the Camino on her own and, in her own words, wanted to "get back to nature and escape the pressures of everyday life". However, Lena then confided in me that, a few days previously, she had been walking along an isolated lane through woods towards a beach. Like me, she preferred to get off the official Camino route at times. She noticed a car parked in a small lay-by. As she approached closer, a middle-aged man suddenly got out of a car and stepped out into the lane about 20 metres ahead of her. The man, according to Lena, was wearing an unbuttoned shirt – and nothing else. She had understandably been very startled and hadn't known what to do. But he just looked at her for a few long seconds and then just walked off into the trees, as if it was a perfectly natural thing to do. After hearing Lena relay this story, I was no longer surprised that she had always appeared a bit wary of strange men, including myself. The funny thing was though, Lena then went on to tell me that when she phoned home that evening to tell her mum about her scary encounter with the flasher in the woods, her mum had found it absolutely hilarious. Despite her mother's casual attitude to what could have been a serious incident, Lena had rather sensibly invested in a panic alarm. I advised her that it might be wise for her to stick to the official Camino route in future, rather than going 'off-piste'. Lena agreed that that was good advice, but she was reluctant to relinquish the freedom of being able to discover some of the beautiful and tranquil places to be found away from the official route. Like me, she had visited Xilo and Aguilar beaches after leaving Muros de Nalon a few days ago and had found it so peaceful and tranquil. I could easily understand her reluctance to forfeit such experiences simply because some local pervert liked flashing at unsuspecting female pilgrims.

After coffee with Lena and then another stroll around town, I met up with the cider drinkers, Angela and Lea, at a little bar beside the river. We shared a couple bottles of the local *sidra* and took it in turns to pour it in the traditional manner, which of course involved pouring small quantities of the amber liquid from the neck of the bottle, held as high as possible, into (or in my case, around) the glasses on the table below. It's supposed to aerate the cider, but, in my case anyway, I think it simply wasted most of it. After a couple of bottles, my attention turned to food. The girls had already eaten and recommended the restaurant they had dined in earlier, so I left them to their cider drinking and headed to get myself a *menu del dia* before it was too late, always conscious of the need to get back to the *albergue* before closing time. I had a pretty decent meal and, despite the large number of beds in the large communal room in the *albergue*, I had a fairly decent rest also.

*****

It was a beautiful morning as I steadily climbed out of the pretty port of Luarca, following my long shadow up through the winding, cobbled streets, until I eventually reached the top of the hill on the opposite side of the town from where I had descended into it yesterday. There were some gorgeous views back over the town as I went, including the multiple tall arches of an old stone viaduct running along the escarpment at the back of the town, as if standing guard over the houses and the townsfolk below. The early morning mist, still lingering in the hills beyond, added to the almost mystical character of the scene. The long climb out of Luarca provided a tough enough start to what was to be another long hike today of 31 kilometres to La Caridad. Whilst very tiring, there was thankfully an ample variety of flora and fauna on show to keep the journey interesting for the most part. I managed to capture some great pictures of birds, butterflies and even lizards as I travelled. The route mainly wound through fairly rural countryside, but unfortunately there were some lengthy spells near busy highways also.

The last few kilometres were pretty tough going and I had been looking forward to arriving at, what was described in my guidebook as, a 'shiny brand new *albergue*' in La Caridad. Well, let's just say that much of

A little sparrow blends in against hte wood grain of a weathered barn door

the shine had already worn off in the short time since my guidebook had been written. It had 18 bunks crowded into a smallish dorm and everything else, including the kitchen, showers and toilets were crammed into a pretty compact building. I didn't really hold out much hope for a comfortable night ahead.

The port in Galicia that the disciples' ship had been guided to was in the kingdom of a pagan queen called Reina Lupa, Queen She-Wolf. It was said she was well named, as she was both powerful and dangerous. The disciples hid the stone sarcophagus containing the remains of James near the port of Padrón and travelled up the coast to Queen Lupa's palace in Mallou. Queen Lupa was intrigued when she heard of the disciples' miraculous journey from Judea to Padrón on a ship that had no rudder or sail and agreed to see them. Joshua told her of the apostle James' beheading in Judea at the hands of the Pharisees and of the angel that had guided their ship to her lands. He continued, "Your majesty, it is clear that the Lord Jesus Christ wishes that his apostle's body is laid to rest in your kingdom. I beg of you to make a suitable place available for James to be buried."

The queen knew of James from his time preaching in Galicia, before he had returned to Judea, and she had always viewed him as a threat to the established customs of her people. She therefore didn't want to help the disciples, but she was wary of this Lord that the disciples talked of. So, wishing to appear helpful, she sent them to King Philotrus in Duio, near Finisterra, to ask for his consent in the matter. Queen Lupa was well aware that the king was renowned for his cruelty and she suspected that, once the king had dealt with the disciples, she would never see them again. The disciples travelled North to Duio and asked to see the king. Once King Philotrus heard of the Christians' arrival, he had them arrested and thrown into prison, planning to put them to death. But the angel of the Lord appeared to the disciples and set them free. When the King learned of their escape, he sent a rout of his knights after them.

The disciples were hurrying across an old wooden bridge spanning a river when they heard the thunder of hooves on the roadway behind. They looked back and were horrified to see six knights on horseback approaching the bridge. With their swords drawn and raised high, they made for a fearsome sight and the disciples started to run in panic towards the roadway at the other end of the bridge. The dull, almost muffled sound of the hooves on the dirt road suddenly switched pitch and became a deafening clatter as the horses reached the wooden planks of the bridge. Joshua, who had been bringing up the rear of the group, turned to face the mounted knights as they charged across the bridge two abreast. They were gaining on them rapidly. Joshua made the sign of the cross and cried out, "Angel of the Lord, protect us."

Almost immediately, a number of loud cracks rang out through the valley and the floor of the bridge began to shudder and shift under his feet. Joshua turned to once again follow his band of disciples and, just as he made it to solid ground, he heard a huge crash of timber intermingled with the terrified screaming of men and horses. Joshua looked back just in time to see the bridge collapsing into the river below and the horses and their riders free falling in a terrible tangle of timber and bodies into the fast flowing waters below. All was quickly swept away downstream by the current of the river and the screams and squeals soon disappeared below the water as men and horses alike drowned - apart from one. He had managed to turn his horse as the bridge was beginning to collapse and had made it safely back to the other side.

Having witnessed the carnage caused to his fellow knights, he galloped back to report the terrible event to his King. Upon hearing of how the disciples had summoned an angel of the Lord to escape the knights, the King repented and prayed for the disciples to return. The disciples came back and subsequently converted the King and his people to the faith of God. The King then told the disciples to return to Queen Lupa and inform her that he had given his consent to the body of James being buried in her lands.

Chapter Eight: Wishing and Dreaming
(Days 35 to 43 – La Caridad to Boimorto)

Unfortunately, the *albergue* in La Caridad proved to be just as uncomfortable as I had feared. There was an elderly Spanish guy in the bunk below me, who seemed to have a very bad case of 'restless legs' syndrome – he hardly stopped tossing and turning on his creaky bed all night. In addition, there were about ten young pilgrims who sat up drinking and partying just outside the front of the *albergue* until about 1am. There seemed to be no *hospitalero* on site to enforce the normal curfew. The dorm was also over-filled – all the bunks were taken and most of the floor space between the bunks, which wasn't much, was filled with spare mattresses that had been put out to cater for the unusually large numbers stopping in La Caridad that night – everyone must have been attracted by the reports of the 'shiny brand new *albergue*' in the guidebooks – like moths to a flame, but one that no longer burned very brightly.

In addition to the noise, the room had also become very hot and sweaty – a combination of lots of bodies and little ventilation. A South Korean couple started to get up in the darkness at 5.30am. Despite all the earlier noise, they were as quiet as mice as they gathered their belongings and made ready for the day ahead – they were like pilgrim ninjas in the darkness. Just then, the Spanish man in the bunk below mine let out a loud groan and bounced himself into a new position on his mattress with all the subtlety of a hippopotamus. At that point, I gave up and decided that there was no point in lying on. So, I stumbled around in the darkness also, trying desperately not to step on any of the pilgrims sleeping on the floor. Between them and their abandoned rucksacks and other belongings cluttering the floor, it made for a very challenging obstacle course at that time of the morning. However, it wasn't too long before everyone else in the dorm had the same idea and pretty soon the early morning 'pilgrim dance' began once again.

I was one of the first to leave the *albergue*, not far behind the South Korean couple, and it was strange stepping out into the half-light and a shroud of early morning mist. Over the last few mornings, I had observed the mist creeping over the distant hillsides, but this morning I was actually in it – in the midst of the mist, if you like. My head was about as clear as the view as I trudged wearily through the town, still not fully alert given my lack of sleep. I really needed a coffee to jump start my system. Fortunately, I came across a café on the main street in La Caridad that was just opening up for business and I stopped there for a light breakfast, including that much needed caffeine fix. Andrés, the Spanish pilgrim I had met in Luarca suffering from bruised ribs from a recent fall, arrived in the café just after me and we sat together over breakfast. He told me that his hospital visit had thankfully shown that there was nothing broken, but it was nevertheless much too painful for him to carry on with his Camino. He was therefore waiting on a bus to take him back home to Madrid. This was very unfortunate indeed, but it certainly seemed to be the right decision for him, as every little move he made saw yet more pain engraved on his face. He hoped to return to the Camino later in the year when he had rested and his ribs had healed sufficiently. His bus wouldn't be along for another half hour, so I finished up my breakfast, wished Andrés well and set off once again along the main street heading out of La Caridad, reflecting on the fact that the Camino certainly claims its fair share of casualties. Many pilgrims come to find some sort of enrichment or enlightenment along the Way, but unfortunately some only discover pain and injury and, dare I say, disappointment. I hoped that I wouldn't be one of them.

About a kilometre out of town, I bumped into Michael and Sabrina, a German couple that I had encountered a couple of times before, and we walked together for a short time. Michael was about 6ft 7in tall and very solidly built, while Sabrina was comparatively petite. They had also stayed in the *albergue* in La Caridad and in addition to the heat and the noise, Michael had also spent the night in fear that the wooden slats under the mattress of his upper bunk wouldn't be able to support his weight and that he would end up crashing through and landing on poor Sabrina below. I think if I had been Sabrina, I would have been the more worried one! Michael and Sabrina stopped off in front of a small church for a snack, as unlike me they had not yet had breakfast, and I decided to press on.

The first half of today's 21.5km walk was through fairly pleasant rural landscapes, but the second half was tough going as it was largely on roads and, by this stage, the mist had burned away to allow the heat of the sun through. I had initially thought that perhaps the misty start to the day had contributed to the melancholy that I carried with me today, but while the sun had burned away the mist and clouds in the sky, it did little to evaporate my sense of longing and the personal dark cloud that followed me on my journey. The song, 'If there was a way', by an old favourite of mine, Dwight Yoakam, came up on my playlist. He sung about his loneliness and how he wanted nobody else but the woman he had lost and how he kept wondering if there was some way he could bring her back. I knew that it was absolutely pointless wishing for some way to have Jacqui back, but it didn't stop me longing. I had read that almost everyone cries on the Camino at least once as they make the pilgrimage to Santiago. I don't think they meant once every day though. Maybe I needed to clear the sad songs from my playlist?

Anyway, I trudged on resolutely, although sometimes it felt like I was making very slow progress indeed. It therefore brought a wry smile to my face when I came across a Camino sign by the side of the road I was travelling along. The sign was made up of a ceramic tile on a wooden plaque and depicted the familiar yellow graphic of a scallop shell on a blue background. However, what drew my attention to this particular sign was the fact that it was covered with snail shells. It seemed that this sign was speaking to me personally as I was indeed progressing along the Camino at a snail's pace today. And such was my pace and my mood on this day, that I decided, for the first time on my pilgrimage, to ignore the option of branching away from the official route and following a coastal variant. It would undoubtedly have been a much more scenic route, passing close to a number of headlands and beaches along the way, but it would have added about five kilometres onto my journey. So, I decided instead to take the shorter official way, which followed an inland route through land mostly given over to agricultural and a number of small rural villages.

The sun was now well and truly out and blazing down from high in the sky. The heat was building, my sunhat was on and the walk was becoming more punishing with every step. I was certainly very glad that I had avoided the longer coastal route on this occasion and it was with great relief that I eventually reached the impressive bridge that crossed the wide Ría de Ribadeo and led to my destination for the day, the town of Ribadeo itself. However, the bridge must have been close to three quarters of a kilometre long and it seemed to take forever to cross. In its favour though was the fact that it had a very safe pedestrian walkway, separated from the busy traffic. It also provided superb views of the wide, sea-blue river, the pretty town of Ribadeo and its large harbour area. The sky behind the town had turned quite misty, giving the impression that the town was detached from the rest of the land that I knew to lie behind it. It almost gave the illusion that I was passing over the sea on this long bridge to reach a mystical island habitation. However, the bridge is no island link, but instead provides a gateway into Galicia, the fourth and final autonomous Spanish region covered by the Camino del Norte, and the homeland of Santiago de Compostela.

When I finally reached the end of the extensive bridge, I still had a lengthy and circuitous route to follow before making it into the centre of Ribadeo itself. I headed for the Tourist Office to get a street map and some advice on places to stay. I found a lovely second floor room in a pension, with French windows and a balcony overlooking the Plaza de España in the heart of the town for only €18 a night. I liked it so much that I decided to book it for an extra night. My feet needed a rest and I'd a number of things I needed to sort out, including rescheduling the remainder of my walk in order to provide my son and daughter with a more accurate itinerary for when they joined me on the Camino in a week's time. We planned to walk the final stretch into Santiago together and then on out to Finisterre ('the end of the earth') on the West Coast of Spain. I was really looking forward to having them with me.

The following day, I spent my time off in Ribadeo wandering round the old town, particularly enjoying the many interesting buildings surrounding the Plaza de España, including the striking 20th century *Torre de los Moreno*. Despite having fallen into a state of disrepair, this multifaceted structure still made for an arresting sight, with its Gaudí-like design, topped with copper coloured tiles. It was a pleasure to sit outside one of the many cafés bordering the Plaza, enjoying a cold beer and *pinchos* and watching life go by. Later, as I relaxed in my room, I enjoyed the simple pleasure of the sound of the children playing in the public park beneath my window. It reminded me so much of 'Jacqui's playground' at Greenisland Primary School and the Roald Dahl quote inscribed on the plaque there dedicated to her memory, *"Life is more fun if you play games".*

*****

It was with some regret that I left the very comfortable and relaxing surroundings of my pension in Ribadeo to embark on the relatively long 27.5km trek to Lourenzá. Nevertheless, I was up early, had my breakfast and was on the streets heading out of town at 7:30am. Now that I was in the region of Galicia, I had to get used to the scallop signs being the opposite way round. Since starting the Camino del Norte in Irún, the converging lines on the scallop shell signs pointed to the direction of travel. This was logical to me as the lines on the scallop shell represent all the various Camino routes converging on Santiago. However, in Galicia, the home region of Santiago, the signs are strangely in reverse and the diverging lines of the scallop shell point you in the correct direction, like a many fingered hand.

It was a damp start and I had to stop after only ten minutes to get my wet gear on, when the rain became a little more persistent. In addition, I soon began to encounter one long ascent after another as the route

An abandoned stone house with a roof of broken slates covered in a pretty pink weed

took me higher into the Galician hills. However, challenging as the Camino may have remained, it also continued to provide plenty of visual rewards as I pressed on through its unique landscape. Mist hanging between the dark green trees of distant forests. Lively little finch-like birds balanced on wires decorated with raindrops. Rows of pastel coloured beehives lining the edge of a forest on a steep hillside. Lanes and pathways through lofty Eucalyptus trees that swayed and whispered in the gentle breeze. Ancient hórreos, now straddling two stone walls, Galician style, rather than four or more pillars as before. Bright red poppies providing little explosions of colour amongst the long meadow grass. And a log pile so neatly stacked under a corrugated tin roof that it resembled a little stone dwelling from a distance. The countryside was also dotted with quite a few old and abandoned stone houses with broken slate roofs covered in clumps of weed, which displayed masses of pretty, tiny pink flowers – the colourful weed adding a certain beauty and sense of renewal to a scene of dilapidation and decay.

And just as this image juxtaposed these two sides of life, the beauty and the decay, so my mind flitted between the wonderful world surrounding me and the sense of hopelessness and despair that often accompanied me on my pilgrimage. I sometimes wondered why I was truly undertaking my Camino. Okay, I was ostensibly doing it in memory of Jacqui and to raise further funds for cancer research. And there was also the notion that I was on a mission – perhaps a mission impossible – to find my place of sanctuary. But at a much more basic level, I was also walking this journey because I simply didn't know what else to do. There was some innate sense driving me forward that held onto the belief that as long as I kept moving then I wouldn't become trapped in the living hell that my life had become. So, there I was plodding along, up a long, steep laneway, with my head down and totally lost in my own thoughts, when I heard a voice call out "Hey, where are you going?" I awoke from my reverie and looked around to where the shout had come from and there was Jane coming up the hill about a hundred metres or so behind me. She was pointing to a sign at the side of the lane and shouting "You've missed the turn off." I turned around and made my way back to where Jane had stopped to wait for me by the sign.

"Thanks. I was in a wee world of my own there," I said, as I joined her and we both turned onto the proper path. "Just as well you spotted me or God knows where I would have ended up."

"Yeah. Do you not think this Camino is long enough without taking unplanned detours?" she asked.

"It certainly is, but I was lost in my thoughts there and just wasn't paying attention to where I was going," I said.

"Were you thinking about your wife?"

"Yes, I'm afraid I was. I think about Jacqui often. Pretty much all the time if I'm being honest. I just miss her so much, you know."

"Yes, I do. I still miss Joe every single day also", she said, "but it's strange; I feel very close to him on the Camino."

"How's that?"

"Oh, I don't know. It's just a feeling I have. It's too hard to explain...yeah, it's just a feeling."

"Well, some people find the Camino to be a very spiritual experience. Maybe that's got something to do with it?"

"Do you? Do you find it a spiritual experience?" The path had levelled off a little, making conversation easier as we walked alongside each other, falling easily into step.

"No. Well, not to begin with. I mean, I didn't come here seeking enlightenment or to get closer to whatever Supreme Being may or may not be up there pulling the strings. But I suppose, if I'm being honest, the longer I've been here the more I feel at peace with things. Being on the Camino certainly strips things back to basics. You don't have too much to worry about other than being able to walk the next stage, finding somewhere to put your head down for the night and getting enough food along the way. And with that, you know, being rid of all the worries and concerns that go along with normal life back home, comes a certain contentment and, yes, even peace. I just wish I was experiencing it all with Jacqui and not on my own."

"But I'm guessing if Jacqui was still around, you would never have found yourself here on the Camino in the first place?"

"That is so true. Friends of mine have been talking to me for years about this wonderful walking experience in Spain and I've always thought 'What? Seriously? Walking day after day in the heat. Carrying all you need on your back. Sharing my sleeping space with 20 sweaty, flatulent strangers. Do I look like I'm nuts?'"

"You do a bit, actually"

"Thanks. Well, you know what they say, 'You don't have to be nuts to be here, but it helps.' Anyway, you're right. It's one of those classic paradoxes. I would love Jacqui to be here with me, but if Jacqui was still around I would never have dreamt of coming here. We would be on a beach in Lanzarote or on the Amalfi coast. I suppose, at the end of the day, I would have been quite happy to never have had experienced the Camino, if it meant that I could have spent the rest of my days with Jacqui. Having said that, I am glad to be on the Camino... under the circumstances that is. If any of that makes sense? I constantly find myself dancing between the 'what if' and 'the way it is'."

"I know exactly what you mean. I faced the same sort of turmoil when I lost Joe. But over time I think you slowly become better at managing it. You don't ever forget and you might never stop asking the 'what if' questions. You simply can't help them popping in, like unwanted guests calling when you're in the middle of something else, but you learn not to dwell on them. You learn how to quickly show them the door, because you know that they will only cause disruption and no good will ever come from them. You eventually realise that the 'what if' questions are pointless – they simply lead nowhere, except down the same cul-de-sac again and again – so you shut them down quickly by focusing on the now – the way it is, not the way you would wish it to be. And eventually you can even start to focus on the future."

"You make it sound very easy."

"Oh, don't get me wrong. It's not easy at all. It's hard work and it takes a long time for it to become natural. You have to learn how to recognise negative thoughts almost before they take form and nip them in the bud before they can take root - if that's not mixing too many metaphors."

"Time is the great healer, eh?"

The simple interior of the church in the hilltop village of Villamartín Pequeño

"Well actually, I prefer to think of time as the great leveller. The wound opened by grief never really heals – not completely anyway. You become stronger for sure and you learn to manage the negative emotions, keeping things on the level as it were. But you will always remain vulnerable and be prone to slipping back. It requires almost constant effort to stay strong and no one, no matter who they are, can remain strong all the time. But over time it does become easier to keep things on the level."

"So, time is the great leveller. I'll have to remember that. I'll tell you one thing though."

"What's that?"

"This flippin' Camino isn't getting any leveller."

We had started to climb again and we eased off on the talking and focused on the walking, our breathing becoming a little more laboured as we went. The sun had now also made an appearance and, although it lit up the farmland and surrounding hilly countryside splendidly, it made our climb that bit harder. We made our way slowly up a long road to reach the tiny, hilltop village of Villamartín Pequeño where we were both equally surprised and delighted to find a small shop serving soft drinks and *bocadillo*s. We were happy to stop and rest at a small table outside the shop and enjoy some food and a cold drink in the bright afternoon sunshine. It was good to slip the walking boots off to let the feet relax and breath for a while. Across the road from us, was a small but unremarkable looking church and after our break we wandered over, not to see the church particularly, but to take in the view of the rural landscape beyond. However, once there we noticed a peephole in the locked door of the church and it provided an unexpected treat. We both, in turn, put an eye to the peephole and were rewarded with a surprisingly clear view of the church's interior. With its modest pine pews, bright white walls, curved pine ceiling and uncharacteristically minimalist adornment, it was quite beautiful in its simplicity.

About 2km beyond Villamartín Pequeño, we passed through its bigger brother, Villamartín Grande, and then another 2.5km brought us into Jane's planned stopping point for today. I tried gently to encourage her to walk on with me to Lourenzá, another six and a half kilometres away, but she said she had done enough walking for today and, besides, she had already booked into the hostel here. I was tempted to see if the hostel still had any beds available, but I didn't want to appear too clingy and so I reluctantly said farewell to Jane again and headed on to complete the final uneventful stretch to Lourenzá alone.

I arrived into Lourenza late afternoon and stopped at a bar along the main street to welcome myself into town with a cold beer. I sat outside with my pint, beside my discarded rucksack and boots, and massaged my tired legs. I was amused to see a shop window display just a few doors along from the bar. The shop sold medical aids of various sorts and in its window, it had a pair of crutches and a range of joint supports nicely displayed alongside a collection of large scallop shells – a not-so-subtle link between the Camino and leg and knee injury. All they were missing was a poster endorsement by Martin Sheen, the actor who had starred in the very popular Camino movie 'The Way' that had undoubtedly contributed to the recent surge of interest in the pilgrimage. A friend of mine had joked that Martin Sheen was probably responsible for more sore legs and blisters than any other actor in the history of Hollywood.

From my position outside the bar, I could also see further up the street towards the town's main square and, after I had slaked my thirst, I wandered up that way to take in the stunning Baroque façade of the tenth century *Benedictine Monasterio de San Salvador*. The elaborate stone façade of the monastery was truly amazing and held me captivated for ages as there was just so much intricate craftsmanship on display. The contrast between this building and the simple, little church in Villamartín Pequeño, could not have been greater. However, despite all the grandeur and splendour of the monastery, my heart still favoured the little village church on the hill.

The *Albergue de Peregrinos* wasn't far from the square and, after the usual registration and credential stamping, washing and cleaning, shopping and eating, reading and typing, I turned in to bed at about 10pm. There were about 24 beds in this clean and tidy *albergue*, but split over three rooms, so there were just eight beds (four bunks) in the room I was in. There were two hippy type guys in the room also – they had arrived late with their wooden staffs and all decked out in loose, flowing robes, beads and ponytails, as if they had just stepped of the ark. I felt that they had a rather arrogant air about them, as if they saw themselves as being more 'pilgrimy' than the rest of us with our conventional hiking garb. After lights out, they kept talking and laughing loudly from their bunks. A few 'shushes' came from the other bunks, but to no effect. Then a German girl in the bunk next to mine asked them politely to be quiet, wishing them good night into the bargain. But they just ignored her and kept on talking. I put up with it for as long as I could, but after a while their behaviour really got on my nerves and I snapped at them, "Look, the girl has asked you very nicely to be quiet. Now I'm telling you to shut the feck up or I'll shove your poncey wooden poles where the sun don't shine." Well, at least that's what I thought about saying, but thankfully I only voiced it within the confines of my own head. They must have detected my silent threat though, as they soon quietened down and we were all finally able to get some sleep. My thoughts were not very becoming of a pilgrim I know, but Jesus, other pilgrims can sure get on your tits sometimes.

*****

The next morning saw a beautiful sunrise over the rooftops and spires of Lourenzá and I watched from the porch of the *albergue* as the two hippies headed off down the street, with their wooden poles safely in their hands. They don't know how lucky they are, I thought to myself, as I recalled my silent 'outburst' from the previous night.

Today's 24km walk was, for the most part, a stunning journey through the verdant hills and valleys of Galicia. The day started of beautifully with very fine weather and even when it got considerably hotter in the afternoon, there was frequently a lovely cooling westerly breeze in my face to keep things on the right side of comfortable. My guidebook gave today's total ascent as 700 metres and, although it was hard work at times, the beautiful surroundings certainly helped make it seem easier. While passing through the pretty little village of Arroxo, just a few kilometres out of Lourenzá, I was met by a very friendly little off-white Terrier-type dog. It just lay down on the brick pathway in front of me, rolled over on its back and waited to have its tummy rubbed. I was only too happy to oblige, but I think it would have quite happily lay there all day if I had been willing to continue. It looked on forlornly, as I continued along the path.

After the first eight and a half kilometres, I reached the charming town of Mondoñedo, nestled in a sheltered valley among the northern outlying hills of the Cantabrian Mountains. I stopped here for a cup of coffee in a café directly across the spacious plaza from the town's stunning thirteenth century cathedral. A young boy, who appeared to be from a very wealthy family and who had just celebrated his first communion, was having his photograph taken by a professional photographer in front of the cathedral. The boy was dressed in a grey and white sailor's outfit and a grey and white classic car, an Opel Kapitan, had been brought in to the normally traffic free plaza as a prop for the photos – obviously the cathedral alone didn't provide a sufficient backdrop.

Mondoñedo's cathedral is known as *catedral arrodillada*, the 'kneeling cathedral', apparently due to its unusual proportions – I suppose it was quite vertically challenged compared to most other cathedrals I had seen. The stone carvings on the exterior were masterful and the frescos and stained-glass windows on the inside were stunning, particularly the huge rose window directly above the entrance, which was a kaleidoscope of colours as the morning sunshine backlit the intricately patterned glass.

Back out in the sunlit plaza, the atmosphere was warm and relaxed, making it hard to set off on the next leg of my journey, which my guidebook warned me would be uphill for the next 11km. But it also spoke of stunning views and there was certainly a lot to see and photograph as I made my way up the mountainside, passing through luscious, green valleys and alongside numerous quaint farm houses of rough stone and moss-covered slate. Even so, the climb was long and exhausting in the afternoon heat and it was therefore with much relief that I made the final 3km descent into Gontán. I had a very welcome cold beer when I arrived at the first (maybe only) bar in this small village and chatted with Michael and Sabrina while sitting outside in the sunshine. They were staying in Gontán, at the *albergue* just around the corner from the bar. I, on the other hand, planned to walk for another kilometre or so to the larger neighbouring town of Abadín to stay in a pension there. But, as decisions went, well, let's just say that the clue was in the name of the town.

As I was entering the town of Abadín, I was met by a German girl coming the other way. She told me that she had just been to the pension and there was no accommodation available. So, we both headed back to Gontán, but only to find that the 26-bed *albergue* there was now also full. I decided to go back once again to Abadín and search around to see if there were any other accommodation options other than the pension, but I had no luck – everywhere was already full. However, a local hostel owner very kindly came to the rescue. He reserved rooms for both me and another stranded pilgrim in a hotel in Vilalba, about 18km away, and arranged for a taxi to take us there. Once again, the Camino had provided. Good Samaritans always seem to come to the rescue of pilgrims needing help on the Way.

*****

I woke early, planning to return to Abadín so I could pick up from where I had finished walking to the day before. After a modest breakfast in the hotel, I went to reception to order a taxi. The hotel receptionist tried at least four different companies before both he and I admitted defeat. I enquired about the public transport options, but there weren't any that wouldn't have involved waiting around for hours. It turned out that returning to Abadín wasn't really a realistic option after all. So instead, I thanked the receptionist for his help and set off out the door to begin my walk to the next stopping point on my schedule, Baamonde, which was roughly 20km south of Vilalba. Although I regretted having to skip the section from Abadín to Vilalba, I certainly wasn't going to beat myself up over it – I would just have to make sure that Maik never got to hear about it. Anyway, the extra kilometres I had already walked, by taking the alternative coastal routes on occasions, more than made up for the kilometres I was skipping on this occasion.

Compared to the hilly terrain of recent days, today's walk was quite a pleasant meander through fairly flat Galician countryside. It started of very cold as I was leaving Vilalba (probably the coldest morning yet) and then there was a light fall of rain. However, I soon warmed up and the rain soon stopped and for most of the journey it remained overcast and pretty comfortable. I took things at a fairly gentle pace today, keeping my eyes open for interesting things to photograph. Near the little hamlet of Ponte de Saa, I crossed a rather evocative medieval stone bridge over the Río Labrada. And I saw quite a few examples of a unique form of stone walling that may be peculiar to the Galician region of Spain. They were formed from a series of thin vertical stone slabs, set on their edges into the ground and carefully interlinked so that no gaps appeared between adjacent stones.

I kept bumping into Ottman from Germany and we walked together on a few occasions. He was due to meet a friend in Baamonde, but not until evening, so he stopped off at practically every bar or café along the way to take a leisurely break and pass the time. However, I was sauntering along at such a relaxed pace that he kept catching up with me again. I finally joined him for a coffee and a small snack at one of the bars we encountered. I told Ottman about my sauntering, not expecting him to understand the word, but he immediately said, "Do you know the origin of that word 'saunter'? Back in the Middle Ages people used to go on pilgrimages to the Holy Land, and when people in the villages asked where they were going, they would reply *'a la sainte terre'*, 'to the Holy Land'. And so they became known as sainte-terre-ers or saunterers." It was an intriguing story even though I wasn't entirely convinced as to its authenticity. The remainder of the journey to Baamonde was uneventful, passing through largely rural landscapes with occasional glimpses of locals out tending the fields or transporting bales of hay stacked precariously on trailers barely visible under their load.

I arrived into the Baamonde *albergue* to encounter a number of familiar faces, including Arnold and Alejandro. The *albergue* catered for a large number of pilgrims, with its 96 beds, but it was well laid out and very well maintained. I had a bed in the huge upstairs open-plan dorm, which was home to about 60 beds.

Later, I enjoyed a very good meal at Restaurant Galicia along with Mírek from the Czech Republic, who was also staying at the same *albergue*. At the end of the meal, I asked for coffee and got more than I bargained for when I was served up with a wonderful experience known as *café pota de madre*. A small caldron of coffee was brought to the table along with a carved wooden pilgrim figure, which opened, sarcophagus like, to reveal a bottle of a local vodka-like spirit. It was the best coffee I had experienced on the Camino so far, but one was quite enough. The spirit was quite strong and walking with a rucksack was tough enough without having to carry a hangover as well.

*****

The following morning, I couldn't believe that I had slept right through the night to 6.30am. Lights were out at 10pm the previous night and despite the number of people in the *albergue*, the place was so quiet you could have heard a pin drop. I had breakfast at a small café next to the *albergue* and then set off from Baamonde under grey skies and light rain.

It was now becoming common for Camino signs to be fixed to short concrete pillars or bollards, which, in addition to giving directions via the usual yellow scallop shell graphic, also often revealed the distance remaining to Santiago. It was quite a 'milestone' therefore to pass a sign on the roadside about 3km out of Baamonde indicating that there were now only 100km to go to Santiago. Not exactly a stone's throw away, but nevertheless it made this key destination finally seem a little more within reach. Of course, I had to remind myself that my journey would not end there, as I then planned to head out to the West Coast of Spain, to Muxía and Finisterre, and back again – a round trip of a further 200 kilometres. However, it was much easier when on the Camino to think of it in terms of short stages rather than risk being overwhelmed by the immensity of the total journey. It was like the old riddle, "How do you eat an elephant?" the answer being, "One bite at a time". So, for today, I concentrated on today's walk, which was a gentle stroll through just 14.5km of relatively flat Galician countryside and, although it remained grey and damp and I had my fleece and cape on for most of the journey, it was still a very pleasant walk. The fourteenth century *Capilla de San Alberte*, partially hidden amongst the trees, and the ancient pathways, corralled by stone walls, coated in thick blankets of soft moss, added a mystical feel to the journey, which was further enhanced by the eerie stillness that gentle rain can bring to a woodland environment. I also passed many more examples of abandoned stone and slate dwellings, slowly being enveloped by nature, as if gradually being drawn back into the enchanted landscape from which they had come.

About a kilometre beyond the village of Raposeira, I took a short diversion off route to visit a charming little café at the *albergue* Witericus, run by a very friendly and hospitable lady. My timing was good as I managed to avoid a very heavy downpour whilst there. It was rather satisfying to sit under the awning, enjoying a *café con leche* and *bocadillo*, while watching the heavy raindrops ricocheting off the pavement – creating thousands of miniature 'crystal ballerinas' that pirouetted for the briefest of moments, almost gone before they were formed. While waiting for the rain to pass, I noticed that on one wall inside the café, pilgrims had taken to leaving coins in the gaps between the stones of the wall. The owner told me that one pilgrim had started it years ago and other pilgrims had since followed suit. Many pilgrims do appear to be very attracted to the notion of leaving something behind on the Camino. Everywhere you go there are little stacks of stones built alongside the trail, old walking boots planted with flowers or makeshift shrines. This coin decorated wall seemed to be another manifestation of this desire to leave something to show others that you had been here. There is actually a very strong tradition of pilgrims carrying a little stone from their home place and leaving it behind somewhere on the Camino. I myself carried a little pebble from a beach on the North Coast of Ireland. It was one of the many that Jacqui had collected over the years and I had found it in the pocket of an old coat of mine that she had borrowed one day for a walk along the beach at Ballycastle,

Jacqui's hometown. I had only discovered it shortly before leaving for my Camino and it seemed as if it had been destined to make the journey along with me. At this stage, I had the vague notion that I might leave it behind me on the Camino at some appropriate location, such as Santiago or Finisterre.

The rain passed and the sun started to make an appearance. I no longer had a good excuse to loiter in the café. So, I wished the owner well and set off to rejoin the Camino. I caught up with Mírek towards the end of the day's journey and we both arrived at the San Martin Albergue in Miraz together. We received a very warm welcome at this hostel, which was run by the British Confraternity of St James. It was an extremely well run *albergue* with excellent facilities – it even had a kettle, which was unheard of in most of the other *albergue*s I had stayed in. The volunteers were all English speaking and it was so nice to be signed in by Paula, a lady originally from Belfast.

After ditching my rucksack beside my allotted bunk, I went to a bar a short distance away for something to eat. The place was very quiet – just me and a couple of bar flies (the ones with wings this time). However, other pilgrims soon started to drift in from the *albergue* and I was delighted to meet Sara from Italy again, along with Freccia, and it was time for a big hug – from Sara of course, not the dog.

*****

The *albergue* in Miraz was definitely one of the best I had stayed in to date, however I didn't sleep particularly well. It was one of those nights when my mind wouldn't allow me to settle, as it kept replaying scenes from Jacqui's final days and revisiting my feelings of hopelessness as her body, and then her spirit, gave up on her. This constant rerunning of memories I would prefer to forget seemed to serve no purpose other than to taunt and deny me the peace I so dearly craved. However, I was thankful that such nights were now much less common than they had been say a year ago, which I suppose indicated some sort of progress.

Anyway, my poor night's sleep was absolutely no reflection on the San Martin Albergue.

The volunteer *hospitalero*s were as hospitable as the name suggests. As well as Paula, there was also Teresa, another volunteer from Belfast, and Liz from Austria. They were all pilgrims themselves, but had taken a two-week break from the Camino to help out at the *albergue*. And they were excellent hosts throughout our stay and made everyone feel very welcome and very special. Importantly, they also ensured that we all had plenty of breakfast before setting off for the day. Sara and I had decided to walk together today and as we stood on the steps at the front of the *albergue* before departing, Paula sprinkled a little bit of magic on our journey by reciting a traditional Irish blessing for us.

> *May the road rise up to meet you.*
> *May the wind always be at your back.*
> *May the sun shine warm upon your face,*
> *and rains fall soft upon your fields.*
> *And until we meet again,*
> *May God hold you in the palm of His hand.*

It was such a lovely, heartfelt touch. Teresa and Liz were also there to see us off. Sara had actually arrived at the San Martin Albergue a day before me and so she had got to know the ladies quite well. She had even helped them out getting the place prepared for yesterday's wave of pilgrims, myself included. So, there were lots of hugs, and even a few tears (but not from me on this occasion), as the farewells were said. As we started up the road with Freccia, through the still sleepy village of Miraz, Sara and I reflected on how such surprisingly strong bonds could be built up so quickly between people on the Camino. There is definitely something about a shared purpose and shared understanding that undoubtedly gives rise to an easy and often immediate affinity between pilgrims.

In spite of Paula's earlier blessing, the weather deteriorated quite quickly today and Sara and I spent a lot of time plodding through the rain, which got progressively heavier as the day went on. I had my black cape on, which kept my top half pretty dry, but my boots, and eventually my socks, became totally saturated. Poor Sara also had a cape, but it looked like it had been through the wars. It was pretty much in tatters and was hopelessly ineffectual in keeping the rain off her, despite my efforts to rearrange it on her as best I could. Freccia was the only one of us that didn't seem too bothered by the miserable conditions. My guidebook recommended that we should savour the early part of today's route which promised some of the last scenic, off-pavement walking on the Camino del Norte. Unfortunately it was lost on us, as visibility was quite restricted due to the rain and mist and the hoods of our capes. Apart from the poor weather, the only other notable thing about the day's journey was the fact that we apparently reached the highest point on the Camino del Norte at a little place called A Marcela, which sat at an altitude of 710 metres.

Just as we were coming into Sobrado dos Monxes, 25.5km from Miraz and our final destination for the day, the heavens decided to bless us with a final deluge. We squelched our way to the entrance of the main *albergue* in the town, which was situated in the town's ancient and imposing Cistercian monastery. It was an incredible place, much of it dating from the tenth and twelfth centuries, although the centrepiece, the dominating façade of the Baroque main church, was much 'younger' having been constructed in the seventeenth century. The façade was in some need of some tender, loving care though, as much of the elaborate stonework was wildly decorated with grass and weeds and splashed with patches of yellow lichen. As we passed below the huge edifice, a flock of black crows, or ravens perhaps, suddenly erupted from one of the bell towers and twisted and swirled around it in an unruly fashion, cawing menacingly high above us. It only needed a flash of lightning and a loud rumble of thunder to complete our ominous welcome to this dark and ancient monastery. As it was, there was no thunder and lightning, but there was a heavy wooden door at

The Cistercian monastery of Sobrado dos Monxes with the twin towers of the Baroque main church in the background

the main entrance, which might very well have creaked theatrically when slowly opened by a wizened medieval monk. However, we soon discovered that the door would not be opening for another two hours at least.

The entrance portico was packed with young Spanish boys also waiting to gain entry to the *albergue*. They were part of a youth group that were walking a section of the Camino in what appeared to be an equivalent venture to the Duke of Edinburgh Award back home. Everyone was wet and cold and sitting around on the bare and unforgiving stone floor of the large porch way, trying their best to pass the time. At least it provided some shelter from the rain, although, contrarily, the rain had by this stage eased off considerably. Sara and I headed across town and found a cafeteria, where we relished the opportunity to gain some warmth and have a hot drink. We then decided to try a private *albergue* about 100 metres up the street. We had spotted a sign for it on the way into Sobrado dos Monxes and it sounded like a nice place. It also had the added attraction of claiming to be the proud owner of a 'boot drying device', which, given the state of our boots, would be very welcome indeed. I managed to get a place okay, but it was with some dismay that I watched poor Sara being turned away as the *albergue* was not able to accommodate Freccia. Sara returned to the monastery to try her luck there, but unfortunately wasn't allowed inside with Freccia either. However, the monks did permit her to pitch her tent in the grounds directly behind the monastery and also granted her access to the showers and toilets for a small fee.

Meanwhile I settled into the private *albergue*, which was pretty decent although the lauded 'boot drying device' turned out to be nothing more than a slatted shelving unit in the hallway with a supply of newspaper to stuff inside the boots. Hardly a unique device and I certainly didn't see my boots being anywhere near dry by the morning. Anyway, after getting cleaned up and at least myself, if not my boots, dried out at my *albergue*, I set off for a wander round town. I spotted a bright, yellow, waterproof poncho on sale in a hardware store which I was given for only €4 – half price to a pilgrim the store owner said. I then sought out Sara's tent behind the monastery and presented her with her gift, which she was delighted with. A little while later, after Sara had fed and settled Freccia, we headed into town again and ducked in and out of a number of bars and cafés until we found one with some fellow pilgrims already ensconced and we joined them for food and a few drinks.

*****

The next morning I met Sara in a café as planned at just after 8am. After a light breakfast, we set off together for Boimorto, which was only about 11.5km away from Sobrada dos Monxes. It was very cold and very wet and both our capes remained on for the whole journey. I'm not sure that Sara was overly keen on the colour of the cape I had given her – bright yellow was the only colour the store had – but she certainly appreciated the protection it provided during some of the downpours we experienced. It certainly did a much better job at covering her than the previous tatters had managed, although together

Sara in her new yellow cape leading Freccia through the rain on the way to Boimorto

we must have looked a right sight with Sara in her big yellow cape and me in my big black one. At one point, we were amused to see a Spanish woman coming down a country road towards us, dressed for the farm in her wellington boots and apron, carrying a large parasol and leading a mule. We greeted each other and she wished us *"Buen Camino"* as we passed. I'm sure that she was probably more amused by our attire than we were by hers. The heaviest downpour of the day, this time accompanied by fierce thunder and lightning, fortunately happened to coincide with our lunch stop in A Casanova, at the Cafe Bar Carreira. We were able to take shelter in the bar and watch the storm play out and wait for it to eventually subside, before we took to the road again. And from here, it was only another 3km to our destination for the day.

A good *albergue* awaited our arrival in Boimorto, although it was quite deserted when we arrived. Fortunately the doors were unlocked and we were able to let ourselves in and make ourselves at home. A few more pilgrims arrived, including Slava from Russia and a few Austrians. After about an hour, the *hospitalero* arrived to register everyone but once this was complete she then left again. There were only about six of us all together and Sara was the only female staying. She managed to secure a two-bed dorm to herself and she then set up her tent outside for Freccia. I had earlier placed my rucksack in another small dorm and had hoped that I might also have it to myself, but one of the Austrian pilgrims also took a bed there. I had no problem with this until he proceeded to gingerly remove his boots and socks and slowly lie down on his bunk, quite obviously in some discomfort. His feet looked an absolute mess and unfortunately, they didn't smell any better. Sara popped in to check on how I was settling in and the look of repulsion on her face probably matched my own, as the unpleasant stench hit her. We both withdrew to the corridor.

"Oh my God, that smell is awful," she whispered, "You can't possibly stay in there." We checked out the other rooms and found that there were certainly plenty of free beds.

"I'm going to move," I said, "There's no way I'm sharing a room with 'Stig of the Dump'. I don't know what that poor guy's done to his feet but they are in a dreadful state and riper than a bunch of overripe bananas."

"You can move into my room if you like" Sara offered.

"Hey, listen, you've been roughing it in a tent with your dog for God knows how long," I replied, "I think you deserve at least one night on your own in some comfort and with some privacy."

"No really, I don't mind at all. I'd be happy for you to share...just so long as you don't snore." she joked.

"Well, I can't guarantee it, but you have permission to wake me up and send me packing if I do," I said with greater confidence than I felt. "Anyway, it would be a shame if you missed out on that important aspect of being a pilgrim. Every pilgrim has to endure the torture of a good snorer before they can really claim to be a true pilgrim. And, to be honest, it's not the snoring you have to worry about."

She stared at me with a quizzical look, before the penny dropped. "Oh God, English humour" she said, rolling her eyes.

"No," I corrected her, "Irish humour."

Later, after I had moved my belongings across to Sara's room, we left the *albergue* and walked the short distance into town. We picked up some food supplies in a supermarket and then enjoyed an excellent meal in the only local restaurant we could find open. While eating, we discussed our walking plans for the following day. The less travelled Camino del Norte merged with the much more popular Camino Frances at a place called Arzúa, 39 kilometres out of Santiago. At this point, the relative peace of the Camino del Norte would be suddenly shot to pieces, as the previous trickle of pilgrims suddenly swelled to literally hundreds. Ray had already alerted me to this unfortunate consequence of the 'meeting of the ways'. His voice messages had clearly conveyed his dismay in typical Ray fashion. "It's feckin crazy here. I've never seen so many feckin pilgrims," were his exact words. Both Sara and I were keen to delay this undesirable experience for as long as possible and so we decided to follow an alternative route outlined in my guidebook that would join the Camino Frances a good 15km beyond Arzúa, at a little place called A Brea. We then planned to walk on to the town of Pedrouzo, which had a pilgrim *albergue* and a range of other accommodation options listed in my guidebook. My son and daughter, Matt and Hannah, would be arriving tomorrow evening to join me and I was hoping that we would all be able to get beds somewhere.

Sara and I probably had a little too much red wine at the restaurant and we were quite merry on the way back to the *albergue*. We crept back into the silent hostel, where everyone seemed to have already turned in, and tiptoed into our room. Sara took the top bunk and I the bottom.

I must have drifted off quite quickly, because the next thing I knew Sara was gently shaking me awake.

"Sorry, was I snoring?" I asked

"No" she replied, "I'm a bit cold though. Would you mind moving over?"

"Come on in" I said as I lifted the blanket and shifted to one side to allow her to climb into the narrow bunk beside me. "I was dreaming that you would join me."

She snorted at that. She actually did. I woke up from my fantasy at that point and Sara continued to snore loudly in the bunk above me, as if mocking the very thought of it.

*****

Interrupted dreams aside, we both had a decent night's sleep in the Boimorto *albergue*, although it certainly had been a bit cold. Dreams do always tend to have an element of reality woven in – I suppose that's what makes them feel so real. Despite my brief fantasy, I had no desire to become romantically involved with anyone. Jacqui was still the love of my life. I had promised to love her until death did us part. And 17 months previously, death had parted us, decisively and permanently. But love doesn't die along with the lover. My love for her was still as strong as it was before, perhaps even stronger. In reality, it was obviously an unreciprocated love, but in my heart and mind Jacqui still loved me from somewhere out there and I couldn't give up on her. That wasn't a conscious decision. I simply just couldn't.

"Well did you hear any snoring last night?" I asked Sara as we were both getting up, unable to keep the smirk off my face.

"No, all quiet" she replied, followed by "What is it?" as I had obviously continued to grin.

"Oh nothing," I replied breezily, "it's just that Freccia probably enjoyed the peace and quiet last night also."

"Oh, more blooming English humour. Ha ha," she mocked.

"Irish humour," I said.

"Whatever," she dismissed what she obviously viewed as a minor detail and then added, "I missed my Freccia last night. It was so cold. Freccia always keeps me lovely and warm at night."

Lucky Freccia, I thought.

When the disciples eventually returned to Queen Lupa and told her about their agreement with the King, she was not pleased but hid her feelings from the disciples. In another act of treachery, she told them that they could take the oxen that she had grazing on a nearby mountain (Pico Sacro, the 'sacred mountain') and yoke them to a cart to transport the body of their master. However, the queen knew very well that there were no oxen in the mountains, only wild bulls, and she suspected that the bulls would never allow themselves to be yoked to a cart, and, if they did, then they would almost certainly run amok, break the cart, throw off the body and slay the disciples. She also knew that the mountain held another great threat to anyone who ventured up its slopes. The disciples, who knew nothing of the queen's cunning, went up the mountain in search of the oxen.

As they climbed up the side of the mountain, they heard a terrible screech echo from the mouth of a deep cave. They rushed to pass the entrance of the cave, but just when they thought that they had safely reached the other side, a huge dragon emerged from the cave, breathing fire into the cold mountain air. Grass and shrubs in its path immediately ignited, flaring and crackling fiercely before the disciples. Joshua turned to face the dragon as it swung its head round to face the petrified group. It seemed infuriated at the sight of the cowering disciples, but even more so at the sight of Joshua standing fearlessly before it. The dragon's head retracted slightly as it prepared to let forth another burst of searing flame directly at the disciples, but Joshua bravely stood his ground and made the sign of the cross before the creature. The dragon's head lunged forward, with its mouth open and so close that Joshua could have reached out and touched its jagged teeth. The other disciples shrunk into the ground and screamed in anticipation of the flames about to engulf them. But nothing came from the dragon's mouth, apart from a strangled croak. Then its eyes started to bulge as if something had lodged in its throat. The dragon began to swell and glow as if its own flames had been turned inward and then suddenly the beast exploded into a dust so fine that every last trace of it was carried away by the wind.

Chapter Nine: Searching
(Days 43 to 50 – Boimorto to Muxia)

Sara headed out to her beloved Freccia to feed him, while I prepared some breakfast with the supplies we had picked up at the supermarket in Boimorto the evening before. We were joined at breakfast by Slava, from Russia, and we shared our food and coffee. Slava was cycling the Camino del Norte to test out a new web-based guide for the route developed specifically for Russian pilgrims. He had been on a number of the Camino routes over the years and had gotten to know his way around Santiago pretty well. He was able to give us lots of helpful hints on where to stay and where to eat. He highly recommended trying to attend a mass in the cathedral in Santiago to witness the swinging of what he referred to as the "big smoky thing". Of course he meant the swinging of the *Botafumeiro*, which dispenses clouds of incense throughout the interior of the building. The name *Botafumeiro* literally means 'smoke expeller' in Galician. I had previously read about this ceremony and was hoping to see it. Slava was sure that it took place at 7.30pm every Friday, which suited us well as that was the very day we were due arrive in Santiago.

Sara, Freccia and I set off from the *albergue* just after 9am and walked into the town of Boimorto again. Here we picked up the alternative route we had chosen to follow in order to avoid meeting the Camino Frances route sooner than we had to. The route we set off on was mainly road based but, with the help of the GPS on my phone, we were able to find some nice lanes and pathways through the forests. This broke up the monotony of the roads and gave all our eight feet a rest from the hard and unforgiving tarmac surfaces. The weather forecast for the day had looked pretty horrendous, but it turned out to be not too bad and at times it even came close to being warm.

Probably because we had ventured away from the official Camino, today's route was pretty bereft of places to stop for refreshments. We had to make do with an improvised picnic with our leftovers from breakfast in the driveway of a private house, at about the halfway point of our trek. We only had water with us to drink and we both craved a cup of coffee. However, it was another 6km before we spotted a café by the roadside, the Pensión O'Mesón Café-Bar, and I dived in to order two cups of coffee, while Sara waited at a table outside with Freccia. We were still 4km from our intended finishing point for the day in Pedrouzo, but stopping at this bar turned out to be a really lucky break.

About a kilometre back we had finally joined the Camino Frances route and had been really surprised by how quiet it was. We certainly didn't see the throngs of pilgrims we had expected to encounter and this led us to believe that we should have no problem finding accommodation in Pedrouzo. However, at the bar we met Paul and Lynette from Australia who had just come back from Pedrouzo. It turned out that every *albergue*, hotel and pension from here on was already full. It would seem that the 'throngs of pilgrims' had already passed through by the time Sara and I had joined the main route. We quickly abandoned our plans to walk any further and asked the owner of the bar/pension if he would be able to accommodate us. Fortunately, he had a room with three beds available, which I jumped at, and he told Sara that she could camp in the football pitch behind the premises and use the showering/washing facilities in the pension for a small fee. And just like that we were sorted – the Camino had provided once again.

We were so pleased at having received the warning of difficulties ahead that we bought Paul and Lynette a drink. They were both in their early 50s and, although they were from Australia, they didn't live there anymore. When we asked them were they did live, they replied in unison with what was obviously a much used and familiar phrase, "Anywhere and everywhere." They had sold up the family home about five years before and now split their time between working in various locations, Lynette as an English teacher and Paul as an engineer, and travelling the world. They had grown up children still living in Australia and so they returned there for a few weeks each year. It was an interesting lifestyle choice, which they admitted wouldn't suit everyone, but it was one that they loved.

Matt and Hannah arrived a few hours later. Hannah had phoned me when they had both arrived in the airport outside Santiago – Hannah from Belfast and Matt from Berlin. I had given her the address of the pension and they had taken a taxi out from the airport. We had a lovely evening together and they got to meet Paul and Lynette and, of course, Sara. Hannah was dying to meet Freccia also, but unfortunately he had turned in for the night. Just after arriving, Hannah picked up an email from Queen's University in Belfast to say that she had been awarded a first degree honours in her psychology finals. So, it was celebrations all round that night. The day had worked out extremely well indeed.

I was so pleased that Matt and Hannah were with me and that tomorrow we would all be walking together into Santiago de Compostela. Sometimes, I tended to overlook the very obvious heartache that they were also feeling at the loss of their mother and it was great that we could now spend some time together. It felt so good to have the remnants of our little family together once again, so we could all share in a part of this very special pilgrimage in Jacqui's memory.

*****

Matt, Hannah and I were down for breakfast at around 8am. We were joined by Sara shortly after and we all set off about half an hour later. Hannah was delighted to finally meet Freccia – like Matt, she had been following my progress on Facebook and so already knew about Sara and her dog. Today's route roughly followed the main roads into Santiago, but thankfully, for the most part, the Camino paths were far enough removed from the roadways, and/or screened by trees, so that any disturbance caused by the heavy traffic on the roads was pretty well minimised. For Sara and me, this was our first real experience of being on the busy Camino Frances route after six weeks of walking the much quieter Camino del Norte.

There was a notable increase in the number of what many, who regard themselves as 'true pilgrims', disparagingly refer to as 'Camino tourists'. These were individuals and groups who chose to walk the minimum distance required, that is the final 100km of the Camino, in order to obtain the coveted *Compostela*, the official certificate issued by the Pilgrim Office in Santiago acknowledging completion of the pilgrimage. A significant proportion were also carrying only the lightest of day packs, reflecting the fact that many people choose to have their luggage transferred for them between hotels that have often been pre-booked by a tour company on their behalf as part of a package deal. It is certainly a much more luxurious and comfortable approach.

Our pace today was fairly leisurely. It was Matt and Hannah's first day after all. Even so we seemed to overtake a fair number of pilgrims, including the 'Camino tourists', as we edged our way closer to Santiago. Today's route took us round the perimeter of Santiago's Labacolla airport that Matt and Hannah had flown into the day before. Soon after this we passed through the small town of Labacolla itself, which is 'famous' for its river in which pilgrims of old used to wash themselves prior to arrival in Santiago. Some claim that the name Labacolla literally translates as 'wash scrotum'. However, today it only seemed to be Freccia that felt the need to take the plunge and rinse his undercarriage. Jokes about the 'dog's bollocks' weren't far behind, although this required a bit of explaining to Sara. "Irish humour", I said.

A few kilometres beyond Labacolla, we came across a bar-cafe at Camping San Marcos and we had some refreshments there. Sara was concerned about finding a place for Freccia closer to Santiago and so decided to stop here and use the camp facilities. We arranged to meet in Santiago the following morning and said our au revoirs. Matt, Hannah and I then headed on towards Monte de Gozo, the final hill before Santiago. The numbers of pilgrims flooding towards the city of Santiago had now grown considerably. On our approach to Monte de Gozo, we passed, and were passed by, pilgrims in varying degrees of fitness or exhaustion. We passed one young Italian girl, who was literally just about managing to shuffle along the roadway, as if faced by the steepest of mountains. We had gone ahead of her by about ten metres, when I felt compelled to first look and then walk back to her to see if she needed help. She smiled through the pain and said that she was okay and that she was only going as far as Monte de Gozo, which was less than a kilometre at that stage. She thanked me for my offer of help but said that she would manage and that I should go on. Her determination to complete the pilgrimage alone, under her own steam, was as clear as it was admirable.

I caught up with Matt and Hannah again and we continued up the relatively gentle incline to arrive at the top of the 370-metre high hill. This was apparently the place from where pilgrims once caught their first sight of the spires of Santiago cathedral ahead and cried out in rapture at finally seeing the end of their path. However, potential views of the cathedral now seemed to be largely obscured by tall eucalyptus trees and the only crying we heard was not in rapture, but distress, as one poor female pilgrim allowed her friend to tend to her badly blistered feet. A small church, the chapel of San Marcos, provided some spiritual comfort to those who needed it, but the top of the hill was dominated by an imposing, but rather neglected, sculpture commemorating a mass said here by Pope John Paul II in 1989. We rested on the hilltop only briefly before setting off on the gentle descent and, less than a kilometre later, we began to enter the fairly nondescript suburbs of the city of Santiago, although we were still about three kilometres from the cathedral itself. It was like entering most modern European cities – busy roads teaming with traffic, streets lined with shops, offices and restaurants, and lots of locals going about their daily lives. The locals seemed well used to the throngs of interlopers streaming through their home town – hardly noticing the constant flow of pilgrims, like human gastropods, following a well-marked trail snaking through the streets, with their possessions on their backs.

We were only about a kilometre out of the city centre, where the old town and cathedral were located, when we came across a sign for an *albergue* and we decided to check it out. To our dismay, the lady at the reception desk informed us that the hostel was full and that everywhere else she knew of going into the city was also 'complete'. She was extremely helpful though and phoned an *albergue* back out on the outskirts of the city and secured beds for us there and sent us off with the phone number and a hand drawn map giving us directions to the San Lázaro Albergue. So, resigned to the fact that we were unlikely to make it to the cathedral today, we reluctantly turned away from the city centre and doubled back for two kilometres to find our accommodation for the night. Although located in a very unpromising looking industrial area on the outskirts of the city, the *albergue* was very clean, spacious and well run. We were shown to a large room containing 12 bunks, but we were the only occupants. I fully expected to be joined by other pilgrims by the time the night was out.

So, the final few kilometres into Santiago de Compostela and Santiago Cathedral would now have to wait another day. It was Friday evening and that meant we would unfortunately miss the Botafumeiro ceremony that Slava had told me about. Of course, we could have gone in specifically to see it, but we had had enough travelling for one day and were content to stay put and visit a nearby restaurant for tea. Fortunately, I would be visiting Santiago for a second time, after my jaunt out to the West Coast and back, and so I might have the opportunity to see the Botafumeiro in action then. The three of us went to a nice Italian restaurant and had a great meal and a few drinks to celebrate Hannah's university success once again.

*****

As it turned out, we were fortunate to have the dorm in the San Lázaro Albergue all to ourselves. Matt and Hannah were having a gentle introduction to the normal nocturnal hardships of being a pilgrim. We packed our rucksacks and left the *albergue* to head over to a café across the street for breakfast at around 8am. We had loosely arranged to meet Sara there if she could make it, but she didn't show. On reflection, I think Sara may have felt that she didn't want to intrude any further on our time together as a family. Or perhaps she just wanted to reach Santiago Cathedral by herself – it is a very personal journey after all. I would certainly have loved to have had her walk with us, but I had to also respect her desire to complete her pilgrimage on her own terms.

Matt, Hannah and I started walking into the centre of Santiago at just before 9am. We only had three kilometres to walk this morning and most of the route we were already pretty familiar with, having tramped it in both directions the day before. It didn't take us too long to reach the old town area and wind our way through the busy, narrow, paved streets to finally reach the entrance to the Plaza del Obradoiro, where the magnificent Cathedral of Santiago de Compostela is located. Along with a steady flow of other pilgrims, we descended the short flight of steps, to the accompaniment of a lone piper playing traditional Galician music in the shadows of the dark tunnel-like passageway.

We stepped out into the daylight again to be met with the sight of a huge open plaza, surrounded by buildings positively brimming with architectural grandeur. The plaza was already busy with numerous smiling pilgrims, happy to have finally reached the end of their long journeys.

The Plaza del Obradoiro was certainly a highly impressive space and the grand buildings standing on all four sides, including the City Hall, the Parador Hotel and the various University buildings, were undeniably majestic. However, it was a little disappointing to find that quite a bit of the Plaza's centrepiece, the magnificent Santiago Cathedral itself, was encapsulated in scaffolding due to extensive refurbishment work taking place. So the cathedral's reputedly stunning facade wasn't exactly looking at its best upon our arrival. But even given these factors, there was no denying that the cathedral, and the square in which it was located, was quite a special place. As we soaked

Hannah, me and Matt very happy to have arrived in Santiago de Compostela

up the atmosphere, pilgrim after pilgrim, some as individuals and some in groups, came through the passageway in the corner of the plaza and spilled into the square – some cheering loudly, others entering in quiet reverence.

We were surprised and delighted to meet up with the young Italian girl we had passed on the way to Monte de Gozo the day before. She had been clearly struggling then, literally looking like she was on her last legs. Her name was Sabrina and it turned out that she had walked close to 50 kilometres by that stage, so it was little wonder that she had looked so exhausted when we had seen her last. However, now, in the square in Santiago, she was like a totally new person – fresh and beaming. She thanked us for stopping to talk to her the previous day. She said that it gave her the necessary encouragement to go on and she was very grateful for that. She took some photos of Matt, Hannah and me together in the square, but politely declined when I offered to take one of her. She said that she preferred to retain her memories of the Camino in her head only. She certainly knew her own mind and I was once again full of admiration for this young girl. We wished her all the best and we made our way to the Pilgrims Office to get my first *Compostela* (Camino certificate). Matt and Hannah also needed to buy their *credentials* (pilgrim passports), which they had fortunately managed without up to now, but would most likely require in the coming days.

They had a very efficient queuing system at the office and before too long I was called forward to Station Number 6 to hand in my nearly full *credential* in order to obtain my *Compostela*. I had been pretty much unmoved by the whole occasion up to this point, but when the Spanish gentleman behind the desk started to complete my certificate my emotions suddenly overtook me and, embarrassingly, I was standing there with tears rolling down my face when he handed me my completed certificate. On the Camino, fellow pilgrims would come and they would go, but grief was my constant walking companion. For most of the time it would remain hidden, as if stored away in my rucksack with my other possessions. But inevitably, it would occasionally make an appearance when my guard was down or my resistance lowered. This was obviously one such occasion. The official looked a little embarrassed and waived the €2 charge for the little tube to store the certificate safely – either that or, in my emotional state, I misunderstood his intentions and simply walked away without paying. Anyway, I got a big hug from Matt and Hannah, who had obtained their *credentials* by this stage, and I was so glad that they were there for me at that moment.

After the melodrama of the Pilgrim Office, we went to find a place to stay for the night, before we set off west again the following day. As expected it was very busy in town, but we managed to get a three-bed room in a pension not too far from the main square. We ditched our bags and went exploring the old town of Santiago and had a much more extensive look round the magnificent cathedral, both inside and out. And there was certainly a lot to see. Apparently the cathedral's construction started in austere Romanesque style in the eleventh century, but significant remodelling during the Baroque era resulted in the elaborate adornment, which was now apparent wherever we looked. Despite the extensive scaffolding spoiling the view of the west façade of the cathedral, reputed to be one of the most beautiful in Europe, there was still much to see. Walking around the cathedral, there was just so much to take in – soaring bell towers, Gothic cloisters, an elegant clock tower, high domes, decorative arches, stone staircases, intricate carvings, extensive balustrades, ornate statues – it was all wonderfully ostentatious. And that was just the exterior.

Unfortunately, the renovation work being undertaken at the cathedral also prevented us accessing the cathedral through its main entrance, the magnificent *Pórtico de la Gloria*, considered one of the finest works of medieval art in Europe. It was there that a very special statue of Saint James was located and unfortunately we couldn't get near it. Since the Middle Ages, it had been the custom of pilgrims to place their right hands on the marble column below Saint James, and apparently, after hundreds of years, five deep indentations had been worn into the marble as a result. However, we were not going to be able to add our wear and tear to the column today and we had to access the cathedral's interior via a side entrance.

However, when we did enter, the interior of the cathedral was absolutely stunning and the *Pórtico de la Gloria* was quickly forgotten. The Baroque high altar was undoubtedly the glorious centrepiece. If it had been designed to dazzle and amaze the onlooker, it certainly achieved its aim. It was a multi-tiered extravaganza, with a huge, golden canopy seemingly held above the altar by four gold-winged angels in flight. On top of the canopy sat more gold clad figures, grouped around the figure of Saint James on his white horse with his sword held aloft and appearing to chase down a number of Moors, who were stumbling and falling in front of his charger. The legend of Saint James enabled the Catholic faithful to bolster support for their stronghold in northern Spain during the Christian crusades against the Moors during the eleventh to thirteenth centuries. The miraculous

The elaborate high altar in Santiago Cathedral with the Botafumeiro hanging in the foreground

armed intervention of Saint James, disguised as a white knight to help the Christians when battling the Muslims, was a recurrent myth during the High Middle Ages and the image of Saint James on horseback, slaying the moors, is much repeated in paintings, carvings and statues. The altar also incorporated two other statues of Saint James, one of him in his pilgrim garb and another representing him as the Apostle James. The whole design was as audacious as it was elaborate. I had never before seen so much gold in the one place.

It was highly impressive, although I really couldn't gaze upon such excess and not at the same time feel a sense of injustice. In the past, pilgrims would have flocked to this cathedral, having endured real hunger and hardship in the name of their religion and yet here was that same religion dripping with such an overabundance of riches. However, it was no time for me to become all virtuous and sanctimonious. I also had to admit that those same poor pilgrims must have truly believed that they had reached a piece of heaven here on earth when they entered this cathedral and knelt in adoration before this lavish spectacle. And that was the whole point of it after all. It was to dazzle and fill congregations with the wonder of God that such elaborate cathedrals and churches were constructed in the first place – early Christian 'shock and awe' tactics.

We joined the queue to climb the stairs behind the altar where pilgrims could touch, hug or simply pass by a medieval statue of Saint James. We then descended into the *Sepulcrum Sancti Jacobi Gloriosum*, the crypt of Saint James, below the altar and saw the decorative silver container, purported to contain the relics of the saint that the cathedral and the city were built around. It was strange to think that what was believed to be in that container was ultimately responsible for drawing hundreds of thousands of pilgrims from across Europe and further afield to make the pilgrimage to this spot over the centuries.

We returned to the transept and saw the famed *Botafumeiro* hanging from the ceiling. This famous silver thurible is the largest censer in the world, weighing over 50kg and measuring 1.5m in height. It was hanging perfectly still when we saw it, but it is used to burn incense during certain pilgrim masses and is swung on a pulley system from one end of the transept to the other, apparently reaching speeds of nearly 70 kmph. Nowadays, it fills the cathedral with a heavenly, woody fragrance purely in an act of symbolism, but apparently in the Middle Ages it was all the Church could do to cover up the stench of the sweaty, unwashed hordes of pilgrims – presumably mainly those who had skipped bathing their parts at Labacolla.

High above the *Botafumeiro*, at the highest point of the dome above the transept, a single large eye painted within a triangle stared down from above as if keeping a watch on everyone below. It immediately brought to mind thoughts of Dan Brown novels, the Illuminati and other secretive organisations. However, it is of course a long-standing and well recognised Christian symbol that represents the all-seeing eye of God watching over humanity.

There was so much more on show inside the cathedral, but after a couple of hours we felt we had overdosed on opulence and reckoned we needed to escape to the real world again. We left by the rear entrance and stepped out into yet another huge square, the Plaza de la Quintana. This square was divided into upper and lower areas by a flight of stone steps running the entire width of the square. The upper area at the top of the steps is known as *Quintana de Vivos*, 'Quintana of the Living', while the more extensive lower area is known as *Quintana de Mortos*, 'Quintana of the Dead.' It takes its name from the burial ground that used to occupy this space, before the city's public cemetery was moved outside the old town in 1780. We climbed the steps and took our place among the living. We found a free table at a café there and relaxed for a time in the glorious afternoon sunshine over a few drinks and snacks, before continuing with our wanderings around the old town.

We later ate at Casa Manolo, which was excellent and obviously popular with pilgrims. While there, I picked up a text message from Fibi, an English girl I had met in Lourenzá a few days before, who was travelling with her boyfriend Felix. Fibi invited us to join her and a few others for pre-birthday drinks for Felix in a nearby bar. We made our way there and were met outside the bar by Fibi, who led us down through a warren of dark corridors to reach a cellar bar, where Felix and Paul and Lynette from Australia were already well ensconced. We probably stayed much later than we should have, but the craic was good and we just had to stay until after midnight to welcome in Felix's 24th birthday.

*****

The following morning, and despite the late night revelry, I got up before Matt and Hannah and headed into the Plaza del Obradoiro in front of the cathedral to enjoy the early morning sunshine and watch a trickle of fresh pilgrims arriving. The Spanish word *obradoiro* means workshop and the Plaza del Obradoiro takes its name from the fact that, when the cathedral was being built, the stonemasons would have had their workshop set up here to prepare the huge blocks of granite and carve their sculptures. The plaza was surrounded by four important buildings, which are said to represent the four powers of the city: the cathedral to the East (the church), the hotel to the North (the capitalists), the city hall to the West (the government) and the college to the South (the university). The floor of the plaza is decorated with eight rays or pathways leading to the centre, where a plaque commemorates the location, the traditional end point of the Camino de Santiago, as a World Heritage Site.

The hotel building, now a five-star Parador hotel, originally served as a hospital, where pilgrims could recover and rejuvenate after completing their pilgrimage – a reminder that, although still arduous, the Camino de Santiago is perhaps not as punishing or dangerous as it was in times gone by. I sat for a while on the stone bench at the hotel end of the square in the warm sunshine and listened again to the special song, 'See you in Santiago', that Hannah had composed and recorded for me. The lyrics were so beautiful and touching and, I must admit, they gave rise to a few more tears.

When I returned to the pension, Matt and Hannah were up and ready to go, so we settled up at reception and headed to a friendly café for breakfast. I ran into a group of familiar faces just outside the café – three German pilgrims, two men and one woman – and we all posed for photos together to mark our arrival in Santiago. I had crossed paths with them on many occasions over the past few weeks but had strangely never got to know their names. One of the men in particular had always been very friendly though. I made no mention of it, but these two men were also the German snoring champions I had encountered in the Soto de Luiña *albergue* a couple of weeks back. They were both great beer drinkers. I think that they must have stopped at every single bar between Irún and Santiago and no doubt that contributed heavily to their nocturnal noises. The woman in this small group was either hard of hearing or thoroughly deserved a medal.

After breakfast, Matt, Hannah and I donned the rucksacks once again and set off out of Santiago and started on the day's trek to Negreira, 20km away. It was a tough walk as it became very hot and there were a few steep climbs along the way, including one particularly long slog up a steep hill that ran for approximately two kilometres. The highlight of the day was without question passing through Ponte Maceira, which was described in my guidebook as possibly the prettiest town on the whole Camino and I wouldn't disagree. The medieval bridge over the Rio Tambre, and the river and buildings either side of the bridge, were incredibly picturesque and we, and many others, stopped here to enjoy the sights and sounds and take loads of photographs. The river had a weir just upstream from the bridge and the almost deafening roar of the water cascading over its length just added to the overall spectacle and atmosphere of this wonderful place. We finally arrived in Negreira

With Matt and Hannah at Ponte Maceira

at around 4pm and headed to the Albergue Lua near the centre of this small, nondescript town and got three beds there in another very large, open plan dorm. The facilities were adequate, but the evening and night that followed amounted to a time we would all prefer to forget.

It was Fathers' Day and Matt and Hannah had planned to treat me out to dinner. However, that evening Hannah said that she wasn't feeling great and so Matt and I left her to rest while we went in search of a restaurant. But we had to cut our evening short when Matt also began to feel unwell. Back in the *albergue* we discovered that Hannah had been very sick. And a few hours later Matt was very sick also. An absolutely horrible night ensued for us all, but especially for Matt and Hannah. Thankfully, I managed to escape any sickness myself. I just hoped that they would both feel better in the morning. For the first time I had to seriously consider having to abandon my Camino.

*****

Thankfully, both Matt and Hannah seemed to be over the worst of their sickness in the morning. However, they were both weakened after their night of illness. There was certainly no way that they were going to be able to walk today. Hannah had fallen ill first and had subsequently gotten over the worst of it soonest. She and I left Matt to sleep on in the Albergue Lua, while we went to get some breakfast and plan our next move. We decided that it would be best for her and Matt to take a taxi on to the next stopping point in Santa Marina, while I would walk and meet them at the *albergue* there later. We could then see how they were doing and plan the next day accordingly. I gave Hannah details of the Casa Pepa Albergue, which appeared to be only one in Santa Marina, and we went back to collect Matt.

A little later, I waved them off from the centre of town, as they left in their taxi for Santa Marina. I then walked out of Negreira, resigned to once again walking solo, to pick up the Camino trail once more. I just hoped that they would be able to rest in the Casa Pepa Albergue and continue to recover from their horrible sickness. Unfortunately, it was very close to 11am by the time I had hit the road and the heat of the day had started to build. There wasn't a cloud in the sky and, while it was beautiful to look at, walking in it for 20km with a heavy rucksack was a different matter entirely. What followed was probably one of the toughest days walking for me so far and that was almost entirely due to the energy sapping heat. It was beautiful countryside that I passed through though and that certainly made the journey more bearable.

I stopped at an *albergue* near the town of Vilaserio for lunch. It was a large two-storey building, which was lying completely open and totally deserted, but it had a few tables and chairs and so I made myself at home. It reminded me of the deserted Blackbird Café in Derrylin I had encountered on my Ulster Way walk the previous year. After my lunch of bread, cheese, ham and fruit, I got on the road again and began to tackle the final seven and a half kilometres of the route to Santa Marina. It was now around 2pm and the temperature had risen to about 26C, which was sweltering to walk through. By the time I reached Santa

Marina, I was bathed in sweat and dying for a cold beer. At a junction in the small village, I was mildly surprised to see a sign for a second *albergue* to the right, as well as a sign for Casa Pepa to the left. I headed for Casa Pepa, which was the one I had given Hannah the details of. However, when I arrived, there was no sign of them and the *hospitalero* claimed not to have seen them. She checked the register for that day, but their names were not recorded in it. She even showed me to the dorm, but again there was no sign of them. I assumed that the taxi driver must have dropped them off at the other *albergue*, which was on the main road heading west out of Santa Marina.

So I headed the extra kilometre to the second *albergue*, which was called Albergue Santa Marina. However, when I got there the *hospitalero* said that Matt and Hannah were definitely not staying at her *albergue* either. At this stage I started to panic a little and crazy scenarios started to run uninvited through my mind. Perhaps the taxi had been involved in some horrendous traffic accident on the road between Negreira and Santa Marina. I had of course tried, but I couldn't reach either of them by phone. Thankfully the *hospitalero* at the Albergue Santa Marina was very helpful. She phoned round the taxi companies in Negreira until she actually tracked down the driver who had driven them to Santa Marina and he confirmed that he had dropped them off at Casa Pepa. She then phoned Casa Pepa and, after much animated conversation, it was finally confirmed that they were indeed in Casa Pepa. By this time I was almost ready to be scraped off the floor. I thanked her for all her help and set off back to Casa Pepa once again. I was met there by the *hospitalero* who I had spoken to earlier and she was so apologetic – it turned out that they were in a second dorm at the *albergue* fast asleep and that they had been registered by another *hospitalero* who had gotten their names wrong. I was presented with an 'on the house' beer, which I graciously accepted while trying my best to brush off the mistake that had added two of the longest kilometres to my already punishing day's journey. "Oh, sure I really felt I hadn't walked quite far enough when I arrived earlier," I declared, with, I fear, not very well disguised sarcasm, much to the great amusement of other pilgrims in the bar who had observed all my comings and goings.

Anyway, I was soon reunited with Matt and Hannah, who had been sleeping off the effects of their illness and, of course, had been blissfully unaware of my frantic searching for them. They were both still feeling rather weak, but we were all glad to be back together again. They had secured me a bed in the bunk next to them in what was a cramped but fairly decent dorm and I soon got settled in and freshened up. However, my travels for the day weren't quite finished yet. For our evening meal we had to walk to a restaurant beside the other *albergue* on the main road. It was only another 2km there and back and sure I felt I needed to stretch my legs anyway. "English humour", as Sara would have said.

I was up at 6am with the early risers, including Michael and Sabrina from Germany, who we had met and dined with at the restaurant the previous evening. Matt and Hannah were still not fully back to form, so I advised them to stay in bed for as long as they could and then get a taxi on to either my next stopping point in Dumbria or the one beyond that in Muxía, where I intended to stop for a day or two myself. I left Casa Pepa and called into the café beside the Albergue Santa Marina, both to have a quick breakfast and also to thank the *hospitalero* once again for her help the previous day in tracking down Matt and Hannah for me.

The weather was very misty for much of the morning, which didn't help with the views, but showed off the cobwebs among the hedgerows very effectively. They were transformed into the most intricate and fine patterns, like layers of delicate, clear-beaded necklaces. I met another Michael, who was from Devon, along the way and we walked together for quite a bit over the next two days. Matt and Hannah had ultimately decided to take a taxi to Muxía, so it was good to have Michael's company until I was reunited with them again. It was Michael's third Camino. He had been on these sections to Dumbria and Muxía before

Chapel, stone cross and hórreo in Dumbria

and so I was able to benefit from his experience and knowledge of the route. Michael was an experienced walker and was also a keen amateur photographer, so we had plenty to talk about.

Just beyond the small community of Hospital, we came to the point where the Camino split between the route to Finisterre and the route to Muxía. It was only another 4km to our stopping point in Dumbria and the *albergue* here was superb. Really modern and clean, with great washing facilities and dorms – everything a pilgrim needed. However, the same could not be said for the town, which really didn't have very much going for it. Michael had warned me that there wasn't a lot to Dumbria, but I had felt compelled to check it out for myself. There was a pretty square at the top of the town, which was home to a little chapel, a stone cross and a hórreo that all looked wonderful together in such close proximity and against the clear blue sky. However, beyond that there was very little to the town – a sparsely stocked supermarket and a small bar and café seemed to be the only public amenities. I bought some snacks in the supermarket, had a drink in the bar and suffered a mediocre meal in the café, before heading back to the *albergue* and telling Michael that he had indeed been correct.

*****

The moon was almost full and still high in the sky as I set off from Dumbria early the next morning. The town had been rather lifeless the previous evening and at this early hour of the morning, it was even quieter, as most of its residents had not yet begun to stir. A ginger and white cat, sleeping with its two front paws resting up on the back of a scruffy little dog, also asleep on the pavement, were practically the only signs of life as I strolled through the still streets to pick up the route to Muxía. The bright moon, still clearly visible against a gradually lightening sky, provided a beautiful backdrop to some photographs I captured of lemons hanging from branches, swallows resting on overhead wires and long scimitar leaves of Eucalyptus trees.

The weather was gorgeous and helped display the Galician countryside at its very best. Grassy lanes, forest trails, stone walled tracks, cultivated fields, roadside shrines, rural homesteads, ancient hórreos, pretty wildflowers, weathered window frames, wooden carts and stone churches, all contributed to the colourful and varied palette on display. Once again, I walked with Michael from Devon for a good part of the route and his memory of the many twists and turns from his previous Camino was impressive. This stretch of the Camino is not travelled by many pilgrims. Only a small proportion of pilgrims walking to Santiago each year choose to walk the additional kilometres out to the West Coast and, those who do, tend to favour going directly to Finisterre rather than via Muxía. As a consequence, the way-marking on the route out to Muxía is not quite as dependable as that found on the other routes. In addition, my guidebook provided scant information on this section. So, having Michael around as a personal guide was pretty handy indeed. We would walk together for a while and then drift apart for a bit, before linking up again at some point further along the trail. We were both very relaxed with this approach and it happened quite naturally throughout the day and without the need for any spoken agreement – we just seemed to mutually understand each other's needs and respected the occasional desire for space, whilst also enjoying each other's company.

Arriving into Muxía during the hot, sunny afternoon was delightful as Michael and I approached the town via a long boardwalk that skirted the bay and its sandy beach. Michael and I parted company for a final time in the town, as he headed off in the direction of the municipal *albergue*, while I headed on to the private one recommended to me by Ray, who had been there a few days earlier. From Santiago, he had walked to Finisterre first and then travelled to Muxía, but he had left a few days ago, taking a bus to Santiago to catch his flight home to Germany. We had hoped to tie up again at some stage along the Camino, but it hadn't proved possible. Anyway, the private *albergue*, Bela Muxía, he had recommended was superb. And it was here that I was once again reunited with Matt and Hannah. It was great to be back with them again and they were certainly looking a lot better than when I had last seen them in Santa Marina.

After I got settled in and freshened up, we headed out for a light lunch before setting off to explore the rocky peninsula behind the small town. There was a sizeable swell rolling in from the Atlantic, which made for quite a dramatic backdrop, as the waves crashed against the rocks sending sea spray high into the air. Muxia is situated on a part of the Spanish coast known as the *Costa da Morte*, the 'Coast of Death', named as such due to the large number of ships that have been wrecked along its rocky shoreline over the years. It was here, back in November 2002, that the tanker ship Prestige sank, spilling millions of gallons of oil into the sea and causing Spain's worst environmental disaster ever. A large monument sits on the peninsula to commemorate this dreadful incident, which resulted in the pollution of thousands of kilometres of Spanish, French and Portuguese coastline, and caused great damage to the local fishing industry and marine life for many years after. The monument is like a huge slab of stone standing upright, but split down the middle in a jagged line, representing the split in the hull of the Prestige, which literally broke in two before disappearing beneath the waves. However, this wasn't the only monument to seafaring voyages associated with the area.

We made our way down to the large church building at the end of the peninsula that Muxía is renowned for. This was the *Santuario da Virxe da Barca*, the Sanctuary of the Virgin of the Boat, and it was built here in honour of a legend relating to Saint James. The legend claims that the Virgin Mary arrived in Muxía in a stone boat, guided by angels, and she appeared to the Apostol James to encourage him in his preaching to the Galicians. This legend was apparently used by the Catholic Church to Christianise existing Neolithic cults relating to a number of the large granite boulders located near the church. In pre-Christian times, *Pedra de Abalar*, the 'Rocking Stone', was believed to predict catastrophes and also have healing powers, while *Pedra dos Cadrís*, the 'Hips Stone', was believed to cure back ailments, rheumatic pains and even help with fertility issues. The *Pedra de Abalar* resembled a boat and the *Pedra dos Cadrís* resembled a sail. Thus, a cunning legend was born to wean the pagans off their crazy stoneage beliefs and onto perhaps an even crazier Christian one involving a stone boat guided by angels. Christianity is littered with examples such as this, where pre-Christian beliefs have been adopted and adapted by the Church in an attempt to guide pagans towards Christianity. Each September, a traditional festival dedicated to the Virgin of the Boat now takes place in this little fishing village by the Atlantic Ocean. So, the Church's strategy certainly appears to have been successful in Muxia.

Unfortunately, as was so often the case on my Camino, the doors of the sanctuary were locked. So, we left the church and followed one of the paths to the top of the hill on the peninsula, Monte Corpiño, where a simple stone cross is erected. From here, we enjoyed the stunning panoramic views southwards over the orange rooftops of Muxía, with its picturesque harbour and sandy beach to the East and yet more rocky coastline stretching off to the West. It was all looking rather resplendent in the evening sunshine, although we could see that clouds were now beginning to approach, being blown in on an on-shore breeze. We made our way down off the hill again and wound our way back towards the Bela Muxía *albergue*, where I remembered to pick up my Muxiana. Just like receiving my *compostela* (pilgrimage certificate) in Santiago, I was entitled to another certificate, called the Muxiana, for walking from Santiago to Muxia.

*****

The following day was quite cloudy and we even had some light rain in the morning. We pottered about between the *albergue* and the town's harbour and beach. It was certainly nice to leave the rucksack and boots behind and enjoy the lightness and freedom that came with being a tourist for the day. Muxía was certainly a pretty little town, but it was also very quiet and, after having seen the sights, there wasn't much else to do. I was very conscious of the fact that Matt and Hannah had come out to Spain to walk on the Camino with me and that their opportunity to do that had been severely limited by their unexpected illness. Unfortunately, Matt had run out of time and was due to return to Berlin the following day. However, Hannah still had another day before having to return to Belfast and so we decided to put that time to good use and walk together from Muxía towards Finisterre. It would at least salvage something positive from the disastrous few days they had experienced.

The disciples continued up the mountain until they reached a green valley nestled between the peaks. Here they saw, not the oxen promised to them by Queen Lupa, but a herd of wild bulls. The bulls were heavy and buffalo like in appearance and many carried fearsome looking horns on their broad heads. The disciples were initially too frightened to approach the wild animals, but, led by Joshua, they slowly made their way towards the herd. As soon as the bulls caught the scent of the disciples on the gentle breeze brushing over the pasture, they raised their heads, now alert to the presence of a threat. However, rather than retreating from the disciples, the wild bulls became angered and rushed towards them. Their hooves thundered across the plain, as the bulls charged with their heads lowered and horns forward.

The disciples were petrified at the sight of the wild bulls stampeding towards them, but emboldened by Joshua's stand against the dragon, they held their nerve and their ground as the bulls drew ever closer. They all raised their arms and made the sign of the cross and prayed aloud, "In the name of James, the holy apostle of Jesus Christ, be calmed."

The wild bulls all suddenly came to a halt and, for a moment, the only visible sign of the earlier uproar was the dust cloud kicked up by the bulls' hooves blowing across the plain. The wild bulls had now become as meek as lambs and the disciples were able to approach them and handle them with ease. They selected the four strongest looking animals and led then down off the mountain and yoked them to the cart they had left there. The bulls then drew the cart, without any guidance or direction from the disciples, directly to the stone sarcophagus containing the body of the apostle James. The disciples lifted the sarcophagus onto the cart and the bulls then once again miraculously drew the cart to the palace of Queen Lupa without any need for direction.

The Queen herself witnessed the arrival of the sarcophagus on the cart drawn by the 'wild' bulls and immediately believed in the Lord and was subsequently christened. She repented for her treachery towards the disciples and provided them with all that they needed. The disciples then brought the apostle's body to a secret location in Galicia to be buried. And there his remains lay hidden for almost eight hundred years.

Chapter Ten: End of the World
(Days 51 to 54 - Muxia to Negreira)

After saying our farewells to Matt, Hannah and I set off out of Muxia at about 8.30am. It was a rather cold, foggy and mizzly start to the day, but it was fine for walking and we soon warmed up as we got going. Unfortunately, we took the wrong road out of town, but we were eventually able to link up with the proper Camino route after a few kilometres.

The going was fairly easy and passed through some very pleasant Galician countryside and lots of forests of both pine and eucalyptus, the forest floors often carpeted with luscious green ferns. It was great to have Hannah's company again, but we had agreed that the full distance from Muxía to Finisterre, which was 31km, would probably be too far for her to walk at this stage, given her recent illness. So we stopped as planned at a cafe in the small town of Lires, which was roughly halfway along the route to Finisterre. We had some lunch here and then I arranged for a taxi to take Hannah on to Finisterre to await my arrival later on foot. I booked a room in a small hotel in Finisterre, and gave Hannah the address. I then gave her a hug and left her to wait on her taxi while I set off on foot again.

I soon began to think that maybe I should have waited on the taxi with Hannah also. The terrain became a lot more challenging beyond Lires and the temperature began to increase steadily. Although it was not as tough as some of the previous days I had experienced, it was a very long section and it seemed to take me forever to get to Finisterre. I felt tired and my walking pace had slowed considerably. For the first time, I really began to wish that my walk was finished. I was tired of living out of a rucksack, tired of carrying all my belongings on my back, tired of sharing rooms, tired of the Spanish food, tired of being away from home and, yes, tired of walking. But after today, I reckoned that I only had another four more days to walk to get back to Santiago. After seven weeks of being on the road, I was now into my eighth and final week. I was too close to my goal of 1,000km to consider throwing in the towel.

So on I plodded to Finisterre, eventually getting into the town at around 6pm, which was much later than I had expected. I made my way to the municipal *albergue*, which also acted as the local information office. Here I got my credential stamped and picked up my third certificate, a Fisterrana, this time to acknowledge my journey from Santiago to Finisterre. I also made some enquiries about Cape Finisterre, which was still another three kilometres beyond the town. I had been in touch with Hannah on my way into Finisterre and by now knew that the room I had booked for us was not actually in Finisterre town, but about six kilometres outside it. I contacted Hannah to say that I was going to walk on out to the Cape and for her to take another taxi and meet me there in about an hour's time. I then set off to 'the end of the world' on foot. Although tired, I was determined to walk the final few kilometres to Cape Finisterre and, thankfully, this part of the journey passed by fairly quickly. I think the romantic lure of this mystical place gave my legs the extra energy they needed to climb to the top of Monte Facho, the mountain on Cape Finisterre.

The name Finisterre, derives from the Latin finis terrae, meaning 'end of the earth', and it achieved this name because, in Roman times, this cape was thought to be the westernmost point on the Iberian Peninsula and hence the end of the world as it was then known. However, this was not quite true. Quite apart from the now obvious fact that there are lands far beyond these Atlantic shores, Cape Finisterre is not actually the westernmost point on the Iberian Peninsula. Cape Roca in Portugal is about 16.5 kilometres further west. There is even some doubt as to whether Cape Finisterre is the westernmost point in Spain, with that accolade also being claimed by Cape Touriñán, further up the coast. However it certainly didn't diminish my enthusiasm for reaching Cape Finisterre and, whatever else it was or was not, it was without a shadow of a doubt the westernmost point on my pilgrimage.

I was intrigued to pass a Celtic looking painting on the side of a stone building on my journey up Monte Facho. It reminded me that Cape Finisterre also had a lot of pre-Christian associations. There was an *Altar Soli*, 'altar to the sun', on the Cape, where the Celts had engaged in sun worship and other pagan rituals. As with Muxia, there are also several rocks at Cape Finisterre associated with pagan rites, such as the 'holy stones', the 'stained wine stones' and the 'stone chair'. A stone known as *Pedra de San Guillerme*, St William's Stone, is reputed to have been used by sterile couples to copulate on, following a Celtic ceremony of fertility, in order to help them conceive. Apparently, so many people took to the 'stone bed' that a bishop had it destroyed, but the two broken pieces of the stone still exist on Monte Facho and some believe it has not lost its miraculous properties.

I arrived in the public car parking area of the cape just a few minutes before Hannah arrived by taxi. We walked the last few metres together towards the cape's lighthouse and the rocks looking out to the seemingly endless ocean beyond. On the way we passed the last waymarker, with its blue and yellow scallop symbol and the distance remaining reading "0,00 KM." For many pilgrims, this was indeed the end of their journey, with some even symbolically burning their walking boots here. However, I still needed my boots for another few kilometres yet, as I had still to return to Santiago to complete my pilgrimage. Standing on the granite rocks high above the blue sea, with the sun now low in the sky and casting a silver path across the ocean towards us and long shadows behind, it was easy to imagine that we were indeed at the end of the earth. And it was equally easy to envisage how pilgrims of old would have stood here, perhaps exactly where we were standing now, and believed, not imagined, but truly believed that they had reached the very end of the world and that beyond the horizon, far out to sea in front of them, there was nothing more. During the Middle Ages, the Atlantic Ocean was known as the *Mare Tenebrosum*, or the 'sea of darkness,' and the Romans believed that the entrance to Hades was just over the horizon. So, it must have felt both frightening and miraculous at the same time to those ancient pilgrims. As I

Final way-marker at Cape Finisterre, which reads "0,00 K.M."

continued to look out into the far distance, with that path of silver streaming in across the surface of the sea, I couldn't help but wonder if similar feelings occurred at the end of one's life. And I wondered if, in her final moments, did Jacqui's fear, as she slipped away from her life here on earth, change into something more wonderful, as some divine light perhaps guided her forward to another better life? I certainly hoped so.

Since losing Jacqui, it had felt in so many ways as if I had reached the end of my world. It had certainly been the end our world – the world we had joyfully shared together for 35 years. At times it felt like there was now nothing but emptiness ahead – without Jacqui the future often seemed pointless. It was difficult for me to even think about the future. It was much easier to just live in the present – and easier still to remain in the past. There was always a burning desire to wish that everything was still as it was – to just put my head down and keep on walking blindly, trying to ignore reality. So long as I was walking across Spain, I could try to forget about the shattered life I had left back at home.

But now I had come to an end in the road, literally, and it forced me to lift my head and confront the reality of my situation.

As I stood at the 'end of the earth', I realised that I had to accept that my and Jacqui's journey through life together had ended. Jacqui had moved on, into the unknown, and I couldn't follow her – not yet anyway. I had to turn around and find my own way through the rest of my life without her. This was what I felt that Finisterre was telling me, loud and clear – you can't go on the way you have been going; you have to change direction; you have to let go of the past; turn away from the void you have been walking towards all this time; turn back towards life. Although it was still very hard to accept, I knew in my heart of hearts that this was the only way for me to go on – either I take a final step over the edge and join Jacqui, or I take a step back, turn around and continue with life, whatever that might bring. I looked over to Hannah, who was sitting on the rocks, enjoying the warmth of the evening sunshine and the dramatic views out to sea, and I knew what I had to do. She and Matt had travelled all the way out to Spain to support me on my walk. It hadn't quite worked out as planned, but that wasn't important. The important thing was that they had come. We were a family; a broken family, but a family nonetheless. It was important that we were there for each other and that also meant me being there for them.

I was ready to move on. I had to step back from the edge and get ready to continue with my journey – back to Santiago first, and then on into the future. Was I ready to let go of the past? That was going to be harder. I reached into my jacket and found and then rolled a familiar shape between my thumb and forefinger. But rather than being cast into the ocean or left hidden in the rocks of the Cape, Jacqui's pebble remained in my pocket. Somehow it just hadn't felt quite right to leave it there. Maybe it had to do with the fact that I knew my journey wasn't yet over. Maybe I needed to cling onto that small talisman for a few more days yet, at least until I reached the very end of my pilgrimage. Perhaps then I would be able to relinquish this small but potent symbol

Hannah at the 'end of the world'

of the life I had lost. I phoned for a taxi and Hannah and I returned to our accommodation for the night, six kilometres on the other side of Finisterre town in the village of Sardineiro.

*****

The following morning, Hannah and I had breakfast in the café next to our pension, before getting a taxi back to Finisterre so Hannah could catch the early bus to Santiago in time for her afternoon flight back to Belfast. I was sorry to see her go, but at least our time together in Finisterre had made up somewhat for the disappointment of the days before. I waited to wave her off and then, as the bus pulled away from the town centre, I turned and set off on my journey once again; only this time heading back towards Santiago and away from the end of the world. After more than seven weeks of walking into the west and away from the morning sun, it now felt slightly peculiar to be walking east, with the sun now on my face. It didn't take me too long to walk back through the bustling streets of Finisterre and then cut down, past an old, stone cross, and onto the beautiful, long, sandy Langosteira beach that stretched away from the edge of town.

The beach was more than a kilometre long and it was simply sublime to walk along the water's edge, stopping to look back every so often towards the picturesque town of Finisterre and Monte Facho rising up behind, both bathed in the glorious morning sunshine. I stopped occasionally to pick up a little shell that caught my eye, something that Jacqui could never resist doing when we walked along a beach together – we have many little containers full of sea shells lovingly selected from beaches across the world and across the years. A happy memory for sure, but a memory that also accentuated the fact that Jacqui was no longer with me. The lessons of Cape Finisterre from the previous evening were all very well, but they couldn't eradicate the feelings of loss. I wondered if I would ever be able to enjoy the beauty of nature without thoughts of my lost love intruding. I didn't think so and, in some ways, I hoped that I would never reach that state. Ideally,

Langosteira beach looking back to Finisterre town and Monte Facho behind

I would have liked to be able to think about Jacqui and remember the times we had together, without the sadness that it inevitably engendered. I longed for the time when smiles would replace the tears, but realised that that would only come with time – and how long, was anyone's guess. I recalled what Jane had told me; that time wasn't necessarily the great healer, but it was the great leveller. I found a small scallop shell and pocketed it to add to the collection of memories back home and as a personal memento of my Camino. Many pilgrims buy scallop shells in one of the numerous tourist shops all vying for the pilgrim pound, but I felt that it was much nicer to find and claim my own shell, fresh from the sea at the end of the world. I think Jacqui would have approved.

When I reached the end of Langosteira beach, I left the fine sands behind to join the network of roads and tracks that turned and twisted and, after about an hour and a half, brought me into the small village of Sardineiro again, where Hannah and I had stayed the night before. I called into the café where we had breakfasted that morning and I decided to treat myself to a *café con leche* and a piece of *Tarta de Santiago*, a traditional Galician almond cake. Then a troop of five local musicians entered the bar for some refreshments. They had been taking part in the ongoing San Juan celebrations, which centre on Saint John's Eve. After this colourful group of musicians, dressed in traditional costume and carrying traditional instruments, had slaked their thirst, they struck up a lively tune. Everyone in the bar was delighted at this unexpected and spontaneous performance. After rapturous applause from their small but appreciative audience, the musicians headed out the door again and marched off down the street, playing joyously as they went. I left also and walked up the street in the opposite direction to the marching band, the music gradually fading into the distance behind me, but the feeling of bonhomie it had engendered staying with me long after the sound had disappeared.

As I continued on my route back towards Santiago, I was met by a steady trickle of pilgrims heading for Finisterre. It was actually quite helpful being able to see where these other pilgrims were coming from, as at times it was quite hard to spot the waymarker signs whilst going in the opposite direction. Another hour and a half brought me past the pretty town of Corcubion and half an hour after that brought me to my final destination for the day, Cee. I'd really had enough of *albergue*s by this stage and so I checked into a nice little hotel near the town centre, called Hotel Larry. I threw my rucksack in my room before going downstairs to the bar area to have one of the nicest meals of my entire Camino – a beautiful fish salad followed by the most wonderful hake, all washed down with a few glasses of a soft red wine.

*****

After breakfast the following morning, Hotel Larry's manager pointed me in the right direction and so, initially anyway, I set off following the actual Camino route. My guidebook said that the directions into the town of Cee when coming from Santiago were not the easiest to follow. Given that I was going in the opposite direction, I didn't have much chance and I lost the route fairly early on. Unfortunately, it was too early in the day for any pilgrims to be coming into town so that method of keeping on track, that had worked well the previous day, was not available to me.

After reaching the outskirts of Cee, I could see a long hill ahead of me, which stretched into the distance before turning a bend to disappear between the trees. This turned out to be just the start of a very long, steep road climb that continued for almost three kilometres and ascended almost 300 metres. There was also a lot more traffic on these country roads than I would have expected on a Sunday morning, all of which resulted in my morning walk being much more demanding than anticipated. It wasn't until 11km and two and a half hours after leaving Cee that I finally encountered the official Camino route once more.

It was good to be back on track again and I knew that there was a good café not far from here, which was great because I was certainly ready for some lunch. It was a sunny but very windy day, so as well as having the sun on my front as I headed east, I also had the strong wind in my face. It was unusual for the wind to blow from the east and I certainly hadn't experienced such strong winds in Spain to date. I had now begun to encounter a few pilgrims going towards Finisterre and I envied them having the wind at their backs; but only a little – I was quite happy to be heading back to Santiago and the end of my two-month pilgrimage.

However, close to my planned lunch stop, I was stopped in my tracks. For here is where I saw a pilgrim coming up the track towards me riding a unicycle. And he had a full rucksack on his back also. What made this even more bizarre was the fact that Sara and I had been talking the previous week about how, if we were to do the Camino again, we should do it in some totally unique way. I had joked that I would like to be the first to complete in on a unicycle. I was flabbergasted and just stood there and stared as he peddled his way up the pathway towards me and then applauded as he whizzed past me.

A pilgrim heading west towards Finisterre or Muxia on his unicycle

One man, one wheel, one Camino. It was an incredible sight and it certainly brightened up my day.

I continued the short distance to the Café O Casteliño in Hospital and had a nice break here that set me up for the remainder of my walk. Now that I was back on the Camino route proper and that I had completed most of the steep climbs for the day, the journey became much more pleasant. And the landscape was much more enjoyable to walk through. The path followed a route high above a river valley and the views down into the river and the surrounding forests were stunning.

Unusually, I hadn't yet decided on my final destination for the day. I could keep on going to Santa Marina, but that would involve quite a bit more walking in the heat of the day and would also mean staying in an *albergue* again, which I was no longer keen on doing. So I preferred to stop sooner if that was possible. When I reached the village of Olveiroa, I called into a café to treat myself to an ice cream. I was about to head on when I noticed that there was a pension next door. On making enquiries, I found that there was a room available, so I immediately booked it and decided to call it a day so far as the walking was concerned. It was a good choice as the room was great and there was a nice restaurant nearby. My plan was to stop here for the night and get away early the next morning to cover the 33km to Negreira.

As I enjoyed my evening meal alone in the restaurant, I reflected on the fact that it was quite a lonely trek back to Santiago from Finisterre. It was a direction rarely travelled on foot by pilgrims. Having walked to 'the end of the world' at Cape Finisterre, most pilgrims felt that they had done enough – they had completed their pilgrimages and were more than happy to return to Santiago by public transport. However, I had my 1,000 kilometres, my 1000K4J, to achieve and so, solitary though it was, I had to keep walking for a few more kilometres yet – a total of 53 to be exact.

*****

I was up early and on the road at just after 7am, after having had breakfast at the café next door to Pension Loncho. It was a beautiful morning. As the sun came up, it bathed everything caught in its light in an incredibly rich and warm glow and cast impossibly long shadows that stretched into the distance. The waning moon, now just a half-moon, was clear in the sky again and both sun and moon provided me with magical scenes as I walked out of Olveiroa. As I watched the skies, I spotted a plane heading for Santiago Airport leaving a white jet stream trail in the blue above. Then as it changed course for its final descent, it transcribed a huge 'J' in the sky and my heart leapt at the sight. It was reminiscent of the 'J' being marked out in the sand of the beach at Zumaia near the start of my Camino. Was this yet another sign of Jacqui's presence or just a plane carrying out a routine manoeuvre?

Regardless of whether it was a sign from above or not, I had felt Jacqui's presence with me right throughout this pilgrimage and the feeling was getting stronger as I neared Santiago for the second time and as I came closer to completing my 1000K4J. I also had a feeling that something special was going to happen in Santiago. I had no idea what this might be or what form it might take. Perhaps it was more a hope than a feeling and there was every likelihood I would end up disappointed. Some pilgrims hope for some sort of epiphany or deeper understanding of themselves, or of life in general, when they reach the end of their Camino, while many others simply just have a sense of relief that their long journey is over. I was certainly looking forward to hanging up my walking boots and rucksack, but I craved for there to be something more; something deeper; something to soothe my troubled soul; some sort of sanctuary. However I would just have to wait to see what my return to Santiago delivered.

Most of today's walk was on roads, as once again I found it very difficult to follow the Camino trail when walking it in reverse. I managed okay early on, as I met dozens of pilgrims, including a young couple with a donkey, all heading for Finisterre or Muxía in the morning. Each pilgrim, or group of pilgrims, as they appeared over the horizon or round the bend ahead of me, provided welcome reassurance that I was still on the right path. They all admirably resisted the temptation to tell me that I was going the wrong way – I had yet to meet a single pilgrim who, like myself, was walking back to Santiago. At one point, I stopped to look back the way I had just come to watch a line of ten or more pilgrims, in a range of trendy outfits and rucksacks, heading towards the coast. They created a vibrant chain of colour, as they stretched out along the dry and dusty track cutting through the verdant Spanish countryside.

Unfortunately, the flow of pilgrims disappeared in the afternoon and it was then back to my phone's GPS to help me find my way. Although I had already walked this part of the Camino, it was still not easy to recognise and locate the numerous turn-offs when going in the opposite direction and I ended up following the main roads for quite a bit. This meant that I had to keep a wary eye out for traffic and also that I was exposed to the heat of the sun for long periods of time without the shade of forest trees to benefit from. There had been a nice breeze earlier in the day, which had kept things pretty comfortable, but it became very hot in the afternoon. And to cap it all, today's walk was a pretty long one for me at nearly 33km. It was therefore with much relief that, at around 3.30pm, I finally reached the outskirts of Negreira. I called into the very first bar I came across, the Bar Porto, and had a beautifully cold beer, served in a frosted glass, sitting on a balcony outside overlooking the Río Barcala – it was heavenly. Suitably refreshed and revived, I headed on into town via its arched and fortified gateway, passing the fateful Albergue Lua, where Matt and Hannah had taken ill, and heading instead for the cheap and cheerful Hotel Millán at the opposite end of town. It had a single room available and it suited me perfectly.

Tomorrow would see me walk the final 20km back into Santiago and complete my second pilgrimage in memory of Jacqui. I wondered what she would have made of all this walking. We had loved going for walks together, but they had always been over quite short distances. Invariably it was me who said that my legs had had enough and that it was time to be turning back, usually only after a few kilometres. So, Jacqui probably would have been amazed at the distances I was now covering. I hoped also that she would have been proud of what I had achieved in her honour – not just the kilometres walked, but the fundraising for cancer research and helping in my own small way to raise awareness of ovarian cancer. Of course, I would never know for sure what she would think, but I couldn't help but wonder. I also couldn't help but wonder if something special was going to happen in Santiago when I returned for the second time. My first visit there, although rewarding in some respects, had ultimately seemed rather underwhelming and lacklustre. I still craved some sort of personal sanctuary; some sort of resolution; some sort of peace. The end was now truly in sight and my sense of anticipation was growing. But I had to admit that it was growing in the shadow of anxiety, as I also feared that all my hopes could just as easily come to nothing. I might only find that I had walked 1,000km and ended up no further forward.

Year 814 AD

The monk Pelayo struggled up the narrow dirt track to his hermitage in the hills of Galicia, bowed under the weight of the bundle of firewood he had been gathering in the woods of Libredón. He dropped the bundle to the ground as he arrived at the door of his humble abode and groaned with relief as he straightened and stretched his aching back. The evenings were getting noticeably colder and he was looking forward to getting a fire going, both to warm up the chilly hermitage and also to heat up some broth for his first and only meal of the day. He pushed open the heavy wooden door and then turned to lift his load once again. As he stooped, he noticed something out of the corner of his eye – something glowing. He stood again and turned to look back in the direction of the woods. There was undoubtedly a strange glow coming from deep in the forest, where he had been earlier collecting branches for his fire. Intrigued, he pulled the hermitage door closed again and set off towards the tree line. As he drew closer, he could see peculiar lights flickering amongst the trees, but he was puzzled as to what they could be. They looked like stars, but surely that was not possible? He was too fearful to enter the forest alone, but suspecting something miraculous, he made his way to the palace of the local bishop, having now totally forgotten all about his earlier desire for warmth and food.

Bishop Theodomir was intrigued by what Pelayo reported to him and he immediately set off with a small party of servants to see what was behind the strange lights. Like Pelayo, the bishop suspected something miraculous at work. On leaving his palace, Bishop Theodomir and his party had their path illuminated by an unusually bright star in the night sky above. The light from the star moved ahead of them and led them into the remoteness of the Galician hills. When they reached the top of the peak, now known as Monte de Gozo, they noticed that the star had come to rest and was shining a shaft of light directly down into the woods of Libredón, located in the valley between the surrounding hills. The bishop's party descended into the valley and made their way to the location, which remained illuminated by the bright star. When they finally arrived, they discovered a clearing in the woods with a large stone slab lying amongst the ferns covering the forest floor. The slab had obviously lain there for centuries, but there was something unnatural about its position given that there were no other rocks in the vicinity. He instructed his servants to drag the slab aside, which they managed with some great difficulty. Once the slab was out of the way, the bishop peered into a shallow chamber illuminated clearly by the light of the star above. Lying in the chamber was a skeleton and it appeared that the skull had been severed from the body before burial. Bishop Theodomir immediately dropped to his knees before the ancient grave and looking skyward cried out, "Thank you for leading us to this holy place Oh Lord." and turning to his servants, he declared, "Behold, the remains of the apostle of Jesus Christ; the holy martyr James."

After learning of the discovery, King Alfonso II journeyed to the site to venerate the relics and ordered that a church be built on the spot in honour of Saint James. The site became known as Santiago de Compostela - Santiago being the local Galician evolution of the Latin 'Sanctus Iacobus', meaning Saint James, and Compostela deriving from the Latin 'Campus Stellae', meaning field of the star. The modest church established by King Alfonso II later grew into the Cathedral of Santiago de Compostela and a city gradually began to grow up around it.

Chapter Eleven: Sanctuary
(Days 55 and 56 – Negreira to Santiago)

I woke early in my basic but comfortable room in the Hotel Millán in Negreira. It was the last day of my pilgrimage and it was time to get cracking. So, I visited the bathroom, got dressed, pulled on my socks and boots, refreshed my water reservoir, repacked my rucksack and I was good to go. I had done it so often now that I think I could have done it in my sleep. In fact, I'm sure that I had done so on a few mornings. With my gear all prepared, I headed down to the hotel's dining room for a quick breakfast prior to setting off. I had some coffee and croissants and just as I was about to get up from my table to leave, I heard a familiar voice behind me.

"Do you mind if I join you?"

I turned around, astonished to see Jane standing there, and quickly answered, "Of course not. Please do," and then added, as she took her seat, "It's lovely to see you again. I thought that you had maybe finished your pilgrimage and headed back home by this stage."

"Oh no, I'm still here. You're not going to get rid of me that easily, you know," she joked.

I was immediately transported back to a moment in time shortly after Jacqui's diagnosis. A time when hope still had a justifiable right to exist and be given voice. Jane's words recalled a conversation I had had with Jacqui just after her diagnosis of ovarian cancer had been confirmed. We were in bed together that night, still trying to take it all in. She was coping with it much better than I was. She had told me not to worry; that she was stubborn; she was a fighter; she was going to do everything she could to beat it; going to do everything in her powers to stay alive. She then kissed me and said, "You're not going to get rid of me that easily, you know."

"Are you okay?" Jane asked, "You look like you've just seen a ghost."

"Yeah...yeah...I'm okay," I replied, feeling anything but okay. I struggled to drag my thoughts back to the present, quickly asking, "So, where have you been? Did you make it out to Finisterre?"

"Oh yes, I made it to the end of the world. And then I decided to come back." We both smiled at that.

"Yeah, me too," I said, before adding, "Sometimes you don't really have a choice."

"That's very true. Anyway, enough chat. It's high time you were hitting the road. I guess you're on the home stretch now."

I lifted my rucksack from under the table and stood up. "You're right, it's time to go. We'd better get a move on if we're ever going to reach Santiago today."

"We?"

"Yeah, I would really love it if you would walk with me today. Will you?"

"To be honest, I was hoping you'd ask. I can't think of anything that I'd rather do more."

"That's great. Let's go then." I settled the bill at reception and then Jane and I stepped out into the early morning sunshine and made our way down the main street to pick up the Camino route back to Santiago.

"I'm certainly not sorry to be leaving Negreira behind," I said, as we walked together through the quiet streets of the town. "It's here that poor Matt and Hannah both fell ill when they were walking with me last week. They had to get taxis from that point, while I walked on and finally caught up with them in Muxia."

"Oh, that was very unfortunate, but it was great that they came out to join you on your Camino and at least they got to walk into Santiago with you the first time, which must have been special."

"It certainly was. It was great to have them there. Although, for me personally, it was a bit of an anticlimax in a way. I'm hoping my second visit to Santiago will be a bit more fulfilling."

"I'm sure it will be," was all Jane said.

We had reached the top of the hill on the way out of town and were now beginning the long descent down towards the valley of the Río Tambre.

"I remember coming up this hill into Negreira with Matt and Hannah. I think they were on their last legs by that stage. They had just walked close to 20 kilometres and it was quite a hot day. It's certainly a lot easier going down in the cool morning air."

We were walking at a good pace, buoyed on by the sunshine and the knowledge that Santiago was within our reach today. We had joined a main road and I was lost in my own thoughts for a bit, walking on autopilot along the verge, when I suddenly realised that Jane had stopped behind me.

"Hang on there, Dermot, you've just missed the turn off. Here, there's an arrow painted on the road. You remember this little dirt track that ran behind these houses and the neighbouring fields?"

"Oh yes, of course. It eventually meets up with the river and follows it upstream to that lovely bridge at Ponte Maceira. Well spotted. I would have missed that turn off if it hadn't been for you. I'm so glad I've traded in my GPS for JPS."

"JPS?"

"Yeah. Jane's Positioning System."

"Oh, very droll. Well, it's not the first time my JPS has helped you out. Remember that time back near Ribadeo when you were nearly wandering off to God knows where, before I shouted to you."

"Oh yes, I remember that. Yeah, you've saved me from heading in the wrong direction a few times. I don't know what I would have done without you – or where I might have ended up."

So, we left the road and joined the little track that meandered peacefully through the fields and followed the banks of the Río Tambre, before entering the small town of Ponte Maceira.

"Stop," I said. "Listen. Can you hear that? It's the sound of the water going over the weir just above the bridge."

We walked on and stopped halfway across the medieval stone bridge to watch and listen to the sights and sounds of the river. Ponte Maceira was built in the thirteenth century on the foundations of a previous Roman bridge and it crosses the Río Tambre with five large and two small arches. It was perfectly idyllic in the late morning sunshine. The surface of the river's waters above the weir was totally smooth and calm, but as it cascaded over the weir, which was only about a metre high, the release of energy in terms of noise and churning white water was as spectacular as it was captivating.

"I really love this place. Matt and Hannah and I spent ages here when we passed through. It's probably one of the prettiest towns I've encountered on my entire walk. This place alone is reason enough to do the Camino Finisterre. And it's lovely to be passing through it again with you."

"It's a beautiful place for sure. A little piece of heaven on earth. You know, the literal translation of the name Ponte Maceira is Apple Tree Bridge. Not sure why it was called that, but it makes me think of the Garden of Eden."

"I think the Garden of Eden was supposed to have been in the Middle East somewhere, but yeah, it could equally be applied to this place. Anyway, nice as it would be to linger here, I think it would be best if we got moving again. Still about 17 kilometres to go."

So, we left that little piece of paradise and after about an hour we passed through the small settlement of Carballo before beginning the steep descent through the forests towards Augapesada. Many of the pilgrims we met coming the other way were so exhausted that they could barely lift their heads to speak as they passed us. Our greetings were frequently ignored – not out of ignorance, but simply because many we spoke to were totally out of breath. We finally reached the bottom of the hill and felt great sympathy for those pilgrims we met who were just about to start the climb, probably having little idea of what lay ahead.

"Gee, I remember coming up that hill with Matt and Hannah," I said to Jane. "It seemed to go on forever and it was a really hot day also. It's not a bit wonder that they found the walk on to Negreira so tiring. Maybe Matt and Hannah faked their sickness to get out of doing any more."

"I very much doubt that. I'm sure they were very disappointed to have their plans to walk with you brought to a premature end in such a horrible way."

"Yeah, of course you're right. I'm only joking. I think one of the places we ate in specialised in 'boke-adillos'."

"Oh please!"

"Sorry," I said, laughing. Then, a few moments later, I added, "I am getting hungry though. There's a nice place near Ventosa, which is only a few kilometres from here. If you want, we can stop there for a break and then it's only another eight kilometres to Santiago."

"Sounds good to me."

However, when we reached the Restaurante Alto Do Vento in Ventosa, they weren't open, so we picked up some bread and cheese in a store and continued walking until we found somewhere to sit and have our lunch. Beyond Ventosa, the route took a path through another wooded area and it was here that we stopped, in a clearing away from the track a bit. We sat on a fallen tree trunk to have our picnic. As we ate, butterflies fluttered around our heads and it was quite magical as they danced through the filtered sunlight seeping through the leaf cover of the trees above. Both of us seemed reluctant to break the spell as we enjoyed our food in silence, but eventually Jane sighed.

"Gee, it's so beautiful and peaceful here," she said softly.

"Yeah, it surely is. I wonder if my sanctuary will turn out to be somewhere like this. If I ever find it that is. I'm no longer sure I will. I've walked almost a thousand kilometres and I haven't found it yet. Two thousand, if you include last year's walk."

"Dermot?"

"Yes?"

"Do you ever stop to think that perhaps all your walking is more about trying to escape, rather than trying to find something? And do you ever feel that your sanctuary may not actually be a place; somewhere that you finally reach at the end of all your walking and enter into, suddenly leaving all your heartache on the outside?"

"If you're suggesting that I may be delusional thinking that I'll find a place of sanctuary, well, I have to concede that you may be perfectly correct. But, I just feel compelled to keep walking, hoping that it will lead me somewhere. Anywhere. Somewhere better."

"No, no, I'm not suggesting that you're delusional at all. What I'm suggesting is that your sanctuary may not be a place, but rather a state of mind; an acceptance of the way things are; contentment even."

"Well, if that's the case, then what the hell am I doing here? If sanctuary is simply a state of mind then I could just as easily have achieved that at home. Why am I wasting my time doing all this bloody walking?" I wasn't getting angry with Jane. Perhaps just a little bit irritated at having something so obvious pointed out to me. Something that I perhaps, in my heart of hearts, already knew to be true, but was too stubborn to admit.

"But you're not wasting your time at all. This walking is your way of dealing with your grief and it does help. Surely you can see that. It gives you space. Space to think; to process; to come to terms with your terrible loss. I really don't think you would have been able to achieve the same by staying at home. You came here because it felt like the right thing to do. You weren't sure why, but that didn't really matter. It felt like the right thing. You followed your instinct. That can never be wrong."

"Good God. Where are you getting all this homespun philosophy from?"

Jane was clearly taken aback by my thoughtless remark. "I'm sorry" she said, "I was only trying to help."

After a brief moment, I relented. "No Jane, it's me who should be sorry. Thing is, I know that there's a lot of truth in what you say. It's just that I suppose I've been unwilling to face that truth. The concept of finding a place is a lot easier to understand and deal with than the concept of having to reach some nebulous state of mind. I mean, how the hell will I even know how to reach it or even realise when I've got there. You can see a place, pinpoint it on a map, walk towards it and step into it, but how in God's name do you do that with a state of mind?"

"Look Dermot, I accept totally that it's not as clear cut and easy, but it can be done. And certainly it is nebulous. It's not finite like a building, or a room, or a forest clearing" she said, sweeping her hand around our little wooded glade. "It's more like a spectrum of emotions that you will continue to slide up and down, but staying within a safe band on that spectrum that lies somewhere between despair and anger and all those negative emotions on one end and total joy on the other. And that band can be thought of as acceptance."

"Jesus. Acceptance. Is that as good as it gets?" I asked, almost dismissively.

"If you're lucky," she replied, which sort of took the wind out of my sails. "And sometimes it will be acceptance tainted with loss and hurt and at other times it will be acceptance tinted with memories and smiles. But often it will just be acceptance. Nothing more, nothing less. Just neutral acceptance."

We sat in silence for a time, giving me time to absorb what Jane had just said.

"You know, the truth is, I already knew all this. I guess I just needed it spelt out for me. These sorts of thoughts buzz around in my mind all the time while I'm walking, but never seem to settle on anything definite. Sometimes I think of my thoughts as little bees in a field of wild flowers, buzzing loudly and moving randomly from one bloom to another – never resting."

"Very poetic. But yes, I know what you mean. And when that happens, it's very hard to make any sense of what's going on. But your buzzing thoughts are just part of the process. That's why I believe that your walking is so valuable. It allows time for all those thoughts to sort themselves out and for you to eventually see the bigger picture."

"The honeycomb you mean?"

"If you like," she said laughing, "Just add a wee bit of milk and you'll have found your promised land."

"Hey, very good. I like that" I said, joining her laughter. The tension had passed now. We were both relaxed and jovial again and the mood of the forest clearing was recaptured. I leaned forward and kissed her gently on the cheek. "Thank you," I said.

"You are very welcome," she replied, not abashed in the slightest at my sudden show of affection.

"Come on. It's time we were moving on again."

I started to gather up the remnants of our lunch and stuff them into one of the outer pockets of my rucksack for disposal later. We left the clearing to pick up the Camino route once again and, as if the enchantment of the woods continued to stay with us, we joined hands as we headed on down the forest track.

The next 5km or so was along a series of dirt tracks and small roads and it was pretty tough going in the afternoon heat. The sky was clear blue and there was little shade from the midday sun high above,

The skyline of Santiago appears in the distance

relentlessly searching us out and finding us at every turn. It was with some relief when the mighty domed spires of Santiago Cathedral appeared over the horizon. We both cheered at the sight ahead of us. This must have been what it was like for the pilgrims of old, when they reached the top of Monte de Gozo on the other side of Santiago and caught their first glimpse of the cathedral's spires. That sight had been denied to me on my initial approach to Santiago with Matt and Hannah due to the tall eucalyptus trees covering Monte de Gozo, but from this vantage point the view was both unobscured and wonderful. The rest of the city's skyline also started to reveal itself as we edged our way over the final rise and ever closer to our goal.

We then began our descent from the hills, eventually crossing the small bridge over the Río Sarela to reach the outskirts of Santiago. We stopped briefly in the small park of Carballeira de San Lorenzo to rest a little and enjoy the shade provided by the ancient oak trees there – *carballeira* is a Galician word meaning oak grove. We also took the opportunity to freshen up, courtesy of the cool water cascading from the park's fountain. Once refreshed we headed on through the busy city streets to cover the final kilometre to the Cathedral de Santiago. This of course was my second arrival in Santiago, although this time I would be approaching the Cathedral and the Plaza del Obradoiro from the west side. We made our way up the long, narrow, stone-paved street of Rúa das Hortas, passing the stunning little church, *Iglesia de San Fructuoso*. It was tucked away at the top of the street and almost in danger of being overlooked against the grandeur of what lay beyond in the plaza. Then, hand in hand, we climbed the gentle slope of Costa do Cristo to once again step into that glorious square that welcomes hundreds of pilgrims from all corners of the world every day. And though I was only but one among millions of pilgrims, who had set foot in the Plaza del Obradoiro over the centuries, it still felt very special indeed. We stood in the centre of the huge square, under the glorious blue sky, and slowly turned full circle again and again to drink in the wonderful atmosphere of the plaza and its buildings, as yet more pilgrims arrived to join the growing throng of ecstatic, exhausted, enraptured and excited pilgrims.

"Wow. I can't quite believe it. I'm here at last. My thousand kilometre Camino de Santiago finally finished."

"Well done Dermot. I never doubted that you would do it. Are you okay?"

"Yes...I'm okay...I've just got something in my eye. Sorry, who am I kidding? I just need a moment. It's all a bit overwhelming. I wasn't expecting my arrival in Santiago a second time to be so emotional."

"Well it is the end of a remarkable journey. It's taken you almost eight weeks to complete it and so much has happened in that time. You've met so many super people and visited so many lovely places. It's hardly surprising that you feel emotional now that you've reached the end."

"Yeah, you're right. It's been a long journey for sure. Hard going at times, but so rewarding. I think I'm going to remember this experience for the rest of my days. You are so right about the lovely people I've met and the places I've seen – so many it's almost unbelievable. And I'm so glad I met you too."

"And me you," Jane responded with a smile.

"Right, let's find somewhere to stay and then we can get something to eat and then see if we can make the evening service in the Cathedral."

"I thought you weren't religious?"

"I'm not, but come on, it Santiago Cathedral and there's a chance the 'the big smokey thing' might be in action tonight."

"Gee, your reverence for the Church really is endearing."

Later, as planned, we were back outside the Cathedral. We then left the bright sunshine and heat of Plaza de la Quintana and stepped into the relative darkness and coolness of the Cathedral's interior. It was still about half an hour before the service was about to begin, but the pews were already beginning to fill up with devout worshipers, devoted pilgrims and dedicated tourists alike. However, we were lucky and found space in a pew only two rows back and off to the side of the altar in the south transept. The Cathedral was filled to capacity by the time Mass began and, as Masses go, I have to admit that this one was pretty impressive. Quite apart from the extraordinary setting, the ceremony itself was presided over by no less than three priests, of different nationalities, and the Mass was said in a mixture of Spanish, Latin and English. After the celebration of the Eucharist, one of the priests announced that the ceremony of the *Botafumeiro* would follow directly after the Mass. Even in the hushed reverence of the Cathedral's interior, a detectable buzz of anticipation passed around the congregation. This was what many, including myself, had been hoping for.

The Mass finished with a traditional blessing from the lead priest, "Go in peace to love and serve the Lord," and the congregation's response, "Thanks be to God." Then eight men dressed in dark maroon robes stepped into the chancel, the area around the altar. These were the eight *tiraboleiros* required to swing the heavy censer, the *Botafumeiro*, that was suspended on a rope hanging from a pulley in the main dome of the cathedral, 20 metres above the chancel. Two of the tiraboleiros opened the top of the censer and the three priests placed the incense inside. Suddenly the censer was smoking. The lid was closed and the priests moved back. While one of the two *tiraboleiros* joined his colleagues to start hoisting on the rope, the other man-handled the censer to guide it into a swinging motion. Once he was satisfied that it was on the correct trajectory, he too joined his robed colleagues and all eight of them then hauled on the rope in a well-practised rhythm, like silent bell ringers. This sent the censer in an ever-increasing arc, swinging through the transept at incredible speed and reaching incredible heights, all the while filling the cathedral with its clouds of perfumed incense.

According to the Cathedral's own literature, the purpose of the *Botafumeiro* is *'to symbolise the true attitude of the believer. In the same way that the smoke from the incense rises to the top of the temple's naves, so must the prayers of the pilgrims rise to reach the heart of God. And in the same manner that the aroma of the incense perfumes the entire basilica, so must Christians, with their virtues and the testimony of their lives, impregnate with the good scent of Christ, the society that they live in.'* I still believe that it must have also proved pretty effective at masking, if not exactly eliminating, *olor del peregrino* in days gone by.

By this stage, everyone in the congregation was on their feet. Cameras, prohibited from filming during the Mass, now appeared en-mass to capture the spectacle. Our viewing position was perfect as the censer travelled almost directly overhead. At one point a woman beside us almost jumped out of her skin as she thought the censer was going to

Three of the tiraboleiros bring the swinging Botafumeiro to rest in Santiago Cathedral

come crashing down on her. The organ played loudly as the *Botafumeiro* swung through the transept at terrific speeds. It almost seemed like it was going to reach the ceiling of the basilica at the end of each arc, only to fall back again to leave another cloud of incense hanging in the already hazy air, cut through with rays of sunlight from the windows high above. It was a tremendous spectacle. It only lasted a few minutes, but would doubtless be etched in people's memories for years to come. The *tiraboleiros* finally brought the *Botafumeiro* to rest and, suddenly, unexpected applause filled the Cathedral to mix with the incense and the filtered sunlight, as the final notes from the organ ebbed away.

As the congregation started to shuffle out of their pews and make their way towards the doors, Jane and I sat on for a few moments, reluctant to allow the experience to suddenly evaporate. Jane turned to me and whispered, "You know that the area around the altar is called the chancel?"

"Yeah, I think I remember that from when I nearly became an altar-boy once."

"I really can't imagine you as an altar-boy. But anyway, what you might not know is that it is also often referred to as the sanctuary."

"Good Lord. Are you serious?"

"One hundred percent. Sanctuary comes from the Latin *sanctuarium*, which literally means a container for keeping holy things in. Over time the meaning has been extended to cover places of holiness or safety. In Europe, Christian churches were sometimes built on land considered to be a particularly holy spot, perhaps where a miracle or martyrdom was believed to have taken place or where a holy person was buried such as St Peter's Basilica in Rome or..."

"Here, in the Cathedral de Santiago – the Cathedral of Saint James."

"Correct. And that spot, and therefore the church built there, was considered to have been sanctified, or made holy, by what happened there. The Catholic Church has continued this practice by placing in the altar of each church, when it is consecrated for use, a box (the sepulcrum) containing relics of a saint. This Cathedral contains a sepulcrum with the relics of Saint James."

"Allegedly."

"Allegedly. Anyway, what I'm telling you is that you are at this very minute probably sitting just a few metres away from one of the most visited sanctuaries in the world."

"My God. So I am. How am I only realising this now?"

"Ahem."

"Sorry. Yes, of course. Thanks. But, sometimes it seems that I can't see the wood for the trees. I certainly knew that churches and the like have long been regarded as 'places of sanctuary', but to my mind that was more associated with people seeking refuge from some threat. Probably from watching too many old war movies when I was young. You know, when members of the French resistance hid out in the town's church, protected by the local priest, until the German soldiers were thrown off the scent. But I never really thought of churches actually containing an area called a sanctuary." After sitting in silent reflection for a moment, I said "Let's go."

We both moved to the end of the pew, but instead of turning towards the doors to leave the now almost empty Cathedral, we turned in unspoken unison towards the altar. We approached the marble altar rail and knelt on the step before what I now recognised as the sanctuary. It had been a long time since I had prayed; I mean, really prayed. But on this occasion, I was filled with such a sense of wonder, such a sense of spirituality, that I felt moved to express my feelings in prayer. Not by way of any formal prayer. No 'Our Fathers' or 'Hail Marys'. Just to simply talk, inwardly, about the things that were on my mind and to hope that someone 'up there' was listening. I prayed that Jacqui had found peace and that she and I would be reunited someday. I prayed that all those who were missing her, particularly our children and her siblings, would also find peace and strength to move on with their lives. And I prayed that I would also find some peace of mind that would allow me to move beyond my loss; allow me to fully accept my circumstances for what they were; allow me to look to the future once again and not be constantly shackled to the past and always wishing that things were different. I didn't really believe that a lapsed Catholic, silently pouring his heart out before the altar of Saint James, was going to change anything. But it certainly felt good to express those things that were eating away at me in this most holy of places, highly adorned and the air still heady with incense. I certainly felt a little lighter, a little less burdened, as I got to my feet again and Jane and I made for the exit. I had contemplated leaving Jacqui's pebble behind on the altar, but once again it had remained steadfastly in my pocket. Once again, it just hadn't felt right to leave it behind, even though my pilgrimage was now complete. We stepped out into the bright evening sunshine that filled the Plaza de la Quintana.

"You appear to have something in your eye again," Jane said softly.

"Hmm. Yes," I replied, laughing a little as I wiped my eyes. "Well, that was more moving than I had been expecting. I thought you said earlier that my sanctuary might not actually be a place?"

"Well, I still believe that. That place, before the altar in the Cathedral, is certainly a sanctuary. But I don't believe it's the sanctuary you are seeking. You have further to go."

"Oh Jesus. I've finished my pilgrimage. Do you not think I've walked far enough. Give me a break."

"No, silly. I mean further to go in your mind. You have to break free from the stranglehold of your past."

"What. You mean just forget about Jacqui. Like, she's gone. Goodbye Jacqui. Hello new life. Now let's get on with it. Shit. What am I waiting for?" My irritation was perhaps just a little too apparent, but the serenity I had felt at the altar only a few minutes ago was quickly evaporating.

"No," Jane replied calmly. "I don't mean for you to forget about your past and I certainly don't mean for you to forget about Jacqui. I sincerely hope you never do that. But you don't want to be shackled to the past life you had with Jacqui forever. Unfortunately, that life is over now and, as much as you may wish for it to, it is never going to return. Not in this world anyway." I held my hands up in a gesture to signal that she should stop, but she pressed on regardless. "You have to accept the way things are now and you have to carve out a new life for yourself, without Jacqui by your side. Your past life with Jacqui may certainly shape your future life, but it shouldn't define it. Accepting and forgetting are two totally different things and you can certainly accept without having to forget anything. You need to throw off that heavy cloak of grief that you carry around with you. It's weighing you down."

"Christ. You really know how to kick a man when he's down."

"Please. Can you not see that you have become so used to being seen as the 'grieving widower' that you have now almost fully embraced that role. You have become that man. It's your default position. All I'm saying is that you need to break free from that gloom and start to live again."

"Jesus, don't you think I would if I could?" my blasphemy in the square outside the Cathedral was unbecoming to say the least, but Jane's words were really getting under my skin. "Do you really think that I like being like this? Trapped by my own memories. Every possible moment of joy dragged down and beaten into the ground before having a chance to flourish. Every moment of delight quickly soured by the thought that Jacqui isn't here to share it with me. Ah.. I've had enough."

And with that I stormed off and left Jane standing in the Quintana of the Dead, while I strode up the steps to the Quintana of the Living. I headed back towards my pension, but stopped along the way to have a couple of beers in a bar on Rúa da Fonte de San Miguel to lick my wounds and reflect on what had just happened. I wasn't worried about Jane. She was more than capable of looking after herself. She didn't need me to chaperone her around Santiago. But I did regret parting from her the way I did. It wasn't like me at all to get so heated and storm off in a strop. I knew that she had of course been talking a lot of sense, even if I didn't want to hear it. I knew deep down in my own mind that her words were true. Very similar thoughts had been going through my own mind after all. It was just that I found them so hard to accept. It was the age old battle of the head versus the heart. Some people say that you should always follow your heart. "Follow your heart and you won't go wrong" they espouse with confidence – the line probably gleamed from the daily message on the page of a desk calendar or some insipid post on Facebook. The problem was my heart was broken and what remained of it was constantly drawn back to Jacqui, the person I loved more than anyone else in the whole world. Is it wrong to love someone so much? Can you love someone too much? The answer to those questions may very well be yes, but that's certainly not how my heart saw it. And what of the head, that part of the body that contains the supposedly more rational organ? Well, I can't claim that mine had been the most rational since Jacqui had been taken from me, but it still did possess the capacity for reasoned thought on occasions. Jane had certainly spelt things out for me quite clearly and I now began to see that she was perhaps being deliberately blunt in order to get by my heart's natural defences. Yes, I could now see that it was time to allow my head to rule my heart for a change. How I was going to manage that exactly, I still didn't know, but I now knew that I needed to try.

I emerged from the darkened corner of the bar, where I had chosen to hide myself in my time of contemplation, and strolled back to my pension. There was no sign of Jane. I went to bed and turned out the lights almost immediately, but sleep eluded me and I struggled through a long, torturous night of conflicting emotions and thoughts.

*****

I must have fallen into a deep sleep at some point and, when I awoke, somehow things had become much clearer. I somehow knew exactly what I wanted to do. I dressed quickly and rushed down to reception. And there waiting for me was Jane. She greeted me with a cheery, "Good morning. I was wondering when you might appear."

"My God," I said, finally understanding.

"Not quite," she replied, with the warmest of smiles.

Then remembering that I owed her an apology, I began, "Listen....", but before I got any further, Jane held her hands up and interjected.

"I know. You're very sorry for stomping off in a huff yesterday evening. No need to apologise. I laid it on a little too heavy."

"Well, I wasn't going to say 'stomping off in a huff' exactly, but I suppose that's not far from the truth and I am very sorry. I did get a bit irritated with you. Well, not with you really. More with what you were saying. But I now realise that there was a lot of truth in what you were telling me."

"That's okay. Apology accepted. You just needed a bit of time to think things through before you finally saw sense and agreed with me."

"That's the workings of a slow brain for you. I should have learned to just accept straightaway that you were always right."

"Yeah, that would have been handier for sure. It could have saved a lot of time over the years", she said, smiling knowingly.

"Right," I said, "let's go to the Pilgrim Office and get our certificate."

"Our certificate?"

"You heard me. Come on."

We made our way back to the Plaza del Obradoiro, down the slope of Costa do Cristo and turned right to make our way along Rúa das Carretas to the *Oficina de Acollida ao Peregrino*, the Pilgrim's Reception Office. It was very busy when we arrived, with a queue lined right around the corridors to the other side of the rectangular building. The queue was moving along slowly but steadily towards the large room where the *Compostelas* were issued. Thankfully, there were a number of helpful and friendly volunteers on hand to keep people informed and distracted with conversations about individuals' journeys – and there was no shortage of stories. It probably took us well over an hour to reach the issuing office and to eventually be summoned forward to one of the many reception desks. The young Spanish man behind the desk introduced himself politely, but in that slightly world weary way that belied the fact that, to him, I was probably just one of many dozens of pilgrims he had already dealt with today.

"Hola. Inglés?" he asked.

"Si," I replied.

"Okay, my name is Alberto. Can I see your passport and credential please. Thank you. What name would you like me to put on the *Compostela* – just Dermot Breen, or your name in full." It was all very formal. Friendly enough, but rather impersonal.

"Actually, I have a special request," I said, realising only then that my heart was racing. "Could you please put Dermot and Jacqui Breen?"

"Did Jacqui walk the Camino with you? Where is she? If she presents her passport and credential, she can also get a *Compostela.*"

"Why, she's right here by my side Alberto."

At first I received a puzzled look from Alberto, but it quickly changed into a look that suggested that he now felt that he was dealing with someone who had been out in the sun for too long.

"I'm sorry. Let me explain," I quickly added. "Jacqui is...sorry...was my wife, but I'm afraid she passed away last year. So she doesn't have a passport or a credential. But she was by my side for the entire journey and she's here with me now. She helped me through the hardest days and kept me company when I was feeling down and lonely. She encouraged me to keep going when I felt like giving up and she guided me back onto the way when I took a wrong turn. She is therefore every bit as deserving of the *Compostela* as I am and that is why I would like her name included. Please."

Alberto's eyes immediately softened and the official behind the desk suddenly transformed into a fellow human being.

"Sir...Dermot...I am very sorry for your loss and I am truly touched by what you have just told me. However, I'm sorry to say that it is not possible to issue a *Compostela* with your wife's name on it in that way. I can only write the names of those who have actually walked the Camino."

"But..." I was about to plead ever further.

"However, there is something that I can do. I can issue you with a second special certificate that will show the total distance walked and I have more flexibility with the names that can be added to it." Alberto looked apprehensive as he said this, perhaps nervous that his suggestion might not be satisfactory, but he had no need to worry.

"You mean you can put 'Dermot and Jacqui Breen' on it?" My heart began to soar.

"It would be my pleasure to do that Dermot. And if you would like, I can also add a dedication to your late wife on your *Compostela* directly under your name."

"Alberto, that would be wonderful. I am delighted. Thank you so much."

I think I stopped breathing as I watched Alberto carefully transcribe Jacqui's name alongside mine onto the special certificate. All the hustle and bustle in the office no doubt continued uninterrupted around me, but I was oblivious to it. It was as if the entire world had suddenly retreated and only Alberto and I remained as this special moment played out. When Alberto handed me my *Compostela* and my very special certificate complete with Jacqui's name, the tears started to come once again. Alberto stood up from behind his desk and reached out his hand.

As we shook hands, he said, "Dermot, I am very honoured to meet you and it is a privilege for me to issue you with your certificates. I am going to request that a special prayer be offered for you and Jacqui at the mid-day service in the Cathedral."

I could see that Alberto was truly touched by this encounter. He was tearing up a little also. Perhaps I had been a little bit different from the dozens of other pilgrims he had already issued with certificates that day. I'm sure that many of them also had their own special stories to tell. Perhaps some of them preferred to keep their stories private. I don't know. All I do know is that my encounter with Alberto in the *Oficina de Acollida ao Peregrino* was one of the most wonderful experiences of my entire Camino de Santiago and I had the feeling that it was a little bit special for Alberto also.

I thanked Alberto and left the office in a bit of a daze, clutching my new *Compostela* and my even more valuable special certificate with Jacqui's name on it. That magical moment that I had been longing for right throughout my Camino had just happened. It's a moment that will live on in my heart for the rest of my days, right alongside the many happy memories of my wonderful wife.

Outside the Office, I turned to Jane and said, "Well, Jacqueline Jane Breen, what did you think of that?"

"That was just wonderful. I feel so proud of you Dermot."

"I think I'm going to remember this experience for the rest of my life.

I'm so glad you joined me on my Camino. I needed your guidance more than I ever realised. It's been just wonderful the way you suddenly appeared when I needed you most. And also the way you gave me space to meet and engage with others along the way. Thank you so much."

"You are very welcome. I'm so glad to have been able to help, even if I'm merely an apparition."

"Oh, you are much more than that. You're my guardian angel. You will never disappear from my life."

"That's okay. And I'll be here for you for as long as you want or as long as you need me. Just so long as you don't allow me to hold you back. Remember what I said about acceptance and allowing yourself to move on."

"Yeah, I know. And acceptance isn't the same as forgetting."

"Exactly. At last. I think he's finally got it."

"Hey, no need to rub it in. By the way," I said, "but you never did explain what happened to your husband, Joe."

"Well, Dermot Joseph Breen, I was very worried about him for a long time there. But you know what? I think he's going to be fine. He's stronger and more resilient than he sometimes thinks he is. I've seen him doing things over the last year or so that have made me very proud. So, yeah, I think he's going to be okay."

"I hope you're right"

"I know I am. Aren't I always?"

"But of course you are dear. Always."

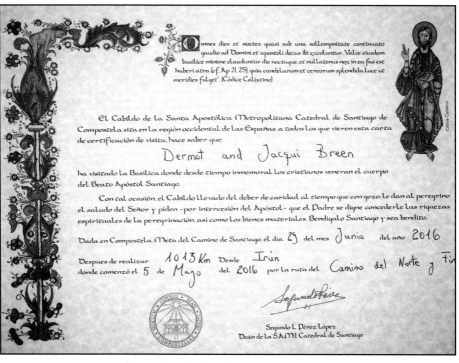

The special certificate made out to me and Jacqui

"Here, I think you deserve a big hug."

Moments later I said, "So that's what it feels like to be wrapped in angels wings."

"Much better than that heavy cloak you've been carrying round with you, eh?"

"Oh yes. That's for sure. Much, much nicer." We embraced for a long time before I noticed we were getting strange looks. "Hey, people are beginning to stare."

"That's okay. They can't see me. Only you."

"I know. I think that's why they're staring."

Epilogue

The metal gate squeaked mournfully on its hinges as I pushed it open and stepped into the grounds of the old stone parish church, with its tall Gothic windows and wildly pitched roof. It was an early morning in late September and the air was crisp and clear. The distinctive profile of Fair Head was just visible ahead of me, over the roofs and spires of Ballycastle town. There was a hint of a much more distant outline of the Mull of Kintyre, across the blue grey sea of Moyle. The scene before me was bathed in soft sunlight and the graveyard was peaceful, its stillness accentuated by the light birdsong accompanying my footsteps. There was still a fresh sparkle of early morning dew on the grass, which gradually darkened the leather of my shoes as I left the stone path and worked my way between the headstones.

As I made my way through the church's graveyard, the weathered names on some of the headstones caught my eye, almost as if their owners were beseeching me to not ignore them as I passed. I could never walk through this graveyard without pausing once or twice to study the names and dates and to wonder as to what sorts of lives and deaths were associated with these inhabitants from across the centuries. But I never paused for long as there was really only one particular plot that kept bringing me back to this place. I walked to the far end of the graveyard and, stopping at my intended spot, I smiled in response to the words engraved in the marble surround of the grave below my deceased wife's name, 'You can shed tears that she is gone or you can smile because she has lived'.

"There have been enough tears," I whispered, as I looked down onto the gravel covered plot that held the remains of Jacqui's mother Annie and father Jack, as well as my wife's ashes. My words were perhaps spoken more in hope than in conviction, but it was certainly the case that the tears were becoming much less and I was surely still heading in the right direction. "Thanks again for your company in Spain, my love. I really don't think I could have done it without your guidance."

I looked up to take in the sight of Jacqui's favourite mountain, Knocklayde, knowing that I would return here in a few months' time to complete what was becoming an annual pilgrimage. That relatively short pilgrimage of only four or five hours, would take me from this very graveside to the summit of Knocklayde and back again and would be undertaken to mark the anniversary of Jacqui's passing.

"I'll see you in January, if not before," I said as I got to my feet once again. And then I remembered something. "Oh, I almost forgot. I've got something for you." I reached into my coat pocket and found Jacqui's little round pebble. I rolled the familiar shape between my fingers for the last time and then I gently placed it amongst the blanket of gravel covering the grave. "I think this is where it rightfully belongs." I stepped back from the graveside and nodded to Jack and Annie, as I always did. "Look after her until I join you all". I turned to head back across the graveyard and towards the gate. *"Adios"* I sighed into myself as I worked my way between the other resting places. As I reached the gate I could have sworn that a *"Buen Camino"* sailed in on the air behind me. But when I turned to look back, there was of course no one there. Only headstones, standing in grim and silent resolution. I smiled again at the tricks my imagination could still play on me. I pulled the gate behind me and left Jacqui to rest again under the watch of the old stone parish church that has stood on this spot since 1849 and just so happens to be called St James.

Author's Note

The legend of Saint James[1] is recounted in a medieval manuscript known as 'The Golden Legend', which was first published in the thirteenth century. The Golden Legend contains what are alleged to be factual accounts of the lives of many of the Saints, including Saint James. James was originally one of the twelve apostles and his legend begins after the death and resurrection of Jesus Christ.

James is believed to have been beheaded in Jerusalem in 44 AD and his remains brought to the region of Galicia in Northern Spain to be buried in a secret place. Here they lay for eight centuries until they were discovered in 814 AD by the monk Pelayo and Bishop Theodomir, after they were guided to the burial site by a star.

The short sections in italics between each chapter are my 'imaginative' reinterpretation of the legend of Saint James as set out in The Golden Legend.

King Alfonso II's journey to the tomb of Saint James after its discovery was considered the first pilgrimage to Santiago de Compostela and it set the example for subsequent generations of pilgrims. Today, the pilgrimage to the shrine of Saint James remains incredibly popular, with over 200,000 pilgrims travelling to the city of Santiago each year from points all over Europe and other parts of the world. The pilgrimage is known in Spanish as the Camino de Santiago, which translates as the Way of Saint James.

In modern times, people walk the Camino de Santiago for all sorts of reasons. Certainly, many still walk it for religious motives, as a form of devotion, penance or atonement. However, others undertake the pilgrimage simply as a form of exercise or a physical challenge, while others walk it for a variety of spiritual or emotional reasons. Many just wish to take time out from their busy lives and give themselves space to think about their futures.

What you have just read was the story of my Camino. I have told it as it actually happened. There has, of course, been some artistic license applied in relation to my conversations with the character of Jane. These conversations really represent the internal dialogue that occurred within my own mind throughout my pilgrimage as I struggled to come to terms with my loss. It only seemed right and appropriate that my guardian angel should be given the voice of reason, just as my wife was always the voice of reason during the 35 years we had been together.

This book contains only a small selection of the photographs that I took during my Camino. If you wish to see more please watch my video 'The Man with the Camino Tattoo' on YouTube at: https://youtu.be/oosXRcTnZtE.

All author profits from sales of this book will be donated to Cancer Research UK[2] to fund its important work in the fight against cancer.

Buen Camino

Dermot Breen

---

1 'The Golden Legend' or 'Lives of the Saints'; compiled by Jacobus de Voragine, Archbishop of Genoa, 1275

2 Cancer Research UK is a registered charity in England and Wales (1089464), Scotland (SCO41666) and the Isle of Man (1103). Northern Ireland charity registration pending.

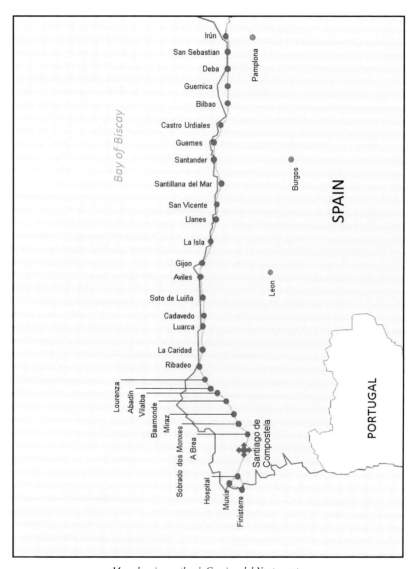

Map showing author's Camino del Norte route